THE HORRIBLE PAWS

DH Lawrence's Australian Nightmare

"It was as if the silvery freedom suddenly turned, and showed the scaly back of a reptile, and the horrible paws."

(*Kangaroo*, p350)

by Robert Darroch

Published in 2022 by

HEAD OFFICE: 11 Rodriguez Avenue, Blackheath 2785
SYDNEY OFFICE: 2/2-4 Notts Avenue Bondi 2026
email: rob@cybersydney.com.au

&

PO Box R1906
Royal Exchange
NSW 1225
AUSTRALIA

ISBN 978-0-9946155-6-5 pb
ISBN 978-1-925706-78-9 e

© Robert Darroch 2019

All rights reserved worldwide. No part of the book may be copied or changed in any format, sold, or used in any way other than what is outlined in this book, under any circumstances, without the prior written permission of the copyright-holder.

CONTENTS

	ACKNOWLEDGEMENTS	i
	SELECT BIBLIOGRAPHY & CUE-TITLES	iii
	EXPLANATORY NOTE	v
	DEDICATION	vi
	PREFACE	vii
	PICTURE INSERT	centre pages
	INTRODUCTION	1
1	*Where It Begins*	20
2	*Sydney & First Impressions*	30
3	*First Contact*	37
4	*Thirroul & "Wyewurk"*	46
5	*The Tangled Skein*	54
6	*The Diggers & the Maggies*	71
7	*Getting Down to Business*	81
8	*Kangaroo*	87
9	*Betwixt & Between*	95
10	*Stuck, Unstuck & Stuck Again*	116

11	*The Worst Day of his Life*	130
12	*The Nightmare*	140
13	*Bits & Pieces*	145
14	*Jack Slaps Back*	149
15	*Interlude, & a Trip to the Zoo*	156
16	*The Row in Town*	161
17	*Thinking of Leaving*	168
18	*Departure, Taos & Second Thoughts*	174
19	*Postscript*	189
Appendix 1	*The Curious Incident of the Red Wooden Heart*	210
Appendix 2	*"Claws in the Arse"*	220
	WHAT HE WROTE EACH DAY	235
	RESEARCH-DIARY 1972-2018	236
	BIBLIOGRAPHIC NOTE	265
	INDEX	267

ACKNOWLEDGEMENTS

IN THE four decades it took for me to come to write this book, I had a lot of help – so much so that I cannot possibly pay tribute, acknowledge, or thank everyone (or every entity) that contributed to its ultimate publication. (See my *Bibliographic Essay*, below.) For those who did assist, you have my sincere appreciation and gratitude. I could not have completed this without your combined help and many contributions.

However, I do want to take this ultimate opportunity to thank four people in particular – my wife and collaborator Sandra (Jobson) Darroch; my research colleague John Ruffels; my secret-army confidant Andrew Moore; and Robert Whitelaw, who came on the scene to make the final breakthrough.

Although this project began as a joint effort, Sandra handed over the research reins to me in early 1976. Nonetheless, she has helped, encouraged, supported – and believed in – the project all along the way. To her goes my greatest thanks and warmest appreciation. Only she and I know how much of this is hers, too.

John Ruffels I met at a cafe in Bondi in 1981 after my first book *DH Lawrence in Australia* was published. He offered his help with the ongoing research, and that help persists to this day. His research skills are of Bletchleyesque dimensions, and much of what follows is the product of his dogged delving and continuing persistence, and support. I owe him a debt of gratitude that I cannot adequately put into words.

Andrew Moore I first met in the Mitchell Library in Sydney one day in 1976, and it was he who coined the term "The Darroch Thesis". Our research went along similar tracks for much of the time, although his was on an academic rail, while mine was more divergent. Despite the slings and arrows of some of his fellow academics, he still believes in The Darroch Thesis, and I take this opportunity to thank him, too, for his help, support and loyalty.

Robert Whitelaw came late on the scene. He helped track down "the end house" *Billabong* at Narrabeen, where Lawrence first met Jack Scott, and to place George Augustine Taylor and Charles Rosenthal – "the two faces of Benjamin Cooley" – there (see a snapshot of Rosenthal and Taylor together at *Billabong* in the *photo-insert* of this present work).

Finally, I would also like to thank and pay tribute to Paul Delprat and Garry Shead, whose images (along with those of Sidney Nolan and Brett Whitley – see *Appendix 2* below) have provided fitting and evocative imagery to the chronicle of Lawrence's 99 days in Australia. (I would also like to thank Edwina Doe, who helped check the manuscripts, and our "techo" Peter Jeffery, who prepared the texts for the printer, and guided us through the digital undergrowth.)

> THE COVER ILLUSTRATION is a reproduction, slightly enhanced, of Sidney Nolan's 1981 painting entitled "Kangaroo", which is a representation of the artist's former friend, the Nobel-prizing-winning Australia author Patrick White, depicted here as the primary character Benjamin Cooley in Lawrence's Australian novel (note the blood-caked "horrible paws") - see *Appendix 2*, "Claws in the Arse"

SELECT BIBLIOGRAPHY & CUE-TITLES

RICHARD ALDINGTON *Kangaroo* (Heinemann Phoenix edition, London, 1950) [*Introduction* to the text] CUE-TITLE: *"Aldington"*
WITTER BYNNER *Journey with Genius – Reflections and Reminiscences Concerning the D. H. Lawrences* (J Day & Co, New York, 1951) CUE-TITLE: *"Bynner"*
ERIC CAMPBELL *The Rallying Point – My Story of the New Guard* (Melbourne University Press, 1965) CUE-TITLE: *"Campbell"*
The DH LAWRENCE REVIEW (various editors) CUE-TITLE: *"DHLR"*
ROBERT DARROCH The day-by-day diary of the research 1972-2016 accessible at: http://www.dhlawrencesocietyaustralia.com.au/ CUE-TITLE: *"Research-Diary"* [dated]
ROBERT DARROCH *D.H Lawrence in Australia* (Macmillan Melbourne, 1981)
ROBERT DARROCH *The Quest for Cooley* The Svengali Press (Sydney, 2016) CUE-TITLE: *"Quest"*
ROBERT DARROCH *DH Lawrence's 99 Days in Australia* (volume 2) CUE-TITLE: *"99 Days"*
ROBERT DARROCH "Not the End of the Story" *DHLR* vol 26, 1-3 (1996) CUE-TITLE: *"Endings"*
BRUCE STEELE Introduction & textual notes to the CUP edition of *Kangaroo* CUE-TITLE: *"Steele"*
JOSEPH DAVIS *DH Lawrence at Thirroul* (Imprint, Sydney, 1989) CUE-TITLE: *"Davis"*
DAVID ELLIS *DH Lawrence – The Dying Game* (Cambridge University Press, 1998) CUE-TITLE: *"Ellis"*
DAVID GAME *D.H Lawrence's Australia – Anxiety at the Edge of Empire* (Ashgate, Farnham [Surrey], 2015) CUE-TITLE: *"Game"*
D.H. LAWRENCE *The Letters of D.H. Lawrence* (Cambridge University Press) 1979-2000 [volume 4, 1989, unless otherwise stated] CUE-TITLE: *"Letters #[numbered]"*
D.H. LAWRENCE *Kangaroo* (the 1922 holograph (hand-written) text [HRC Texas]) CUE-TITLE: *"holograph"*
D.H. LAWRENCE *Kangaroo* (Cambridge University Press, 1994) CUE-TITLE: *"K"* [+CUP page]
D.H. LAWRENCE *Fantasia of the Unconscious* (Heinemann, London, 1961) CUE-TITLE: *"Fantasia"*
FRIEDA LAWRENCE *Not I But the Wind* (The Viking Press, New York, 1934) CUE-TITLE: *"Frieda"*
ANDREW MOORE *The Secret Army and The Premier – Conservative*

Paramilitary Organisations in NSW 1930-32 (University of NSW Press, 1989) CUE-TITLE: *"Moore"*

EDWARD NEHLS ***DH Lawrence: A Composite Biography*** (The University of Wisconsin Press, 1957) CUE-TITLE: *"Nehls"*

RANANIM The Journal of the DH Lawrence Society of Australia http://www.dhlawrencesocietyaustralia.com.au/ CUE-TITLE: *"Rananim"*

"The Spy Episode in *Kangaroo* – the Kershaw/Aldington/Lawlor Letters" *Rananim* vol 3, no 2 (June 1995) CUE-TITLE: *"Spy Letters"*

M.S. ("Mollie") SKINNER ***The Fifth Sparrow*** (Sydney University Press, 1971) CUE-TITLE: *"Fifth Sparrow"*

THE SYDNEY MORNING HERALD (Sydney, 1831-) CUE-TITLE: *"SMH"* [+ date]

GEORGE AUGUSTINE TAYLOR ***The Sequel*** (Building Limited, Sydney 1915) CUE-TITLE: *"Sequel"*

EXPLANATORY NOTE TO THE TEXT

This is a second, revised and updated version of my Svengali text, published in 2016. This new edition was made necessary by the emergence of fresh information[1]; by the opportunity to correct errors and solecisms; but also because of my decision to now combine the original two 2016 books (volume 1, *The Quest for Cooley*; & volume 2, *The Silvery Freedom…& the Horrible Paws*) in this single 2018 updated-edition. (The original *Quest* text has been condensed and truncated to provide an extended *Introduction* to this new volume.) Extracts from *Kangaroo* are cited as from the Cambridge University Press 1994 edition, although the actual text reproduced in this volume comes from the Gutenberg [or Secker] version, but with individual CUP-edition page-numbers. The primary textual apparatus – citing specific references and providing further explanatory information – are in the footnotes at the bottom of each page (instead, as in the first edition, *Endnotes*). Yet by far the bulk of the background information is to be found in the *Kangaroo* Research-Diary, which chronicles the progress of my research from when it began in 1972 – day-by-day, month-by-month, year-by-year, decade-by-decade – culminating in its (initial) denouement in 2011-12. This Research-Diary can be seen at: http://www.dhlawrenceinaustralia.com.au/ But for ease of access, relevant diary entries specifically-cited in the text are reproduced (cross-referenced by date) at the end of the main text. Our DH Lawrence Society website (which we started in 1992 – see http://www.dhlawrencesocietyaustralia.com.au/) – has reproductions of each edition of our DHLA journal, *Rananim* (articles from which are also cited in the following text) and which can be accessed via both our DHLA websites.

---

[1] specifically, my post-2016 realisation about the homoerotic sub-theme in *Kangaroo* (see below & *Appendix 1*, "The Curious Incident of the Red Wooden Heart")

DEDICATION

This book is gratefully dedicated to the memory of the late Dr Warren Roberts, the distinguished Lawrence scholar who first put my nose on to the track of *Kangaroo*

PREFACE

THIS IS a book going on for almost half a century in the making.[2] The reason it took so long was that its underlying tenet[3] – that *Kangaroo* is based on D. H. Lawrence's encounter with a secret army[4] in Sydney in 1922 – while easy to arrive at, was difficult to prove. There were many obstacles along the way, and many interests who did not want the truth to come out.

It is the second edition of my third book about Lawrence's 99 days in Australia. The first, *D. H. Lawrence in Australia* (Macmillan [Melbourne 1981]), was the interim product of the first six years of my research. My second book, *The Quest for Cooley* (now also incorporated into the new *Introduction* in this volume) tells the story of the search for the truth about Lawrence and *Kangaroo*…from its start in the Fall of 1972 at the University of Texas at Austin, when Dr Warren Roberts, Lawrence's bibliographer, put my nose on the track of *Kangaroo*, to its initial denouement, starting in 2012.[5] The third is the original 2016 edition of this work, originally entitled *DH Lawrence's 99 Days in Australia*, but now in this fourth (much-revised second edition) iteration retitled – for reasons that will become clear – *The Horrible Paws*.[6]

Take especial note of this present volume's cover illustration, which is a reproduction of Sir Sidney Nolan's 1981 image of Australian Nobel-laureate novelist Patrick

---

[2] in 1972 I was helping my wife Sandra with her research (at the Humanities Research Center [HRC] in Austin, Texas) on Lady Ottoline Morrell
[3] that "underlying tenet" came to be called "The Darroch Thesis", a term coined by Australian historian Dr Andrew Moore
[4] There is no settled or accepted definition of the term "secret army". The consensus, such as it is, seems to be of a large-scale clandestine paramilitary organisation.
[5] see my *Introduction* below
[6] For more than 40 years they were not "*paws*" but "*jaws*". In 1950 the original Penguin editor, unable to see how a reptile could have paws, changed what became the standard text to "*jaws*" – not realising Lawrence was describing, not the claws of a reptile, but something much more human.

White as the eponymous, anthropomorphic reptile, with its horrible, blood-caked paws. Why Nolan, Australia's most famous painter, chose to portray Patrick White, Australia's greatest writer and his once close-friend, as a blood-soaked fascist is explained by my wife Sandra Jobson Darroch in the "Claws in the Arse" *Appendix 2* below.

A question that could occur to the reader of what follows is: how do we <u>know</u> this is what happened to Lawrence and Frieda during the 99 days they were in Australia? I will endeavour to answer that question in the following text. But the short answer is that, while not everything in *Kangaroo* happened to Lawrence in Australia, almost everything that happened to Lawrence in Australia is in *Kangaroo*. (However, a word of caution to the reader. *Kangaroo* is not a novel in the accepted sense of the term, but an unorthodox form of "fictionalised" autobiography, set within a traditional fictional framework.)

INTRODUCTION

"The Quest for Cooley"

MY QUEST FOR COOLEY began in 1972 with a murder. My wife Sandra and I had travelled to the U.S. to the University of Texas at Austin to read the 8000-or-so letters the daughter of Lady Ottoline Morrell had sold to the Humanities Research Center at the university. (Sandra was writing the first biography of the famous literary hostess.) After a month of intensive research, we were about to leave when the Director of the HRC, Dr Warren Roberts, called us in to his office. "What are you going to do after Ottoline?" he asked. We confessed we had no future plans. "You're Australian. Why don't you look into the time Lawrence spent in Australia?"

It wasn't until five years later that we learned why Dr Roberts had picked two young Australian journalists to undertake research into Lawrence in Australia, and Lawrence's Australian novel *Kangaroo*. In fact, he himself never told us the reason for his unconventional choice. It wasn't until October 1977, when I received a letter from Gerald Pollinger, the agent for the Lawrence Estate, that I learnt the reason why Dr Roberts had asked us to undertake research into *Kangaroo*. Pollinger informed me[7] that the American academic, Dr F.P. Jarvis, whom Dr Roberts had originally chosen to edit *Kangaroo*, had been murdered[8], and that this was why we were later approached by the CUP "in

---

[7] by then I had assumed the main research role into Lawrence's time in Australia (a reversal of our roles in *Ottoline*, where I was my wife Sandra's research assistant)
[8] Gerald Pollinger-RD [26/10/77]. He told me: "As I understand it, the professor who was to edit KANGAROO, namely Dr F.P. Jarvis, was murdered..." (I never found out the circumstances of his demise.)

1

regard to editing *Kangaroo* for their critical edition"⁹.

After we returned to Sydney in late 1975, we began looking into the 99 days Lawrence spent in Australia. We read the available literature, which was disappointedly scant as far as Australia was concerned. We travelled down to Thirroul to see *Wyewurk*; then began perusing the local newspapers of the period (May to August 1922). We wanted to get a picture of what Sydney was like when Lawrence was there, and what was happening in Australia at the time. (As a result of our *Ottoline* experience, we had come to mistrust secondary sources.) The newspapers, when cross-referenced to the text of *Kangaroo*, were especially informative. It quickly became apparent to us that much of *Kangaroo* was based on Lawrence's own experiences in Australia, and what was happening around him in Sydney and Thirroul. In this we were encouraged by what Lawrence's first post-war biographer Richard Aldington (who knew him well) had said in his Introduction to the 1950 Heinemann edition of *Kangaroo*:

> Although some characters and episodes in the book are imaginary or transferred to Australia from elsewhere, much of the writing deals with Lawrence's experiences in Australia – with the unique result that he was remembering and setting down with extreme accuracy and vividness one set of experiences while actually undergoing others, themselves designed to be remembered and written as he found new ones.[10]

Our ongoing newspaper research tended to confirm what Aldington wrote about *Kangaroo* in the late 1940s.[11]

---

[9] Gerald Pollinger-RD *ibid*
[10] Aldington p7
[11] One of the first to attempt to correlate local events with *Kangaroo* was the Rev. John Alexander ("DH Lawrence's *Kangaroo*: Fantasy, Fact or Fiction?" [*Meanjin*, June 1965]). Alexander undertook some early research into *Kangaroo* & Lawrence's time in Australia. In particular, he made an effort, most valuably, to correlate events in *Kangaroo* with such things as the weather, local politics, daily newspaper items, etc. He concluded: "It can be said with

"The Quest for Cooley"

Early in 1976 I was at a journalists' Australia Day party when I found myself sitting next to a local finance writer, Tom Fitzgerald. I knew he had written an early article on Lawrence in Australia[12], so we began chatting about my current project. "I'm running across a surprising number of correlations between the text and what was happening in Sydney at the time," I told him. "I'm even beginning to entertain the possibility that the secret-army plot might have some reality in it." He replied: "Strange you should say that. I interviewed Eric Campbell before he died. Campbell asked me: 'Do you know why we called ourselves the New Guard?' When I said no, he said: 'Because there was an Old Guard.'" Fitzgerald said to me: "I would look into that if I were you."

Having read history and political science at university, I knew about Campbell and the New Guard. During a political crisis in NSW in 1930, a paramilitary organisation emerged, initially in Sydney, calling itself "the New Guard". Its proclaimed purpose was to confront the (left-wing) Labor Government which had won a recent State election.[13] Many years later Campbell wrote a book about the New Guard in which he described how in 1930 he and a fellow militia officer, Major John Scott, had decide to revive a "force of 500 stalwart ex-servicemen" that they had recruited during a waterfront dispute in Sydney in 1925.[14] In 1930, after Labor leader Jack Lang became NSW Premier (with a radical socialist agenda), they began recruiting "stalwart ex-servicemen" again, starting with the secret soldiers they had "signed up" in 1925. Soon after, however, Campbell, impatient to be more active in the current crisis, decided to "go public" with the men he had recruited and form a breakaway, non-secret "New Guard". Scott, he recorded, decided to remain behind with the more

---

confidence that he is closer to the facts than almost all critics to date recognised" [Alexander op cit p189]).
[12] "The Beard of the Prophet" [Nation, Sydney 1958]
[13] its main claim to fame, or infamy, was to cut the ribbon at the opening of the Sydney Harbour Bridge in 1932 before the Labor Premier, Jack Lang, could do so
[14] The Rallying Point [Melbourne University Press 1965] p16

secretive group (which Campbell's men afterwards called, derisively, "the Old Guard"). I already knew that a secret paramilitary group called "the White Guard" had been active in Melbourne during a police strike in 1923. That was only a few months after Lawrence was in Australia. From then on, Major Scott's "Old Guard" began to take on increasing relevance to my research into the background of Lawrence's Australian novel.

In mid-1976 I wrote an article for my then newspaper, *The Australian,* entitled "THE MYSTERY OF KANGAROO" in which I speculated that, had Lawrence run across a secret army activist called Scott after he arrived in Sydney in May 1922, it might explain a lot. A week or so later we were at a tennis afternoon on Sydney's verdant North Shore when a schoolfriend of Sandra's said: "We were very interested in Rob's article at the weekend. Did you know that my father is Jack Scott's stepson?" Two weeks later I interviewed not only the stepson but also his brother. To me they confirmed the parallels between their step-father John (known as Jack) Scott and the character I knew as Jack Callcott in *Kangaroo*.[15] Physically Scott and Callcott were identical; both were attractive to women[16]; both had the same specific "special interest" – Japan[17]; both were keen gamblers[18]; both were interested in literature[19]; and most indicatively of all, neither could father children, Scott being rendered impotent by a wartime trauma (shellshock)[20]. From that moment I was convinced that Lawrence had based some at least of his

---

[15] see my report of my meeting with them at *Research-Diary* 9/6/76 entry below
[16] Scott was "a ladies' man" (Lawrence says of Callcott [in his alternative guise of "Jaz"] "he'd make any woman like him" [*K* p64]
[17] (oddly) – see Lawrence's description of Jack Callcott at *K* p40 re his "special subject", Japan
[18] Callcott had "spurts of gambling excitement" [*K* p179]; Scott, according to his stepsons, was an almost fanatical gambler.
[19] Scott was a book collector & had autographed copies of Galsworthy in his library (including books by Lawrence); Callcott shows a keen interest in what Somers writes [see *K* p31]
[20] In *Kangaroo*, one of the several characters based on Scott, "Fred Wilmott, "can't get his pecker up". This aspect of Scott was portrayed even more graphically when Lawrence recycled Scott as the impotent Jack Strangeways in *John Thomas & Lady Jane* [Penguin 1954] (see *Research-Diary* entry 15/8/94 below re this).

character Jack Callcott on Willian John ("Jack") Scott.[21]

It was at the Mitchell Library in Sydney (in whose manuscript collection I was carrying out much of my research) in mid-1976 that the next breakthrough came. In the papers of a local union activist I found a copy of a magazine he had picked up at a political meeting in the Domain (Sydney's "Speakers' Corner") in 1921. It was called *King and Empire* and it was the monthly journal of a right-wing patriotic organisation named the King and Empire Alliance. It listed the Alliance's main officer-bearers. Its treasurer was Major William John Scott, and its secretary was Major-General Sir Charles Rosenthal. The library had the complete "run" of *King and Empire* (January 1921-January 1923), which I read. An early issue said that "the inspirers and founders" of the alliance were Rosenthal and Scott. Could the Alliance's Major William John Scott be Campbell's "John Scott"? More intriguingly, could Major-General Charles Rosenthal have any connection with Benjamin Cooley, the leader of the secret fictional paramilitary organisation Lawrence portrays in *Kangaroo* as "the Diggers and the Maggies"? Could there indeed have been (as Campbell implied) an active secret army in Sydney when Lawrence was there on which he could have based the plot of *Kangaroo*? As the research progressed, that began to appear increasingly likely.

Next, I was directed to a box of manuscripts called "the secret bundles". (The staff at the library was very supportive of my research, and were doing their best to assist me.) These, it turned out, were police reports on clandestine paramilitary activity in NSW during the Lang crisis (the bundles were secret because of what they revealed about prominent people involved in such activity). The bundles confirmed the existence of the 1930-32 Old Guard and named one of their

---

[21] many other parallels emerged out of the ensuing months of research – see in particular Callcott's "job" as, firstly, "*foreman in a motor-works place*". [K p24] then as "*a partner in a motor-works place*" [K p75]; see *Research-Diary* 23/2/97 entry below re Scott & "The Garage"

leaders as Major William John Scott. Then I was directed to a folder called the Haughton James Papers. In the early 1960s, a young (Marxist) student called John Haughton James had looked into the background of what I now called the Old Guard and found that it had predecessors going back into the 1920s. The names of those involved included leading citizens and business leaders in Sydney. It also had a country or rural dimension[22] – in fact, there were apparently similar bodies in the other States.[23]

One day when I put in a slip requesting another secret bundle, the librarian said: "Do you know that someone else has been asking for those folders?" And so I was introduced to a young left-wing historian, Andrew Moore (later Professor Andrew Moore), who was writing a doctoral thesis on the Old Guard in country NSW. Thereafter our research ran along parallel tracks, and he later wrote the definitive book on the Old Guard, *The Premier and the Secret Army*.

It was Andrew who introduced me to another left-wing historian, Humphrey McQueen, who had undertaken significant research into secret armies in Australia. It was Humphrey who told me about the Australian Protective League and its *eminence grise*, Herbert Brookes. He believed that the APL, which had been based on the 1917-18 American Protective League[24], may have been the forerunner of Scott and Rosenthal's King and Empire Alliance (both having a distinctive dual-public/secret structure, as described in the Brookes papers – see below – in the National Library in Canberra).

In September 1977, I was contacted by a gentleman in Melbourne called Ernest Whiting who had read my Lawrence articles in *The Australian*. He told me that he knew I was right about Lawrence and *Kangaroo* because of a conversation he

---

[22] see *K* p92 "...*in Sydney – and in the other towns as well*"
[23] in *Kangaroo* Lawrence mentions "the five", apparently the leaders of the Australia-wide secret army in other States (see *Moore* variously re Australia's paramilitary organisations)
[24] see Joan Jensen's *The Price of Vigilance* [Rand McNally (Chicago 1968)], specifically p234

had overheard at one of his mother's literary conversaziones in the 1930s. He recalled that a leading Australian business figure had told the gathering that Lawrence had based *Kangaroo* on an actual secret army that the author had run across in Sydney in the early 1920s. When asked how a visiting writer like Lawrence (of all people) could have run across such a secret organisation, the business figure, according to Whiting, replied: "To know the answer to that question you must consult the passenger list of the boat that brought Lawrence to Sydney."[25] (I shall return to that remark, and what it led to, when I describe how my other research-helper, John Ruffels, swam into my ken in 1981.)

Over in Texas, Dr Roberts had been very supportive of what I was doing in Sydney, and it was he who recommended to the CUP that I be given the opportunity to put in a proposal to edit *Kangaroo* for the forthcoming critical edition. The CUP's Michael Black then arranged for film of the *holograph* manuscript and the several typescripts of *Kangaroo* to be sent to me in Australia. Ingenuously, I spent some time and effort putting my proposal together, then posted it off to Cambridge. It was rejected, immediately. (A young unknown Australian journalist being chosen to edit a major Lawrence novel? Out of the question.) Undaunted by this rebuff – indeed, spurred on – I decided to continue with my work on *Kangaroo* and Lawrence in Australia.

Between 1977 and 1979 much of my time was spent trying to track down Major Jack Scott. I had already discovered that he had been Rosenthal's deputy organising the return to Australia of its WW1 troops, which was no doubt why he had been chosen by Rosenthal as his deputy in the King and Empire Alliance (KEA). The crucial thing I needed to discover was where Scott had lived in Sydney in 1922. In *Kangaroo* Lawrence describes many excursions his *alter ego*

---

[25] see *Research-Diary* 8/8/77 entry below for Whiting's letter

Somers has in and around Sydney. What I needed was an address where I might place Scott and Lawrence together, and where their paths could then have crossed. But although I could place Scott in 1921 (from the relevant electoral roll) and later in 1925, he was absent from any roll, or other record, in 1922.

In early 1979 I was preparing to return to London, where we still had a home. I planned to be away some time, so I spent my last few weeks in Sydney tidying up some local loose-ends in my research. Lawrence in *Kangaroo* mentions an address, 51 Murdoch Street, where Somers goes early in his stay in Sydney. I had identified a building (called the Canberra Flats) in the Sydney suburb of Neutral Bay that fitted Lawrence's description of "51 Murdoch Street" (moreover, number 51 was indeed an actual address in that street). The local electoral roll listed those then living at that address, but the names (on initial inspection) meant nothing to me. Jack Scott was certainly not among them. So one of my final tasks was to go back to the electoral roll and check those names again, for I was convinced that Lawrence could not have dreamt up such a specific address – it had to have some significance to the novel. Yet when the library assistant brought out the roll for that area, it was not the one I had perused so closely before. What I had not realised was that there were *two* sets of electoral rolls, one State and the other Federal. Moreover, the State roll that I had now been given had been made up in March 1922, for the State election, and in it I finally found Jack Scott's address: 112 Wycombe Road, Neutral Bay.

Next day I drove up to 112. It turned out to be a convalescent home. I spoke to the manager, explaining I was doing some research into a literary work. He invited me in and from an upstairs window I could see a lighthouse, which Lawrence mentions was in sight from "51 Murdoch Street". We then went down into the back-garden. I was looking for the distinctive feature of "51 Murdoch Street" which Lawrence describes in the novel, a "tub-top" lookout that Somers mounts to view the Harbour below. There was nothing like that there now, so I asked the manager if he could recall a flowering tree in the garden (which Lawrence also mentions in *Kangaroo*). "No," he replied, "but perhaps Norm might." He called over an elderly man who was pottering nearby. Yes, he did recall such a tree. He used to lop it for the two ladies who ran the place when it was a guesthouse. Did he also recall some sort of lookout? Yes, he did. There used to be a fern-house in the garden which had a ladder going up to a lookout on top of it, built so guests could see over the house next door to the Harbour below. I now quote from *Kangaroo*:

> *There was a little round summer-house also, with a flat roof and steps going up. Somers mounted, and found that from the lead-covered roof of the little round place he could look down the middle harbour, and even see the low gateway, the low headlands with the lighthouse, opening to the full Pacific.* [K p12]

There was now no doubt in my mind that Lawrence had visited 112 Wycombe Road, and there encountered Jack Scott. Their paths had indeed crossed, probably within days of Lawrence's arrival in Sydney. The Quest for Cooley[26] was well-and-truly afoot.

I was also catching up on my reading of local source-material (which I would no longer have access to in London). To my considerable surprise, I discovered that the Rev John Alexander was not the first Australian to suspect that there was more to *Kangaroo* than had hitherto been assumed. In an article in 1968, Australian historian Don Rawson had

---

[26] I will explain below where Lawrence got the name "*Cooley*"

suggested[27] that Lawrence might have derived his fictional secret army from a local patriotic organisation, the King & Empire Alliance, and that the Alliance's leader Sir Charles Rosenthal might have been the inspiration for Benjamin Cooley in *Kangaroo*.

On my way back to London in February 1979, I made a detour to Austin, Texas, to see the manuscript (the *holograph*) of *Kangaroo* which the HRC there had recently acquired. (Among other things, I wanted to see the stubs of the "missing chapter" – see below.) Dr Roberts took me to a Tex-Mex lunch and we discussed *Kangaroo*. He was sorry about the CUP rejection, but was interested in what I had said in my proposal about the variant endings[28] of the novel. He regarded this as the major unanswered question hanging over the novel. He promised to send me an article[29] on the subject.[30]

Convinced now that I knew where Lawrence got the plot of *Kangaroo* from, I decided to bring together the interim results of my research for a book about Lawrence in Australia, to coincide with him coming out of copyright in 1981. I thought it was time to put my research cards on the table. Called *DH Lawrence in Australia*, it was published by Macmillan Australia in early 1981. I called it "a provisional hypothesis" because I knew that much more needed to be done before the full story of the composition of *Kangaroo* could finally be revealed. Shortly after the book-launch I was contacted by a researcher called John Ruffels who was interested in the area I was looking into (secret armies). He offered his help in the ongoing research. As I say in my acknowledgements above, his research skills proved to be of Bletchleyesque proportions, and he was responsible for many of the subsequent discoveries and insights. It was John who,

---

[27] in his "Political Violence in Australia" article [*Dissent* (autumn) Canberra pp 18-27]
[28] the UK Secker & the U.S. Seltzer endings (the latter ending 375 words short of the former)
[29] this was Dr F.P. Jarvis's 1965 article on the variant texts (see Research-Dairy 31/5/79 below)
[30] see my article "Not the End of the Story" *DHLR* vol 26, 1-3 [1996])

while I was away working in London for much of the 1980s, pushed the research forward in Australia. His main focus was the identity of the person on the "passenger list of the boat that brought Lawrence to Sydney" who was, according to my Melbourne informant Ernest Whiting [see above], Lawrence's original contact in Sydney, and who introduced him to those involved in the secret army. John obtained the passenger lists of the three boats that took Lawrence to Sydney (*Osterley* from Naples to Colombo; *Orsova* from Colombo to Perth; and *Malwa* from Perth to Sydney). He started cross-referencing the names with people Lawrence might have come in contact with in Sydney who could have been involved with political plotting. And for almost a decade we thought we had a likely suspect. We knew[31] that a passenger on *Malwa*, Captain Bertie Scrivener, was met on the wharf in Sydney by his mother, a local society figure, whose main cause was the Harbour Lights Guild, the female auxiliary of an Anglican charity that arranged concerts for visiting seamen. What alerted our particular interest was that chapter 3 of *Kangaroo* is called "Larboard-Watch Ahoy!" because that is the name of a sea-shanty Jack Callcott had sung, according to the text, at a "*Habour Lights concert*" K p43. Yet, try as we may (and we tried very, very hard), we could find no link between the Scriveners and secret armies in Sydney. It turned out to be one of the many false trails – red herrings – that John and I were drawn down in the 1980s.

However, an important breakthrough came when I obtained from a collection of Frieda's papers at the University of California at Berkeley a copy of the address-book Lawrence had kept at this period in his life. In it, at last, we found a Sydney contact (moreover, it was the <u>only</u> Sydney-based name in the address-book). It was of a "DG Hum", and his name proved to have been on the *Osterley* [Naples-Colombo]

---

[31] from a report in a contemporary issue of *The Bulletin*

passenger list, along with the Lawrences.[32] John started tracking down everything he could about David Gerald Hum, a travelling salesman from Chatswood, Sydney. Given that he was almost certainly Lawrence's only contact in Sydney, it seemed likely that they renewed their acquaintance when the Lawrences came ashore from *Malwa*.

In 1989 Joe Davis, a school-teacher who grew up in Thirroul, published his *DH Lawrence at Thirroul,* an account of Lawrence's time in that South Coast township. Joe went on to write a doctoral thesis on Lawrence and Thirroul, and his local knowledge and research advanced the cause of Lawrence studies in Australia. In 1992, Joe and other local Lawrentians joined us in a campaign to save *Wyewurk,* Lawrence's "cottage by the sea" in Thirroul. We managed to get a preservation order put on the bungalow, and soon after that we harnessed the support we had received to start the DH Lawrence Society of Australia. (I became its vice-president and Sandra its secretary. Joe Davis declined to join our committee.) The society publishes a journal called *Rananim,* which continues until today, but is now online.[33]

In 1994 I was sent over to Perth to take charge of some mining publications, and while there Sandra in particular did some valuable research. We visited Leithdale, "Mollie" Skinner's guest-house at Darlington, where the Lawrences stayed while in Western Australia. We saw where Lawrence probably had his evening walk and encountered *"the spirit of the bush"*[34]. Through a contact at the State library, Sandra tracked down relatives of "Maudie" Cohen whom Lawrence sat next to at Leithdale and who was to provide some of the

---

[32] they both boarded the boat at Naples (& may have been put at the same dining table)
[33] Copies of *Rananim* can be accessed at http://www.dhlawrencesocietyaustralia.com.au/ One of its first articles explained the paradox of Lawrence & Frieda's repeated insistence that they "knew no one" in Australia. The article ("Letters of Introduction" [*Rananim* vol 1 no 1 1993 pp 4-9]) explained that what they meant was that no one knew who they were.
[34] the holograph wording, subsequently changed by Lawrence to "the spirit of the place" [*K* p14]

background of Victoria Callcott in *Kangaroo*.[35] Sandra also traced Mrs Frances Zabel, the proprietor of the Booklovers Library in Perth, where in 1922 Lawrence had held court (and where he met a local literary identity, William Siebenhaar[36], whose book he later helped to get published).

It was while we were in Perth that I obtained a copy of the new CUP edition of *Kangaroo*, edited by Melbourne academic Dr Bruce Steele. I was not surprised to learn that Dr Steele, who had already edited another Lawrence work for the CUP (and was going to go on to edit another), had – as we say in Australia – rubbished my research on Lawrence and *Kangaroo*.[37] Although I did not fully realise it at the time, the world of Lawrence scholarship was beginning to turn against me.

On the other hand, it was while I was in Perth, for those few brief months in 1974, that events (outside academia) began, paradoxically, to move in my direction. Before we went to Perth I had received a phone call from my secret-army research colleague, Andrew Moore (Dr Moore by now was a lecturer in Australian history at the University of Western Sydney). His publishers had passed on a letter from the archivist at the King's School in Sydney, Peter Yeend. Its gravamen was startling. In May 1974 – 18 months before we came back to Sydney to begin our Lawrence/*Kangaroo* research – Yeend had spoken to a King's old boy (he was interviewing former students for the school records) who told him that in the 1930s he had belonged to "the secret organisation that 'the Lady Chatterley author' had portrayed [in *Kangaroo*]". In a follow-up interview, Yeend said his

---

[35] the relatives of "Maudie" Cohen confirmed that some of the family-background Lawrence attached to Victoria Callcott (father a surveyor, etc) was in fact the family-background of "Maudie" Cohen – see "Take Me to Your Liedertafel" by Sandra Jobson (Darroch) [*Rananim* vol 6, no 2 October 1998 pp 8-12].
[36] Siebenhaar, a supporter of the banned IWW, apparently furnished Lawrence with a letter-of-introduction to "Jock" Garden in Sydney, who was to become the character "Willie" Struthers in *Kangaroo* (see below).
[37] which, he said, "had now been shown to be without foundation" (*Steele* p xxviii)

informant told him that Lawrence had "stayed in a cottage provided by the Friend family in Thirroul" (see below - the cottage was obviously *Wyewurk*) "who publicly denied they told Lawrence about the rural army". From Perth I then took over corresponding with Yeend. In the ensuing months and years, he did his best to extract from the paranoiacally-reticent Friend family more about their involvement with Lawrence in 1922. (With little success, for although Yeend did manage to obtain more about "the Friend connection", it wasn't until 2011 – almost 15 years later – that I finally managed to prise open that final door, and reach the penultimate end of my Quest for Cooley – see my final Introduction-paragraph below.)

As I read the CUP *Kangaroo* in Perth, I was particularly interested to see what ending Bruce Steele had chosen for his edition of the novel (or rather what argument he had brought to bear on that choice). It quickly became obvious to me[38] that he had blundered. He had chosen the wrong ending for *Kangaroo* (the Seltzer rather than the longer Secker). I told Dr Roberts this and he encouraged me to write an article for the *DHLR* about it, which he later arranged to be published.[39] (These events in Perth – the Yeend letters and the CUP blunder – did much to raise my flagging spirits.)

They were further elevated by a letter I received from Andrew Moore soon after I returned to Sydney, enclosing a thesis written by a student in (of all things) town-planning at (of all places) the University of New England in northern NSW. (If ever something came out of left-field, this was it.)

---

[38] See *Research-Diary* 6/10/94: "I have now analysed Steele's argument for the Seltzer ending, & although I myself originally cleaved to this ending, I now suspect that he is wrong, mainly because of his explanation of how Lawrence's 'last page' came about. It is inconceivable that this Secker 'last page' is not the same last page Lawrence sent Seltzer on 4/1/23, yet Steele alleges just that [indeed, his argument for the shorter Seltzer ending depends on it]. I am convinced he has blundered. Moreover, I think I now know what happened: how the different endings did come about. I may do an article on this."

[39] Without his imprimatur, it would never have been published. (I may be wrong, but I got the impression that the American end of the Lawrence world was not altogether happy with what was happening at its British end.)

The thesis was about a man called George Augustine Taylor, the editor/publisher of a journal called *Building*, who (according to the student) had espoused fascist beliefs. What had alerted Andrew's attention was that Taylor was a close friend and colleague of Sir Charles Rosenthal. Apparently, Taylor had written a book in 1915 called *The Sequel* in which the main character was called Cooley. The (perceptive, not to say prescient) student wondered if the author of *Kangaroo* had read *The Sequel* and had got the surname of the novel's secret-army leader Benjamin Cooley from it. That was certainly a possibility that called to be followed up.

In fact, there were a number of things about Taylor that deserved further investigation. A man of many talents, he was the first man in Australia to fly in a heavier-than-air aircraft. Yet it was where that flight happened in December 1909 that particularly interested me. For it took place off some sand-dunes near the entrance to Narrabeen lagoon, a matter of yards from where Lawrence and Frieda had lain on that same sand on their first full day in Sydney in May 1922. Surely, that could not have been coincidence.

However, it is here that my third research colleague (see Acknowledgements above) in my Quest for Cooley came on the scene. A fellow-member of my club in Sydney, Robert Whitelaw had become interested in my Lawrence research, and volunteered to help. He focussed on the passage in *Kangaroo* in which Lawrence described his visit to Narrrabeen that late autumn Sunday in 1922, and the house where, according to the novel, Richard Lovatt Somers and his wife Harriett had afternoon-tea, and first meet "Jack Callcott" (aka Jack Scott[40]).

> *Harriet sat up and began dusting the sand from her coat--Lovat did likewise. Then they rose to be going back to the*

---

[40] Callcott [mark #2] – see below for this dual categorisation

> tram-car. There was a motor-car standing on the sand of the road near the gate of <u>the end house</u>...It was quite a nice little place, standing on a bluff of sand sideways above the lagoon. [K p29, my emphasis]

I had long believed that the *"end house"* held an important clue which might lead to the end of my Quest for Cooley. For it was at such an *"end house"* where Lawrence, I was now convinced, first encountered Jack Scott (in the guise of Jack Callcott), and which then gave him the beginning of his storyline for his Australian "romance". However, for more than 20 years I had believed the *"end house"* was a bungalow called *Hinemoa*, not at Narrabeen, but in the next suburb south, Collaroy. My belief, which I had thought was rock-solid, was founded on what Scott's stepsons had told me [in 1976] about the house Scott had visit them in 1922. In *Kangaroo*, Lawrence described the *"end house"* in some detail...

> The bungalow was pleasant, a large room facing the sea, with verandahs and other little rooms opening off. There were many family photographs, and a framed medal and ribbon and letter praising the first Trewhella. [K ibid]

...and the stepsons assured me that was a precise description (when I read it out to them) of *Hinemoa* at Collaroy.[41] Yet I could find no way to get Lawrence and Frieda back from Narrabeen to Collaroy, more than five miles away, to have an opportunity to observe (and for Lawrence to describe) the interior of *Hinemoa*. Aware of my dilemma, Robert Whitelaw tried to find out if there could also have been an *"end house"* at Narrabeen (where Lawrence had so ostentatiously positioned it), and whom might have lived there. After some

---

[41] that photograph, medal, ribbon & letter could not have been viewed anywhere else than in *Hinemoa* at Collaroy

diligent research, he discovered that there had indeed been an *"end house"* at Narrabeen, opposite where Harriett and Somers had fictionally reclined in the sand. Moreover, it was not only (as Lawrence described it) *"sideways above the lagoon"*, but matched Lawrence's description of it in every respect – apart from its interior (the framed photograph, etc). Much more significantly, Robert could place not only George Augustine Taylor there, but (vastly more importantly) also Charles Rosenthal – the Benjamin Cooley in Lawrence's novel.[42]

But now, before I conclude, I have to digress. Early in my research I had come across a memoir of Lawrence written by his childhood friend, George Neville.[43] In it Neville described some of the transformation techniques Lawrence deployed to disguise the real people and actual events he was portraying in his fiction. Neville wrote: "...he deliberately mixed up a portion of an experience he underwent...His works are full of such transpositions." Back in 1974 in Perth I had come to believe that many events and characters in *Kangaroo* were probably a combination of real events and real people, conflated by Lawrence using various transformation techniques when he wanted to write about real people and actual places (yet felt he could not use actual names, for fear of offending – or identifying – people). For example, I had come to believe that Jack Callcott was not only modelled on Jack Scott, but on a second person as well (who was a member of the Friend family, whom Lawrence turned into Jack Callcott [mark #1][44]).

Yet a seemingly intractable problem now faced me. How did what I knew to be the interior of *Hinemoa* come to be put into the *"end house"* five miles away at Narrabeen? What was the connection? It turned out that the connecting link was

---

[42] see photo of Taylor & Rosenthal at "*the end house*" at Narrabeen in the *photo-insert* (also see "The Man Who Wasn't There" [*Rananim* vol 10, no 2 May 2002]).
[43] *A Memoir of DH Lawrence (The Betrayal)* [CUP 1981]
[44] see main text below about the Callcott [mark#1] & [mark #2] categorisation

the car parked outside the end-house that Sunday afternoon (*There was a motor-car standing on the sand of the road* [K p28]). It was the big Nash tourer that belonged to Gerald Hum, who had invited the Lawrences to afternoon-tea that Sunday at Narrabeen, and who had a holiday cottage at neighbouring Collaroy.   In *Kangaroo*, at the conclusion of the afternoon-tea at Narrabeen (*"where they first met Jaz"*), Somers is offered a "lift" back to town by car, and the narrative goes on to describe that return trip.   Yet as Hum was staying the weekend at nearby Collaroy, he could not have driven Lawrence and Frieda all the way back to Sydney (for he would have wanted to return that evening to his holiday house in Collaroy Basin). So he must have first driven them the one suburb back to Collaroy, where they must have changed cars, then to be driven back into town by someone else (whose [Friend] car was parked at a nearby address). To get from Hum's holiday address in Seaview Parade to that other person's address in Beach Road, they must have walked along a beach-track that went past *Hinemoa*, where Jack Scott's future wife (and two stepsons) were now living. Scott, who had accompanied them back to Hum's holiday address that afternoon, must have suggested they pop in to *Hinemoa*, along the beach-track, to be introduced to the future Mrs Scott[45], and to wait there until the Friends' car blew its horn outside. And it was there, waiting in the living-room of *Hinemoa*, that Lawrence obtained his description for the interior of the *"end house"* at Narrabeen (thus "fictionalising" it, using his customary amalgamation/conflation techniques).

This also gave me, as an unexpected bonus, not only the identity of "the other half" of Jack Callcott (Adrian Friend – see main text below), but also "the other half" of his wife Victoria[46], they being the two members of the Friend family

---

[45] &, no doubt, also to pick up his things (he had probably been staying there over the weekend), as he may have wanted to spend more time with Lawrence on the drive back to town
[46] *ie*, "Fanny" Friend (the "other half" being "Maudie" Cohen in Western Australia)

(Adrian and "Fanny"[47] Friend) whom the Lawrences had also met earlier that Sunday afternoon at Narrabeen (and who told them that *Wyewurk* was vacant, and who next day took them down to Thirroul, where they then became their next-door neighbours in *Wyewurrie*).

My long Quest for Cooley apparently concluded with the death in 2011 of the member of the Friend family who had latterly come to be my main source of information about the reclusive Friends. In an email to me, his widow confirmed the identity of Adrian and "Fanny" Friend as the hitherto unnamed young married couple who, as the Kings School archivist had told me in 1974,[48] took Lawrence and Frieda down to Thirroul, and installed them in *Wyewurk*.

My four-decade-long quest had come to its end, at last (or so I thought[49]). It was time to tell the rest of the world how *Kangaroo* came to be written (so now read on).

---

[47] on p21 of the holograph manuscript of *Kangaroo* Lawrence wrote what appears to be the name "Fanny", but immediately crossed it out (replacing it with "Harriett")
[48] see *Research-Diary* 20/10/93 below
[49] however, at the time I wrote those words – in 2016 – I had yet to appreciate the full homoerotic implications of "The Curious Incident of the Red Wooden Heart" (see *Appendix 1*)

CHAPTER 1

Where it Begins

AUSTRALIA, for Lawrence, is[50] a detour on his way from Europe to America.[51] He was in Ceylon, staying with some American friends, when the local climate became too hot and oppressive[52], so he decided to revert to his original intention to travel on to America, where his writing was beginning to be appreciated, and which offered the prospect of providing him with the income – primarily from the sales of his recently-published novel *Women in Love* – he so desperately needs to continue his struggling writing career.[53] He has two choices: to travel back westwards to Europe, and leave for America from there; or go in the other direction, and approach America via the Pacific. The latter seemed the more convenient route, as boats leave regularly from Colombo on their way to Australia and Sydney, from where it is relatively easy to take passage to the west coast of America, which is closer to his ultimate destination – Taos in New Mexico.

Earlier, on the voyage from Naples to Colombo aboard RMS *Osterley*, he encountered some Australian fellow-passengers, and struck up an acquaintance with several of them.[54] "The people on board are mostly simple Australians.

---

[50] where possible I will preference the present tense when referring to Lawrence's daily activities in Australia – as they happen – & reserve the past tense for what occurred earlier
[51] Lawrence wrote to his literary friend Koteliansky on April 17 informing him of his intention to go to Australia, saying "it seems to me en route" [*Letters* #2496]
[52] "We…find Ceylon too hot & enervating." [*Letters* #2500 (to fellow writer Catherine Carswell)]
[53] While he was in Australia, Lawrence's hitherto precarious financial position changed (though he was yet to realise this), due to the increasing American royalties from *Women in Love*. Thereafter, he never had to worry much about money.
[54] John Ruffels (see Acknowledgements) tracked down the passenger lists of the three boats that took Lawrence to Australia. On the first, RMS *Osterley* (Naples-Colombo), Lawrence met two Australians who were to prove useful to him – David Gerald Hum (who, like Lawrence, boarded at Naples, & was to be Lawrence's initial contact in Sydney) & Mrs Annie Louisa

I believe Australia is a good country, full of life and energy...I shall go to Australia if we can manage it," he told a friend.[55] Thus the possibility of travelling on to Australia from Ceylon was already forming in his mind on his "passage to India". Before disembarking in Colombo, two of the Australians gave him their addresses in Australia, should he decide to go in that direction. He writes to both of them from Kandy, telling them of his intention to do so, and giving one of them, his fellow *Osterley* passenger Mrs A.L. "Pussy" Jenkins, as his forwarding address in Western Australia. He and Frieda board the P&O liner *Orsova* on April 24 and arrive at Fremantle – the port for Perth, the State capital of Western Australia – in late autumn, after a 10-day voyage.

Lawrence knows a good deal more about Australia than the average – even well-informed – Englishman. He has some picture of where it was and what sort of place it is. His omnivorous reading would have turned up numerous references to Australia (he had read at least one Australian novel, Rolf Boldrewood's *Robbery Under Arms*, and was also familiar with the poetry of the bush-balladist Henry Lawson).[56] At one point, Lawrence and Frieda even considered emigrating, or perhaps even eloping, to Australia. Around the same time, he wrote to a friend, who was herself planning to go to Australia, telling her: "Australia is a new country, new morals: it is not a split from England, but a new nation."[57] Alas, this positive image was tarnished when he came to put an Australian into his 1920 novel, *The Lost Girl*. The Australian, Alexander Graham, a doctor gaining experience in England, is described as *"creepy"*, with a body *"which seemed to move inside his clothing"*. He also has *"a strong*

"Pussy" Jenkins (a 49-year-old widow & member of one of Western Australia's most prominent families, who made regular trips to the UK, often following the Australian cricket team).

[55] DHL-Rosalind Baynes [*Letters* #2472 (8/3/22)]

[56] see David Game's *D.H. Lawrence's Australia* [Ashgate (UK) 2015] for a survey of Lawrence's Australian reading

[57] [*Letters* #468 (Lawrence-May Holbrook 13/7/12)] at that time Lawrence & Frieda were enjoying something of a honeymoon, travelling from Germany to Italy

mouthful of cruel compact teeth"[58], a man, the heroine's mother observed, not to be trusted. On whom this reptilian creature was based is not known. He may have been suggested by an Australian that Lawrence could have encountered at one of the musical evenings he attended at the Australian pianist Florence Wood's home in London in 1910.

On his arrival in Western Australia he is interviewed at the wharf by a local freelance journalist, Frances Zabel.[59] He told her, she reported next day, that he planned to stay some time, and hoped to visit the apple-growing regions south of Perth, which Mrs Jenkins had apparently told him about. Mrs Zabel also ran the local Booklovers' Library in Perth, and she invited him to visit her bookshop, which was something of a meeting place for the local literati. That night he and Frieda are put up at the pricey Savoy Hotel in Perth – he remarked about the cost – where Mrs Jenkins had booked them in (a few pounds meant little to the well-off "Pussy" Jenkins). Two days later Mrs Jenkins' chauffeur-driven car takes them to Darlington in the hills a short distance outside the city, where they have a "bush-picnic" by the side of the road, before going on to *Leithdale*, a guesthouse-cum-convalescent-home run by a nurse, "Mollie" Skinner[60], who is a distant relative of Mrs Jenkins. By now Lawrence had picked up his mail from Mrs Jenkins, including, almost certainly, a letter of reply from his other *Osterley* fellow-passenger Gerald Hum, which no doubt reiterated an earlier offer to assist him if he were to come on to Sydney.[61] If Lawrence were to spend time in Australia (he needs to wait for funds from his American agent Mountsier to be forwarded to him), he would no doubt prefer to spend it at

---

[58] *The Lost Girl* [CUP 1981 (John Worthen ed.)] p22
[59] Mrs Zabel was a "stringer" for a local Perth newspaper, & her interview with Lawrence appeared in the next day's paper (see "Take Me to Your Liedertafel" [*Rananim* vol 6, no 2 (October 1998) pp 8-12])
[60] see *Fifth Sparrow* for details about "Mollie" Skinner, & specifically p110 for her account of Lawrence's arrival at *Leithdale*
[61] When Lawrence wrote to Hum from Kandy, he knew he could not receive a reply from him before he left Ceylon. So Hum's response would have had to be sent to Lawrence's forwarding address in Perth (*ie*, care of Mrs Jenkins at her home in Perth, "Strawberry Hills").

his ultimate port of departure. So instead of going south to see the apple-growing regions, he books passage on the next available boat to Sydney, due to sail a week hence.

The week or so Lawrence and Frieda spend in Western Australia, mostly with "Mollie" Skinner at *Leithdale*, is significant, and will play a role in the new novel he will decide to write while in Australia. He went to Ceylon with a vague intention to write "a Ceylon novel", but there is no evidence that he came to Australia with any intention of writing "an Australian novel". However, he did arrive with a problem. After his sixth novel – *The Lost Girl*, completed in 1920 – he was having problems composing a major new fictional work (as distinct from his travel-writing, essays, poetry, short stories, and translations). His next novel, *Aaron's Rod*, (his seventh) had caused him many worries.[62] Earlier he had attempted to write a novel about Robert Burns, but that did not get very far. He then tried to write what he called "his Venice novel", but that too came to nothing. One difficulty seems to be that he had run out of, or exhausted, his autobiographical, or first-hand, material. *Sons and Lovers* took care of his childhood, and *The Rainbow* and *Women in Love* his early adult life. He had used some of his post-war and travel experiences in *Aaron's Rod* (and also in the then-unfinished *Mr Noon*[63]). Now, Ceylon having failed to inspire his muse, he was no doubt looking forward to America to provide him with the ingredients he might need for a new fictional work. Although he didn't go to Australia intending to write an Australian novel, the problem of what he might write next was certainly on his mind. (He is also, on and off, translating from Italian the works of the Sicilian author Giovanni Verga, and he continues with this task in Australia.)

---

[62] he claimed that he had only managed to finish *Aaron* while sitting under a tree in the Black Forest [see *Fantasia* chapter 4, "Trees & Babies & Papas & Mamas" & *Letters* iv p133 & p259]
[63] he had abandoned this autobiographical novel in early 1921 (in part ii of which the Lawrence character, Gilbert Noon, is to all intents the same person as Richard Lovatt Somers in *Kangaroo*)

He is also, apparently, considering what sort of writing he might do next, for the workings of his creative mind had exercised his thoughts recently. The major work he wrote before he arrived in Australia, *Fantasia of the Unconscious*, is an exploration into his literary processes, and is a very odd book. It seems to reflect the difficulties he is having composing new fiction. Perhaps of equal interest is his earlier book of travel-writing, *Sea and Sardinia*, which he composed in the form of a diary. He apparently regarded the diary technique as successful[64], for while at Darlington he recommended a diary-method of novel-writing to "Mollie" Skinner. Most fortunately, Miss Skinner has left a record of Lawrence's advice on novel-writing, which turns out to be especially germane in the context the novel he himself was to start composing a few weeks later.

In her autobiography, *The Fifth Sparrow*[65], she tells how Lawrence accosted her while she was hanging out sheets in the backyard of *Leithdale*. He urged her, if she wanted to be an author, to write an account of her early life in colony. She told him she didn't think she could do that, because she had so little education, and would need to work to support herself. He told her that she could do it if she put aside a time each day to write. "What about the story?" she asked him. "You need no story," he told her. "What about construction?" she asked. "You need none," he replied, telling her to just "splash down reality"…

> …you can take an hour – the same hour – that's very important – daily. Write bit by bit of the scenes you have witnessed, the people you know, describing their reactions as you know they do react, not as you imagine they should….Write and build up from day to day.

---

[64] he later tells fellow-novelist Catherine Carswell: "Myself I like that letter-diary form." (by "letter-diary" he was probably referring to a diarist's daily recording of events, etc) [*Letters* #2548 (22/6/22) p270]

[65] *Fifth Sparrow*, pp 115-116

> When you've done 80,000 words, throw down your pen.
> [*The Fifth Sparrow*, pp 115-116]

"Mollie" Skinner did not follow this advice. When she came to contribute her part of the novel she and Lawrence were to co-author some time later (*The Boy in the Bush*[66]), it carried no relationship to quotidian events. There was no "splashing down of reality". Yet this technique was precisely the approach Lawrence himself chose to adopt when he started writing *Kangaroo* some weeks later (down to setting aside the same writing-hour each day).

It is indicative – given what happens later in Sydney (where he kept his literary identity under wraps) – that Lawrence in Perth basked in what notoriety that came with him.[67] He held court in Mrs Zabel's Booklovers Library, and makes contact with several local writers. One of them, William Siebenhaar, a local public servant and a supporter of the banned Industrial Workers of the World (IWW), shows him some of his literary efforts, and Lawrence later helps him publish his *magnum opus*.

Several incidents in Western Australia were to become part of *Kangaroo*, Lawrence's main Australian novel (and his eighth major work of fiction). Perhaps his most vivid experience is a walk in the bush at night. Suddenly he feels afraid, as if there is something sinister in the tall, white gums around him, *"like naked pale Aborigines"*[K p14]. He hurries back to *Leithdale*, deciding that what he encountered in the bush is *"the spirit of the place"*[68]. He will put his description of this incident into the opening chapter of *Kangaroo*.[K pp 14-15]

At *Leithdale*, "Mollie" Skinner put the Lawrences at the

---

[66] Seltzer [New York 1924] & CUP [1990.(Paul Eggert, ed.)].
[67] see "Letters of Introduction" [*Rananim* vol 1 no 1 (1993) pp 4-9]
[68] This is an expression much used by Lawrence, before & after *Kangaroo*. Later in 1923, when he revised what became *Studies in Classic American Literature*, he called the first chapter "The Spirit of Place". However, in the original *holograph* text of *Kangaroo* he initially wrote "the spirit of the <u>bush</u>" – hence the word "the" in what would otherwise have been, as it later was, the "spirit of place".

same dining-room table as a young honeymooning couple, the Eustace Cohens, thinking that, as she believed the Cohens were "intellectual", they might prove interesting companions for Lawrence.[69] He strikes up a casual friendship with "Maudie" Cohen and chats with her in the evening on the verandah of *Leithdale,* as she waits for her husband to return on his motorcycle[70] from his architect's office in Perth. Lawrence has an ability to draw people out, and what "Maudie" tells him about her background will provide some of the ingredients for the principal Australian female character in *Kangaroo*, Victoria Callcott.[71]

Kangaroo apart, the major source of information about Lawrence's time in Australia – he arrived in Western Australia on May 4, 1922, and left from Sydney 99 days later on August 11 – are the 52 surviving letters he writes there, some to local Australians like Mrs Jenkins. Significantly, the letters he posts from Perth give no indication that he intends to write anything in, or about, Australia. In fact, over a week later (in a letter apparently written aboard ship to Sydney, but posted from Thirroul) he tells one correspondent he has "sent his muse to a nunnery".[72]

Yet five days later, on Friday May 26, he tells his American agent Mountsier (in a postscript written aboard *Malwa*, also later posted from Thirroul): "I shall try New South Wales, to see if I want to stop there & write a novel."[73] This sudden change of mind was probably made between his arrival in Melbourne[74] on Tuesday May 23 and Friday May 26, the day before he arrived in Sydney. The abruptness, indeed

---

[69] "Mollie" Skinner described Eustace as "a brilliant artist & musician" (he was an architect by profession) & "Maudie" as "delightful…& vivacious" [*Fifth Sparrow*, p111]
[70] Lawrence will borrow Eustace Cohen's motorcycle from Darlington & give it to Jack Callcott [mark 1, *ie* Adrian Friend] in chapter 1 of his new novel [*K* p16]
[71] for more about "Maudie" Cohen, see "Pussy Jenkins & Her Circle" by Sandra Darroch [*Rananim* vol 4, no 2-3 p20]
[72] He tells Amy Lowell: "I am enjoying the face of the earth & letting my Muse, dear hussy, repent her ways. 'Get thee to a nunnery' I said to her. Heaven knows if we shall ever see her face again, unveiled, uncoiffed." [*Letters* #2520 (20/5/22)]
[73] [*Letters* #2523 (26/5/22 misdated "25 May")]
[74] *en route* to Sydney, *Malwa* stops briefly in Adelaide & then two days & one night in Melbourne

the unexpectedness, of this decision may imply that something had occurred in Melbourne that changed or obliged him to change his mind about sending his muse to a nunnery. The likelihood is that aboard ship he received a letter[75] from Mountsier informing him that there were insufficient funds in his U.S. bank account to pay for onward fares. To him, that meant that he would probably need to stay in Australia some considerable time until sufficient money could accumulate in his New York bank account to finance his onward travel. The decision to launch into writing a novel in Australia seems to have been the result, or consequence, of such a letter from Mountsier.[76]

Usefully, we may now be able to pinpoint precisely when Lawrence decided to write something in Australia. The clue here is his letter to Mountsier dated May 25. It was written on *Malwa* notepaper and in it he wrote: "The human life [here] seems to me to very barren: one could never make a novel our of these people, they haven't got any insides to them, to write about." Yet in the very next paragraph of the same initially-dated letter he wrote (as mentioned above): "I shall try New South Wales, to see if I want to stop there and write a novel." It is highly likely that in fact these two paragraphs were written on different days – the first on May 25 in Melbourne, as originally dated, and the second (and the remainder of the letter) <u>after</u> he opened Mountsier's letter posted to the ship in Melbourne. Indeed, this scenario is confirmed in the second paragraph of the letter, which began: "We arrive in Sydney tomorrow morning."[77] So we may now deduce that his decision to write a novel in Australia – the genesis of *Kangaroo* – was taken between leaving Melbourne on May 25 and arriving in Sydney on May 27.[78]

---

[75] in those days of ship-travel it was the custom for letters to passengers on board to be sent to the various ports on their route, to be distributed after the ship left that port
[76] the correspondence between Mountsier & Lawrence has not survived
[77] *ie*, Saturday, May 27
[78] probably on Thursday, May 26

Lawrence in fact added two postscripts to his "May 25" letter, both misdated "Thirroul 28 May"[79]. In one of the postscripts he elaborated on what sort of novel he had in mind, telling Mountsier: "I am going to write a romance – or begin one – while I'm here & we are alone."[80] It may be that the key to what Lawrence intended to do with his new novel is to be found in what he meant by the term "a romance". In his CUP edition, Bruce Steele cites Nathaniel Hawthorne's Preface to *The House of Seven Gables* where Hawthorne – one of the authors Lawrence wrote about in his *Studies in Classic in American Literature* – said that, when a writer calls his work a romance, "he wishes to claim a certain latitude, both as to its fashion & material"[81]. I believe that Steele was perceptive to focus on those words "certain latitude" in the context of *Kangaroo*. Steele, however, did not go on to venture an opinion as to what sort of latitude Lawrence might have had in mind.

Given Lawrence's previous problems completing a novel, for him to suddenly launch into writing a new novel was a bold **decision** for him to have taken, and up till now it has been something of a mystery why his muse had decided to emerge from her cloisters. Not much had happened to Lawrence in Western Australia, nor on the voyage around the bottom of the continent, that might provide him with the ingredients he would need for a new fictional work. Although he had his recent Italian and Ceylon experiences to call on, he doesn't.[82] Yet he now tells his American agent that he will only *try* to write a romance. Maybe he is considering some new approach – indeed, some "latitude" – that he might help him compose a new work of fiction…perhaps the "splash-down-reality" advice he had recommended to

---

[79] for they were almost certainly written on Tuesday, May 30, as a footnote in CUP *Letters* perceptively pointed out [vol 4, p244]
[80] [*Letters* #2530]
[81] [Steele p xxii]
[82] substantively, that is (for he later writes a poem, "Elephant", about his time in Ceylon)

"Mollie" Skinner before he left Perth.

Nevertheless, whatever he was planning to write would have to be slapped down pretty quickly, if he intended to finish it in Australia (which apparently he did). In his Tuesday May 30 postscript to Mountsier, Lawrence informed him that he was planning to sail to America either by the *Marama*, leaving on July 6, or the *Sonoma*, leaving on July 12 (the former departure date being only 37 days hence). If he were – as it now seems he likely – to follow the novel-writing advice he had given to "Mollie" Skinner ("write 80,000 words...and throw down your pen"), he would have needed to write around 2200 words a day to finish his new Australian novel before he departed. As we shall see, that rate was well within his compass, even if he did not write each day. So he was by no means setting himself an impossible task...assuming that he could find something to write about.

Malwa arrives off Sydney Heads before dawn on Saturday May 27, and docks at east Circular Quay about 7.30 am.

CHAPTER 2

Sydney and First Impressions

LAWRENCE in *Kangaroo* – the new "romance" he will start writing five days later on Wednesday, May 31 – describes Frieda's first glimpse of Sydney Harbour, in the words of Harriett Somers, his fictional wife:

I remember looking out of the porthole and seeing that Lighthouse, just as we came in – and those little brown cliffs. Oh, but it's a wonderful harbour. What it must have been when it was first discovered. [K p12]

Later in the novel Lawrence also recalls that first morning in Sydney:

For some reason he felt absolutely wretched and dismal on that Saturday morning when the ship came into Sydney harbour…When he came on deck after breakfast and the ship had stopped, it was pouring with rain, the P. and O. wharf looked black and dismal, empty. It might almost have been an abandoned city. He walked round to the starboard side, to look towards the unimposing hillock of the city and the Circular Quay. Black, all black and unutterably dismal in the pouring rain, even the green grass of the Botanical Gardens, and the bits of battlement of the Conservatorium. Unspeakably forlorn. Yet over it all, spanning the harbour, the most magnificent great rainbow. His mood was so miserable he didn't want to see it. But it was unavoidable. A huge, brilliant, supernatural rainbow, spanning all Sydney. [K p156]

Sydney and First Impressions

After disembarking, they are almost certainly met at the wharf by Gerald Hum, their former *Osterley* shipboard acquaintance, and the only person they know in Sydney.[83] Lawrence probably wrote to him from Perth giving him their arrival details. No doubt it was Hum who has booked them into a private hotel[84] in nearby Macquarie Street. Yet he does not accompany them there, as Saturday in Sydney is a working day, and he would need to be at his office that morning (he sells hats, wholesale). He probably tells them, when the various arrival formalities are eventually completed, to engage a taxi at the rank outside the P&O wharf – they would have had their cabin baggage with them – and ask to be taken to Mrs Scott's establishment at 126 Macquarie Street.

Sydney taxi drivers are, notoriously, a rapacious breed, and new arrivals by boat provide fresh victims for them. Lawrence is overcharged for the short trip, the taxi-driver demanding "'Shilling apiece, them bags'"[K p9] for each item of luggage – four times the normal tariff of thrippence. No doubt the cabbie, having queued for some time at the rank outside the wharf waiting for a "fare", is miffed that they only want to be taken a few hundred yards up Macquarie Street. But Lawrence is in no position to argue, being as yet unversed in local customs (and Sydney cabbies counted on that). So the cabbie deposits them outside 126 and leaves them to carry their bags up the entrance steps into Mrs Scott's homely "budget" accommodation. (Lawrence had probably warned Hum that they could not afford to stay at expensive hotels, like the Savoy in Perth.)

After settling in, it seems that Lawrence took a walk

---

[83] Lawrence's decision in Perth to go on to Sydney straight away is best explained by having opened a letter waiting for him (with Mrs Jenkins) from Hum promising help in Sydney. So it is likely that Hum would have been at the wharf to meet Lawrence & Frieda. (Lawrence has his Chatswood home-address in the address-book he carries with him.)
[84] in essence, a guesthouse (Lawrence's description in *Kangaroo* of Somers' accommodation in Macquarie Street matches Mrs Scott's establishment at number 126, as listed in *Sands* [Sydney-street] *Directory*, & in contemporary photographs – *eg*, the steps up from the street)

further up Macquarie Street and down Martin Place to the local Thomas Cooks office, opposite the GPO (Sydney's main post office). By now he would have given Cooks as his Sydney forwarding-address, so he would have wanted to pick up what mail might be waiting for him.[85] (Lawrence is an experienced traveller, and always makes careful preparations for his onward journeys.[86]) He returns to Mrs Scott's for lunch and to read his letters. Suddenly there is the noise of a band in the street outside, and Frieda, who comes from a military family, insists on going out and seeing what's happening. Detachments of Boy Scouts are marching along Macquarie Street to a vice-regal reception at Government House, further down in the Domain.[87]

> The day was Saturday. Early in the afternoon Harriet went to the little front gate because she heard a band: or the rudiments of a band. Nothing would have kept her indoors when she heard a trumpet, not six wild Somerses. It was some very spanking Boy Scouts marching out. There were only six of them, but the road was hardly big enough to hold them. Harriet leaned on the gate in admiration of their dashing broad hats and thick calves. [K p17]

Lawrence, too, was to marvel at those Australian calves, later remarking: "*Somers wondered at the thick legs. They seemed to run to leg, these people.*"[K ibid]

After lunch they start exploring their new city, as any tourists might. Lawrence records his initial impressions –

---

[85] he no doubt also made inquiries about onward travel to America (hence the *Marama* & *Sonoma* sailing dates he mentions in footnotes next week)

[86] it was, for example, his practice to solicit letters-of-introduction to people in foreign places he intended to visit (again see "Letters of Introduction" [*Rananim* vol 1, no 1 (October 1993) pp 4-9])

[87] As reported in the *Sydney Morning Herald* [*SMH*] the following Monday [29/5/22 p10]. The event was in fact a parade & inspection (probably a hangover from the Empire Day celebrations the previous Thursday) attended by detachments of Boy Scouts from all over Sydney, some of whom no doubt did march down Macquarie Street to the Domain, where more than 1500 of them were addressed, in the Governor's absence, by the Lieutenant-Governor & Chief Scout, Sir William Cullen. (There must have been more than six, but that was probably just the band.)

which are not particularly favourable – in chapter 1 of *Kangaroo*:

> *Somers wandered disconsolate through the streets of Sydney, forced to admit that there were fine streets, like Birmingham for example; that the parks and the Botanical Gardens were handsome and well-kept; that the harbour, with all the two-Decker brown ferry-boats sliding continuously from the Circular Quay, was an extraordinary place. But oh, what did he care about it all! In Martin Place he longed for Westminster, in Sussex Street he almost wept for Covent Garden and St. Martin's Lane.* [K p20] [88]

Sussex Street is by no means a main thoroughfare in Sydney – lined as it was (and still is) with offices and commercial buildings – so it is an odd place for two tourists to go on their first day in town. However, at its bottom end, 10 or more city blocks back from the Harbour, are the main Sydney markets, called locally "the Haymarket" (hence Lawrence's reference to Covent Garden and St Martin's Lane – London's Haymarket precinct). The reason why Lawrence and Frieda go in that direction may be because he has in his pocket a letter-of-introduction to someone whose address is in Sydney's Haymarket, and he wants to check out where that address is. Apparently in Perth at least two people offered to provide him with onward contacts that might prove useful when he arrived in Sydney. Mrs Jenkins, for her part, provided him with a letter-of-introduction to Bert Toy[89], a staff member at the Sydney *Bulletin*, then Australia's national news/features magazine. (Lawrence is to use Bert Toy's Sydney address on that letter-of-introduction – 51 Murdoch

---

[88] note that Lawrence is already starting to "slap down reality"
[89] we know Mrs Jenkins gave Lawrence a letter-of-introduction to Toy, because he told her [*Letters* #2528] that he had found her letter to "Mr Toy" but he didn't know if he would present it

Street – in the text of *Kangaroo*.) The other letter-of-introduction was almost certainly given to him by his West Australian literary contact William Siebenhaar, and is no doubt addressed to "Jock" Garden, the secretary of the NSW Trades and Council, whose headquarters is the Trades Hall in the Haymarket. (Siebenhaar knows Garden because they are both involved in an ongoing campaign to free from gaol a number of IWW activists. Garden will play a significant role in the composition of *Kangaroo*, for he will come to be portrayed in the novel as the radical union leader, "Willie" Struthers.[90])

Lawrence and Frieda would have returned to 126 Macquarie Street for the evening meal and where Lawrence writes several letters, before retiring. He is already thinking – processing in his mind – what might go into his new "splash-down-reality" romance, starting with his first day in town. The first chapter, which he starts writing the following Wednesday, has his early observations of the Australian landscape. Sydney's blue harbour impresses him. He likens it to

> ...*a lake among the land, so pale blue and heavenly, with its hidden and half-hidden lobes intruding among the low, dark-brown cliffs, and among the dark-looking tree-covered shores, and up to the bright red suburbs. But the land, the ever-dark bush that was allowed to come to the shores of the harbour! It was strange that, with the finest of new air dimming to a lovely pale blue in the distance, and with the loveliest stretches of pale blue water, the tree-covered land should be so gloomy and lightless. It is the sun-refusing*

---

[90] It is deduction that his other contact in Perth, William Siebenhaar, also provided him with a letter-of-introduction, in his case to his fellow IWW-supporter "Jock" Garden (probably the only person of note in Sydney that Siebenhaar would have been in a position to address a letter-of-introduction to). The fact that Lawrence did go to see Garden (see my chapter 16 *The Row in Town*) makes it probable that Lawrence had such a letter, & moreover that he did "present it" (his identification as Struthers is confirmed, *inter alia*, by Garden's biographer as well as Garden's nephew ["Was Willie Struthers was My Uncle Jock?", *Ranamim* vol 2, no 1, 1994]).

> *leaves of the gum-trees that are like dark, hardened flakes of rubber.* [K p19]

During his first few days in Sydney, Lawrence seems to be searching for *"the spirit of the place"*.[91] He contrasts the new country with Europe, and finds the former wanting:

> *He was not happy; there was no pretending he was. He longed for Europe with hungry longing: Florence, with Giotto's pale tower: or the Pinkie at Rome: or the woods in Berkshire – heavens, the English spring with primroses under the bare hazel bushes, and thatched cottages among plum blossom. He felt he would have given anything on earth to be in England. It was May – end of May – almost bluebell time, and the green leaves coming out on the hedges. Or the tall corn under the olives in Sicily. Or London Bridge, with all the traffic on the river. Or Bavaria with gentian and yellow globe flowers, and the Alps still icy. Oh God, to be in Europe, lovely, lovely Europe.* [K pp 19-20] [92]

One thing that does impinge on him about his new country is its politics, or at least its political/social system:

> *Somers for the first time felt himself immersed in real democracy — in spite of all disparity in wealth. The instinct of the place was absolutely and flatly democratic, a terre democratic.*[93] *Demos was here his own master, undisputed, and therefore quite calm about it. No need to get the wind up at all over it; it was a granted condition of Australia, that Demos was his own master.* [K pp 21-22]

---

[91] see above re Lawrence's walk in the bush at Darlington where he encounters what he initially called *"the spirit of the bush"*
[92] now he is adding comment & other embellishments to the reality he is slapping down

Here, perhaps, might be a possible theme for his new "romance": the social and political differences between the old world and the new, seen from "Down Under" in New South Wales, observed by someone very much like himself. (This can also be taken as Lawrence's only substantive reference to "class" in Australia. By *"Demos was his own master"* he implies a classless society, or at least one without a formal class-structure, like England.)

Yet Lawrence has more pressing matters on his mind, the primary one being where he is going to stay in the coming days and weeks. (He now intends to stay at least five weeks.) By the time he arrived in Sydney he would not have much more than £50 in the *"little brown handbag"* he carries with him, probably in cash and Cooks travellers-cheques.[94] Accommodation in hotels and guest-houses in Sydney could be upwards of £1 a night. As he cannot afford to stay at such places any longer than strictly necessary, he must find cheaper accommodation, urgently. This is his most pressing need. Gerald Hum, his sole Sydney contact, is no doubt aware of this imperative. Which is probably why Hum – who has a holiday cottage north of the Harbour – has invited Lawrence and Frieda to come up to the northern beaches area of Sydney the following day to explore accommodation possibilities there (and perhaps to meet a few Sydneysiders).

---

[94] In mid-April Mountsier cabled $US1000 to him in Ceylon. On April 22 he told Mountsier he had only £90 of the $1000 left (having paid their onward fares to Sydney). He would have incurred expenses during his last few days in Ceylon, then on the boat & subsequently in Perth. He could not have had much more than £50 left by the time he arrived in Sydney,

CHAPTER 3

First Contact

ON SUNDAY May 28, their first full day in Sydney, Lawrence and Frieda take the Manly Ferry across Sydney Harbour, presumably departing from Circular Quay about 10am, arriving at Manly wharf around 11am. The autumn school holidays are just about to end, and Hum and his young family are staying at their regular holiday place at Collaroy, one of Sydney's northern beaches[95]. Hum has apparently invited the Lawrences to join them for afternoon tea at a friend's beach-house at nearby Narrabeen, an area where there are (in contrast to the more upmarket Collaroy) many inexpensive holiday cottages available for rent. Hum may have issued this invitation when he called in to Mrs Scott's later on Saturday to see how the Lawrences were settling in.

A pleasant way to go to Collaroy is by ferry to Manly, and then by tram up past the various northern beaches to the terminus at Narrabeen. But on arrival at Manly it is too early to board the tram, so Lawrence and Frieda pass some time in this popular beach location.[96]

> *It was Sunday, and a lovely sunny day of Australian winter. Manly is the bathing suburb of Sydney – one of them. You pass quite close to the wide harbour gate, The Heads, on the ferry steamer. Then you land on the wharf, and walk up the street, like a bit of Margate with sea-side shops and restaurants.* [K p28]

---

[95] as identified to John Ruffels by Gerald Hum's son in 1988 (see *Research-Diary* 21/5/88 below)
[96] promoted locally as being "Seven Miles from Sydney, and a Thousand Miles from Care"

The street they walk up is the Corso, which links Manly's wharf and Harbour beach to the surf beach at its other end. A big surf – what Lawrence describes as *"a heavy swell"* – is running, and impresses him with its unPacific nature. Frieda is even more struck, and expresses a desire to stay somewhere by the sea, which seaside preference she might have mentioned to Hum the previous day, leading to the afternoon-tea invitation at Narrabeen[97], another of Sydney's northern beach-suburbs. Lawrence will write about Manly and their Sunday house-hunting expedition in the second chapter of *Kangaroo*, attributing Frieda's thoughts to his fictional wife Harriett.

> *Harriet[98], of course, was enraptured, and declared she could not be happy till she had lived beside the Pacific. They bought food and ate it by the sea. Then Harriet was chilled, so they went to a restaurant for a cup of soup. When they were again in the street Harriet realised that she hadn't got her yellow scarf: her big, silky yellow scarf that was so warm and lovely. She declared she had left it in the eating-house, and they went back at once for it. The girls in the eating-house – the waitresses – said, in their cheeky Cockney Australian that they "hedn't seen it", and that the "next people who kyme arfter must 'ev tyken it".* [K p25]

This is one of the few attempts Lawrence makes to convey "the Australian accent", which he describes as *"pronounced…a bad cockney"*[99].

It is a long tram trip from Manly to Narrabeen, and glimpses of the ocean are to be caught along the way.

---

[97] Lawrence, however, does not mention the name "Narrabeen" until the end of the novel (in the Secker & later UK texts - but not the mistakenly-truncated Seltzer & CUP texts [see my chapter 18 *Departure, Taos & Second Thoughts*])
[98] the incorrect single-t spelling in the Secker edition (which is the Gutenberg text I am citing)
[99] Lawrence also gives this "*bad cockney*" accent to "Willie" Struthers, who is [see *Introduction* above] based on "Jock" Garden (yet who had a strong Scottish-accent)

Lawrence, in contrast to Frieda, is not impressed, describing the ragged bush and bits of swamp they are passing through as *"loused over with thousands of small promiscuous bungalows"*.[K p25] The further they go, the more scattered and wanton the bungalows become, as brick gives way to timber, and roof tiles to corrugated iron – to what Sydneysiders call "beach shacks". At the terminus at Narrabeen they buy what serves as a late lunch, which they consume on the dunes of nearby Narrabeen ocean beach. But they have also arrived there too early, and have an hour or more to fill in before they are due at the rendezvous address they have been given. So they take a leisurely stroll up the long[100], sandy road that runs beside the ocean towards the entrance to Narrabeen Lagoon – their destination – looking at accommodation possibilities along the way.

> *Harriet absolutely wanted to live by the sea, so they stopped before each bungalow that was to be let furnished. The estate agents went in for abbreviations. On the boards at the corner of the fences it said either "4 Sale" or "2 Let". Probably there was a colonial intention of jocularity. But it was almost enough for Somers. He would have died rather than have put himself into one of those cottages.* [K p26]

The road ends at a lagoon *"where the sea had got in and couldn't get out"*.[K ibid] There they lie on the warm sand and observe the Australians skylarking along the water's edge. Again, Lawrence is struck with the contrast with the Europe he is so familiar with. Here the sense of freedom is almost tangible.

> *There is a great relief in the atmosphere, a relief from tension, from pressure, an absence of control or will or form.*

---

[100] it is a very long "stroll" up a road that runs more than a mile beside the sea to a destination that has no public transport at its end – thus it would have been a long return trek had they had to walk back

> *The sky is open above you, and the air is open around you. Not the old closing-in of Europe.* [K p27]

At first, he finds this new atmosphere of freedom off-putting, frightening even.[101] As he reclines in the sand he begins to analyse his first impressions of his new country.

> *This was Sunday afternoon, but with none of the surfeited dreariness of English Sunday afternoons. It was still a raw loose world. All Sydney would be out by the sea or in the bush, a roving, unbroken world. They all rushed from where they were to somewhere else, on holidays. And to-morrow they'd all be working away, with just as little meaning, working without any meaning, playing without any meaning; and yet quite strenuous at it all. It was just dazing. Even the rush for money had no real pip in it. They really cared very little for the power that money can give. And except for the sense of power, that had no real significance here. When all is said and done, even money is not much good where there is no genuine culture.*[102] *Money is a means to rising to a higher, subtler, fuller state of consciousness, or nothing. And when you flatly don't want a fuller consciousness, what good is your money to you? Just to chuck about and gamble with. Even money is a European invention – European and American. It has no real magic in Australia.* [K ibid]

It is soon time to get up and go across to the large house at the end of the road to where they have been invited to join Hum and his family for Sunday tea, which is a serious middle-class rite in post-colonial Sydney. Lawrence, keen observer that he is, makes mental notes of those present (which he later uses in

---

[101] a feeling that will revisit him later in the novel
[102] that "no genuine culture" slur did not go down well with early Australian reviewers of *Kangaroo*

chapter 3 when he comes to describe this Sunday excursion). Among those there are a young man called Adrian Friend and his young wife Mwfanwy ("Fanny").[103] Also present is a man called Jack Scott[104], as well as the owners of the house, Mr and Mrs Charles Schultz. Schultz is a prominent Sydney building contractor with links to the local architectural and construction business-community. He is almost certainly a Mason, as are, probably, some of the others present. His big house, *Billabong*, at the end of Ocean Street overlooking the lagoon (see *photo-insert* in this volume), is a regular Sunday meeting-place, not only for business people, but also those with artistic or intellectual interests (some of whom have their own "weekenders" nearby). Hum and his family are themselves renting a weekender in the adjacent suburb, Collaroy.

Throughout the novel Lawrence makes extensive use of the principal "disguise" (or fact-into-fiction) transformation technique he deploys throughout the text – mixing or amalgamating two or more "real" incidents and personalities to create fictional ones. Hum, his wife Lillian, and their daughter Enid, he portrays as James ("Jaz") Trewhella, Rose[105], and Gladys respectively. One of the other people present may have been a man called George Sutherland, whose father is a leading Sydney architect, and who has a connection with the Sydney engineering firm Cameron Sutherland, whose managing director died recently, and whose Masonic funeral was held the previous Wednesday. It

---

[103] Who turn out to be two of Lawrence's main contacts in Sydney & Thirroul [see *Introduction* above] & will provide elements of several of his characters in the novel. (It is worth noting that into his next major literary work, his 1925 novella *St Mawr*, he inserted a character called "Fanny", whom he described as "A shy little blonde thing".)

[104] Scott will come to be portrayed in *Kangaroo* in various guises: as Jack Callcott (primarily) & "Jaz" Trewhella (occasionally – see below). However, when he appears as "Jack Callcott" he is in fact two people: an amalgam of Jack Scott & Adrian Friend. To help the reader disentangle Lawrence's confusing conflating of "the two Callcotts", I will footnote each of these two manifestations when they occur: as [Callcott mark #1] for Adrian Friend & [Callcott mark #2] for Scott.

[105] it is not difficult to guess why Lawrence transformed "Lillian" into "Rose" (see below re "Gladys")

is likely that when Lawrence arrived at the Schultz house, that Wednesday funeral was being talked about, for he borrows the name of the deceased, Joshua Trewheelar[106], when he begins writing *Kangaroo* a few days later.

However, the fellow guest who makes the strongest impression on Lawrence is Jack Scott, who is to become one of the two main Australian male characters in the novel, and the source of much of its plot (and who will be portrayed in the text as the primary element of the fictional character "Jack Callcott"[107]). The first image of Scott is at this lagoon-side afternoon tea-party, when he, as Jack Callcott[108], engages Somers/Lawrence in some light-hearted, but half-serious, banter. (From now on we can assume that when in *Kangaroo* Lawrence refers to "Somers" he is referring to himself, for no one doubts that the character Somers in the novel is based on Lawrence.) Someone asks the inevitable question: how does Somers like Australia? Lawrence gives his standard response: "'The harbour, I think, is wonderful.'"[109] Jack Callcott[110] then asks him why he has come to Sydney, and what his writing intentions might be. As we shall see later, the real-life Jack Scott has a particular reason for asking this question.

> "Do you mind if I ask you what sort of things you do write?" said Jack, with some delicacy.
> "Oh – poetry – essays."
> "Essays about what?"
> "Oh – rubbish mostly."

---

[106] Once Lawrence decided to portray Hum in the novel he would have needed a fictional name for him. Lawrence's mind would have cast round for someone or something he associated with the name "Hum" (the associative 'switch' being his most common transformation technique). At this Sunday afternoon-tea party the name "Trewheelar" would have rung a bell with him, for, as Bruce Steele pointed out: "DHL probably knew of the legendary chorister Matthew Trewhella [sic] of Zennor, Cornwall, who was seduced by a mermaid" [*Steele* p365] (the Cornwall reference apart, choristers often have to hum, as in, *eg*, Puccini's *Madama Butterfly*).
[107] Lawrence borrowed the name Callcott from the local letting agent in Thirroul, AF Callcott.
[108] [ie, Callcott mark #2]
[109] the quotations in this & the following extract are from *K* p31
[110] [Callcott mark #2], *ie* Jack Scott

According to the text, Harriett/Frieda interrupts, telling Jack that the essays are about "'*life, democracy and equality, and all that sort of thing*'". Callcott[111] says he would like to read some of them. Grudgingly, Lawrence agrees to send him one, adding that it would only bore him. Jack replies:

"*I might rise up to it, you know,*" said Jack laconically, "*if I bring all my mental weight to bear on it.*"
Somers flushed, and laughed at the contradiction in metaphor.
"It's not the loftiness," he said, rather amused. "It's that people just don't care to hear some things."
"Well, let me try," said Jack. "We're a new country – and we're out to learn...there's a minority that knows we've got to learn a big lesson – and that's willing to learn it."
"There's one thing," thought Somers to himself, "when these Colonials DO speak seriously, they speak like men, not like babies." He looked up at Jack.
"It's the world that's got to learn a lesson," he said. "Not only Australia."
"Possibly it is," he said. "But my job is Australia."

Somers' apparent reluctance to talk about what he does (note his off-hand reference to "Oh – poetry – essays") is the consequence of the decision Lawrence has already taken to write a new novel, using an innovative "splash-down-reality" technique, for which it will be helpful if the actual people he is going to be writing about do not realise what use he is making of them. (During this afternoon tea-party Lawrence is already gathering more material for his intended "romance" set, initially, in Sydney.)

The tea-party breaks up some time after 4pm and Lawrence and Frieda are offered a "lift" back to town. Hum

---

[111] [mark #2] Scott

had no doubt pre-arranged this return trip to the city, as he would not have expected them to make their own way back to town via tram and ferry. They cram into his large open car[112] – there could have been as many as eight in the vehicle[113] – and Hum drives them back to his holiday place in Seaview Parade in nearby Collaroy Basin. Apparently the plan is for them to change cars there, and be taken back to Macquarie Street (via the Milson's Point vehicular ferry) in the Austin driven by Adrian Friend. The Friend car is no doubt parked outside the Friends' holiday weekender in nearby Beach Road.[114] (In all probability, Adrian and "Fanny" Friend, together with Jack Scott, had been driven to Narrabeen earlier that afternoon in Hum's big Nash.)

It now seems likely that Lawrence, Frieda and Jack Scott walked from Seaview Parade to Beach Road along an unmade beachside track between the adjacent houses and the rock-pool that gives its name to "the Basin". This unorthodox route, which only a local would know, is probably taken at the suggestion of Scott, who wants to introduce his English visitors to his future wife, who is living in a large bungalow called *Hinemoa* at the end of the beach-track.[115] So while Adrian Friend and "Fanny" get their things and fetch the Friend car, Lawrence, Frieda and Scott drop in to *Hinemoa* to meet the recently-widowed Andree Adelaide Oatley and her young family. They *"sit around in the basket chairs and on the settles under the windows"* in her living-room facing the sea, waiting for the Friends' car-horn.

On the way back to town they drop Jack Scott off at his accommodation[116] in the harbourside suburb of Neutral Bay.

---

[112] Hum owned a big touring car – a Nash (John Ruffels' research)

[113] ie, Hum, his wife Lillian, daughter Enid, Lawrence, Frieda, Adrian & "Fanny" Friend, & Jack Scott (three in front & four in the back, with Enid sitting on someone's knee, probably Scott's)

[114] The "weekender" that the Friend family rented in Beach Road was identified by the Archivist at The King's School Parramatta, Peter Yeend, during an exchange of correspondence in October 1993 (see *Research-Diary* 13/10/93 entry below)

[115] for many years I thought *Hinemoa* was where Lawrence had first met Jack Scott (see *Introduction* above how Lawrence conflated the interiors of *Billabong* & *Hinemoa*)

[116] a guest-house at 112 Wycombe Road, Neutral Bay (see *Introduction* re this address)

Then Adrian Friend conveys Lawrence and Frieda back to Macquarie Street, before taking the Friend car to its garage in another part of town (he had only borrowed the family Austin for the weekend).

It had been a busy day for the Lawrences, but their accommodation quest has been successful, for they were told by Adrian and "Fanny" Friend that they know of a seaside house in a coastal town south of Sydney that has just become vacant. It could be just what they are looking for.[117] The Friends offer to take them down to Thirroul tomorrow, Monday, to inspect it. It is called *Wyewurk*.

---

[117] moreover at "winter rates", 30 shillings a week

CHAPTER 4

Thirroul and "Wyewurk"

THE SOCIAL stratum that the Lawrences have walked into in Australia, both in Perth and Sydney, is not that of the then average – predominantly working-class – Australian. Lawrence had left the working class behind some years ago, and the former Baroness Frieda von Richthofen is definitely not one of the *hoi polloi*. Whatever class-consciousness Lawrence inherited from his upbringing in the Midlands mining town of Eastwood, he has now sloughed off. Mrs Jenkins, Miss Skinner and "Maudie" Cohen, together with the people he met at the afternoon tea-party at Narrabeen, would have assumed he is one of them, which by now he is. These people speak "educated Australian", send their children to private schools, and regard themselves as much British as they are Australian. To them England is "home". It is among these conservative, well-off Anglophile social circles that Lawrence moves while in Australia.

Yet he is wrong about Australia. It is not a classless society. Demos in Australia is not its own master. While the bulk of the population may think of themselves as "working class", a significant minority identifies – steadfastly – with what in England is "the middle class". These are also imperialist circles. Loyalty to King and Empire, at that time, meant a lot to such people. Lawrence's sympathies also lie in that direction. While in Kandy he witnessed a major imperialist event, when the visiting Prince of Wales presided over a Raja[118] Pera-Hera, a local Buddhist festival put on especially for the occasion of his Royal tour of Ceylon. As

---

[118] the word "Raja" implies here a "royal" or special occasion (I am indebted to our late DHLA Society President John Lacey for pointing this out)

Lawrence makes manifest in "Elephant" – the poem he will later write about the Pera-Hera – his sympathies are with the young Prince, and the empire he represents.[119]

The train for Thirroul is due to depart from Central Railway Station around 2pm on Monday afternoon.[120] The Lawrences had apparently arranged to meet Adrian and "Fanny" Friend there. After packing up in Macquarie Street, they take a stroll in the Botanic Garden, across the road from Mrs Scott's accommodation. This becomes the opening slapping-down-reality scene in *Kangaroo*.

> *A bunch of workmen were lying on the grass of the park beside Macquarie Street, in the dinner hour. It was winter, the end of May, but the sun was warm, and they lay there in shirt-sleeves, talking. Some were eating food from paper packages. They were a mixed lot – taxi drivers, a group of builders who were putting a new inside into one of the big houses opposite, and then two men in blue overalls, some sort of mechanics. Squatting and lying on the grassy bank beside the broad tarred road where taxis and hansom cabs passed continually, they had that air of owning the city which belongs to a good Australian.*
>
> *Sometimes, from the distance behind them, came the faintest squeal of singing from out of the "fortified" Conservatorium of Music. Perhaps it was one of these faintly wafted squeals that made a blue-overalled fellow look round, lifting his thick eyebrows vacantly. His eyes immediately rested on two figures approaching from the direction of the*

---

[119] see my "It Was a Hot & Steamy Night" [*Rananim* vol 4, no 1 (April 1996) pp 17-22]

[120] Dr Joseph ("Joe") Davis in his book cited above questioned this scenario [see *Davis* pp 28-37], saying it was likely Lawrence went down to Thirroul on Sunday May 28. He put forward a hypothesis in which Lawrence & Frieda explore accommodation possibilities in Mosman/Neutral Bay on the afternoon of their arrival on Saturday May 27, then next morning catch a ferry to Manly, where they board a tram up to Narrabeen, before returning to town to catch a train to Thirroul that afternoon. But in the diary Lawrence kept while in Australia he made the following entry, written in Thirroul on July 3: "Landed in Sydney on Saturday May 26th – came here on the Monday." (Actually it was May 27.) This, frustratingly, is the only Australian entry in the diary.

conservatorium, across the grass-lawn. One was a mature, handsome, fresh-faced woman, who might have been Russian. Her companion was a smallish man, pale-faced, with a dark beard. Both were well-dressed, and quiet, with that quiet self-possession which is almost unnatural nowadays. They looked different from other people. [K p7] [121]

The degree or extent to which passages like this in *Kangaroo* are pure fiction, or something else, is the underlying conundrum about Lawrence's time in Australia, and the novel he writes there. Obviously, much of it is based on actuality. The following passage rings very true, when Lawrence describes Somers trying to catch a taxi; remonstrating with the driver about the tariff for their luggage; then finally engaging a hansom cab to take them and their disputed items of luggage, not to "51 Murdoch Street" (on, as the text implies, the day they arrived), but in fact to Central Station the following Monday afternoon.

> *The hansom-driver looked down from his Olympus. He was very red-faced, and a little bit humble.*
> *"Them three? Oh yes! Easy! Easy! Get 'em on easy. Get them on easy, no trouble at all." And he clambered down from his perch, and resolved into a little red-faced man, rather beery and henpecked-looking. He stood gazing at the bags. On one was printed the name: "R.L. Somers."*
> *"R.L. SOMERS! All right, you get in, sir and madam. You get in. Where d'you want to go? Station?"*
> *"No. Fifty-one Murdoch Street.*[122]*"* [K pp 8-9]

---

[121] this opening sequence is pure reportage
[122] A significant address – number 51 (today 31) Murdoch Street was on the corner of Florence Avenue, Neutral Bay. It was the "Canberra Flats" & in 1922 was occupied by various people, including Bert Toy, a member of the staff of *The Bulletin*. Mrs Jenkins in Perth had given Lawrence a letter-of-introduction to Toy (as mentioned above), though he did not "present it". As Lawrence did not like inventing things, he borrowed the address on the letter-of-introduction to Toy for the address Somers asks a hansom-cab driver to take him to in Sydney.

When Richard Aldington – Lawrence's first post-war biographer and close friend – composed his Introduction to the 1950 Heinemann edition of *Kangaroo,* he commented on the apparent verisimilitude of what Lawrence wrote ("much of the writing deals with Lawrence's experiences in Australia"[123]). It is the belief, the thesis, of this account of Lawrence's 99 days in Australia that *Kangaroo* is a thinly-fictionalised day-by-day record of what happened to him in Sydney and Thirroul in May, June, July, and August of 1922.

The Friends, Adrian and "Fanny", who rendezvous with the Lawrences on or near the railway platform from where the train to Thirroul departs, are junior members of the local Friend clan.[124] They have come up to Thirroul and Sydney from where they live in the country for the autumn school-holiday period. The Friends inhabit a "large compound" on the outskirts of Thirroul,[125] and one member of the family, Lucy May Friend – Adrian's aunt – had until recently owned the entire other side of the street opposite *Wyewurk.* The Friend family are prominent in Sydney commercial affairs. Their firm W.S. Friend & Co is the largest wholesale hardware and building-supplies business in NSW. Friends are on the boards of banks and insurance companies, and the family is also prominent in Church of England circles. Adrian and "Fanny" are familiar with the street – Craig Street – where *Wyewurk* is, and know the letting-agent who looks after *Wyewurk,* Mrs AF Callcott.[126] One reason why the Friends – whose family also has extensive rural interests – were at the Schultz's afternoon tea-party is that their firm is a major supplier to the building and construction sector in NSW.[127]

"Fanny", now aged 25, is the daughter of an Anglican

---

[123] *Aldington* p7(the full quote is cited in my *Introduction* above)
[124] as explained below (& throughout the *Research-Diary*), the Friend family played a major role in the circumstances of the composition of *Kangaroo*
[125] see *Davis* pp 52-54 re the Friends & their "large compound"
[126] they attend the same Anglican church in Thirroul
[127] they also stock such handy items as guns & ammunition

clergyman in Hunters Hill in Sydney.[128] Her family is Welsh, and she is also a member of the Harbour Lights Guild, an Anglican charity that regularly puts on concerts for visiting seamen. A chapter in *Kangaroo* is called "Larboard Watch Ahoy!", so named because that is the name of a sea-shanty which is sung at a "singalong" in Thirroul, and which had earlier been sung at a Harbour Lights concert up in Sydney.[K p43] As a recently-married couple, Adrian and "Fanny" probably wanted to be independent of the rest of the Friend clan that had gathered in Thirroul for the school holidays, and so have taken the cottage next to *Wyewurk*, called, equally delightfully, *Wyewurrie*.[129] This is how they know that the place next door to them in Craig Street was vacated as recently as the previous Saturday.

The two-hour train trip down to Thirroul ("*The town took almost as much leaving as London does*"[130]) ran through a different type of "bush" to that which Lawrence encountered at Darlington. It is dreary rather than threatening, "*with its pale stemmed dull-leaved gum-trees standing graceful, but spreading over the passing landscape grey for miles and miles*". Lawrence is struck by what he calls "*the invisible beauty of Australia*".

> ...*which seems to lurk just beyond the range of our white vision. You feel you can't see — as if your eyes hadn't the vision in them to correspond with the outside landscape. For the landscape is so unimpressive, like a face with little or no features, a dark face. It is so aboriginal, out of our ken, and it hangs back so aloof. Somers always felt he looked at it through a cleft in the atmosphere; as one looks at one of the*

---

[128] for more details about Myfanwy ("Fanny") Friend see *Research-Diary* 2/11/92 below

[129] There has been a lot of research into the houses in Craig Street, Thirroul, mainly by Joe Davis & John Ruffels. Probably the best information we have on this comes from a 1957 magazine article – see *Research-Diary* 3/6/02 below – which said *Wyewurk*'s neighbouring houses were *Chirrup* to the south & *Wyewurrie* to the north.

[130] the several quotations in this sequence of my text are from *K* p76 (the word "bush" in Australia means the countryside in which the main vegetation is eucalypts, or gum-trees)

ugly-faced, distorted aborigines with his wonderful dark eyes that have such an incomprehensible ancient shine in them, across gulfs of unbridged centuries. And yet, when you don't have the feeling of ugliness or monotony, in landscape or in nigger[131]*, you get a sense of subtle, remote, formless beauty*

The Lawrences and their Friend guides arrive at Thirroul station around 4.30pm. They walk from the station, in the shadow of the "Dark Tor" that looms over the town, towards the ocean. "Fanny" has to go to the estate agent Mrs Callcott[132] to get the key, and so the three of them – Lawrence, Frieda and Adrian – wait on a corner for her to return. The four then walk a few blocks and arrive at the rear entrance[133] of *Wyewurk* at number 3 Craig Street. Lawrence and Frieda go down the side-passage and see, for the first time, its seaward prospect. Frieda is entranced (and Lawrence must have been pretty impressed too).

...the great Pacific right there and rolling in huge white thunderous rollers not forty yards away, under her grassy platform of a garden. She walked to the edge of the grass. Yes, just down the low cliff, really only a bank, went her own little path, as down a steep bank, and then was smooth yellow sand, and the long sea swishing up its incline, and rocks to the left, and incredible long rollers furling over and crushing down on the shore. At her feet! At her very feet, the huge rhythmic Pacific [K p81]

---

[131] reading *Kangaroo*, one has to put up with what would today be condemned as politically-incorrect expressions when Lawrence is referring to indigenous Australians & people of the Jewish faith, & take into account contemporary standards then prevalent

[132] Mrs AF Callcott acted as a local letting-agent in Thirroul. She was the sister of the owner of *Wyewurk*, Mrs Beatrice Southwell, who lived up in Sydney. Her daughter was later interviewed (by Sydney journalist Fred Esch) about her mother's contact with Lawrence for Nehls's *DH Lawrence: A Composite Biography* [Nehls vol 2 pp 144-145].

[133] actually it is the main street-entrance

(The *"forty yards"* refers to the fact that *Wyewurk* is sited on a small cliff above a rock shelf, and the adjacent beach, McCauley's Beach, is a short distance away below and to the right of the seaside holiday-bungalow.)

They decide straight away to take the place, and Lawrence and "Fanny" return to Mrs Callcott to settle the rental details. At first she is reluctant to let them have it, as it was vacated only two days ago, and is in something of a mess, having been occupied by a family with seven children. Mrs Callcott has to ring the owner Mrs Southwell in Sydney to waive the customary formalities[134]. In normal circumstances their occupancy would have been refused, had not "Fanny" been present. But the Friends have a lot of local clout,[135] and their imprimatur overrides any proprietorial caveats. By dusk the Lawrences are securely ensconced in *Wyewurk*. (The Friends must have earlier assured the Lawrences that they would be able to move into *Wyewurk* that Monday afternoon, as there was no possibility of them going back to Sydney that day.[136])

The next day Tuesday is largely spent cleaning up the bungalow, which had not been touched since the previous untidy tenants moved out on Saturday. "F is happy for the moment tidying the house," Lawrence told Mrs Jenkins back in Perth.[137] It is likely that Adrian and "Fanny" Friend lend a hand in the cleaning up, which involves polishing *Wyewurk's* jarrah floors *"with a stuff called Glowax"*.K p82 They probably also assist with local shopping and arranging for the various deliveries – milk, firewood, newspapers, etc – to be made.

With his accommodation settled, Lawrence's mind is turning to the "romance" he now intends to start in Thirroul. He begins the first chapter, entitled [later] "Torestin", next

---

[134] Mrs Southwell had wanted the place cleaned, inventoried, & properly prepared for new tenants [*Nehls ibid*]
[135] see above re the Friends & their local "clout" (& particularly *Davis* pp 52-54)
[136] indeed, they had probably rung Mrs Callcott to alert her to the arrival of prospective tenants
[137] *Letters* #2528 [to Mrs Jenkins]

morning, Wednesday May 31. (The name "Torestin" is intended as a play on words[138] for *Wyewurk*, though the name actually comes from Ceylon, where there are numerous "Rest Inns" which Lawrence could have seen during his stay there.)

---

[138] I am indebted to Lawrence scholar the late Keith Sagar for suggesting this to me in 1986 (see *Research-Dairy* 31/8/86 below).

CHAPTER 5

The Tangled Skein

USING THE *holograph* text[139] of *Kangaroo* we can tell approximately what Lawrence wrote each day, primarily from the variations in his handwriting. At the start of each writing-session his script tends to be tight and even cramped, but flows more freely as he goes on. Using this insight, and correlating it with other clues – such as the dates and content of his letters; his references to the weather, tides, surf conditions, etc; phases of the sun and the moon; news items in the local newspapers; mail-boat arrivals and departures; and other sources (including, most importantly, the number of words he writes each session[140]) – we can deduce that it took him 29 or 30 writing-sessions between May 31 and July 15 to compose and commit to paper the first "Thirroul" *holograph*-version of the text (*ie*, about 46 days – over half the 99 days he spent in Australia). His first writing-session, put down on Wednesday May 31, took the narrative from the Macquarie-Street opening of the novel, to jogging through town in the hansom cab [section #1 MS pp 1-9a[141] c2000 words].

Again, this raises the question of the diary, or autobiographical aspect of the novel. How much of this is "slapping down reality", and what due to invention and creative writing? No one denies that Lawrence was an

---

[139] this is the original hand-written text Lawrence wrote in Thirroul between May 31 & July 15, 1922, & later revised in Taos on typescript the following October (the *holograph* manuscript, apart from the final chapter, is at the Harry Ransom Center in Austin, Texas)

[140] Lawrence usually wrote between 3500-4500 words per session, initially at a rate of around 210-230 words per page in four school-notebooks, two bought in Ceylon & two on June 24 in Sydney

[141] There are two page-9s in the manuscript text of *Kangaroo*. This is not the only instance of Lawrence misnumbering his written & typescript pages.

intensely autobiographical writer, who makes extensive use of incidents from his life in his literary works. He put a great deal of his earlier experiences into *Sons and Lovers*, *The Rainbow*, and *Women in Love* (and later into *The Lost Girl*, *Aaron's Rod* and the then-unpublished *Mr Noon*). Normally, this would not be a particularly important aspect of the novel, and might be covered in an Introduction and some footnotes. But in *Kangaroo* it becomes a much more significant – indeed crucial – matter because of the nature of the plot, or storyline. For *Kangaroo* purportedly tells the story of a British writer Richard Lovatt Somers and his foreign-born wife Harriett – who are obviously Lawrence and Frieda – arriving in Australia and encountering a secret army[142] there. How much of that is "real"? Did Lawrence in fact run across a secret army in Australia, as Somers does in the novel? This is not yet the place to offer a definitive answer to that question, and the other considerations it inevitably raises (this will be addressed below). It is something that should be kept in mind at this early stage in the composition of the novel as the provenance of Lawrence's Australian "romance" unfolds.

Tuesday, the Lawrences' first full day at *Wyewurk*, is a busy one. In the afternoon – probably after a morning's shopping – they walk, accompanied[143] by their now neighbours Adrian and "Fanny" Friend, along McCauley's Beach to Sandon Point, a headland park a half a mile or so to the south of *Wyewurk*, where a joyride aircraft had crash-landed the previous Sunday.[144] The aircraft (when airborne) is a local tourist attraction, as Lawrence goes on to explain, quoting a local Thirroulian:

"*Yes, he's carrying passengers. Oh, quite a fair trade.*

---

[142] the expression "secret army" is explained in my *Introduction* above

[143] so we assume

[144] Its pilot Lieutenant Barkell conducted "joy flights" from Thirroul Beach & Bulli Park (as Lawrence describes below). The "crash" was reported in local & Sydney newspapers (*eg*, *SMH* 30/5/22 p7: "Lieut. Barkell, who has been conducting aeroplane flights from Bulli Park, had a narrow escape from serious injury yesterday afternoon...").

> *Thirty-five shillings a time. Yes, it seems a lot, but he has to make his money while he can. No, I've not been up myself, but my boy has. No, you see, there was four boys, and they had a sweepstake: eight-and-six apiece, and my boy won. He's just eleven. Yes, he liked it. But they was only up about four minutes: I timed them myself. Well, you know, it's hardly worth it. But he gets plenty to go. I heard he made over forty pounds on Whit Monday, here on this beach. It seems to me, though, he favours some more than others. There's some he flies round with for ten minutes, and that last chap now, I'm sure he wasn't up a second more than three minutes. No, not quite fair. Yes, he's a man from Bulli: was a flying-man all through the war. Now he's got this machine of his own, he's quite right to make something for himself if he can. No, I don't know that he has any licence or anything. But a chap like that, who went through the war – why, who's going to interfere with his doing the best for himself?"* [K p192]

Note that Lawrence has abandoned any ongoing attempt to convey this "quote" in the spoken vernacular (nevertheless, he takes another stab at it in *K* chapter 10 "Diggers" when a young girl comes into the local School of Arts library and asks for a book: "*Y'aven' got a new Zaine Greye, have yer?*" [K p190]).

Some of the next day Wednesday is devoted to further setting up house and local familiarisation. In the morning, however, Lawrence opens a school exercise-book he had purchased in Ceylon and begins his first writing-session in Thirroul (*ie*, section #1 MS pp 1-9a [see above]). We know that this first session stopped at page 9a, partly from the change in handwriting, and partly because there are further elements in this first chapter that refer to events that are yet to occur, later in the week. This first writing-session may have been followed by a visit to the letting-agent Mrs Callcott, whose daughter remembered that her mother offered to cut some flowers for Frieda,[145] an incident that Lawrence recreates in chapter 1. *"But did ever you see such dahlias! Are you sure they're dahlias?'"*[K p17] he quotes Harriett/Frieda as saying.

The following day, Thursday June 1, Lawrence returns, alone, to Sydney, ostensibly to arrange for the rest of their substantial travelling-luggage (four trunks) to be sent down to Thirroul. But his main reason for going back to Sydney would have been to see Jack Scott again. (A telephone call to the shipping agents would have sufficed.) Clearly the two men had "hit it off" the previous weekend, and an appointment to meet up that Thursday in Sydney was probably made during the drive back to town on Sunday. At Circular Quay Lawrence catches, no doubt at Scott's instruction, the ferry across to Mosman Bay, their rendezvous venue. On the trip across the Harbour he witnesses a ferry collision, which he describes in the novel as having occurred (erroneously) on the trip to Manly four days earlier.

> *One day their ferry steamer bumped into a collier that was heading for the harbour outlet – or rather, their ferry boat headed across the nose of the collier, so the collier bumped into them and had his nose put out of joint. There was a considerable amount of yelling, but the ferry boat slid flatly away towards Manly, and Harriet's excitement subsided.* [K p25]

(The newspapers on Friday reported that the ferry collision on the Harbour occurred about 10am that Thursday morning.[146])

Scott, as mentioned above, has a particular motive for wanting to see Lawrence again. He is the treasurer of a local

---

[145] the daughter, interviewed in the1950s by *SMH* journalist Fred Esch, was Mrs Clarice Farraher [*Nehls* vol 2 pp 144-145 (& also *Davis* pp 75-76)]
[146] as reported in, for example, the [Sydney] *Daily Telegraph* 2/6/22 [p5 col 8]

patriotic organisation called the King and Empire Alliance.[147] Precisely one week before Lawrence arrived in Sydney – the previous Saturday in fact – one of its leading lights left for overseas. His name was George Augustine Taylor,[148] a local journalist who helped put the Alliance's monthly magazine, also called *King and Empire,* together. Scott, who co-founded the Alliance in mid-1920, is aware that Taylor's departure has left a gap or vacancy, and that *King and Empire* might be in the market for some additional writing assistance. This was no doubt why Scott questioned Lawrence on Sunday about his writing intentions while in Sydney. On that drive back to town late on Sunday he may have intimated to Lawrence that he might be able to put some writing-work his way. No doubt this was his reason for arranging today's meeting at Mosman Bay. (Lawrence, however, has his own reasons for wanting to see Scott again – to collect material for the "romance" he has already started to compose, and commit to paper). We know Lawrence had been on the lookout for extra writing-work. Why else would Mrs Jenkins give him a letter of introduction to Bert Toy on *The Bulletin*? (Lawrence, however, did not "present" that letter-of-introduction, nor make any attempt to contact *The Bulletin*, which he nevertheless praises – and later borrows excerpts from – in *Kangaroo*.[149])

Scott must have been waiting on the wharf for Lawrence that morning at Mosman Bay. They then walk around the bottom of the bay, over a footbridge, to a bench across from the wharf in what is today Harnett Park. This early-Thursday meeting in June marks a significant change, or rather departure-point, in the novel. For it introduces what will turn

---

[147] the Alliance (portrayed in the novel as "the Digger clubs") was formed about 18 months previously after the election in March 1920 of the left-wing Storey/Dooley Labor government
[148] This is a vital name in the story of how *Kangaroo* came to be written, first mentioned in my *Research-Diary* 4/4/02 & then the subject of a major article "The Man Who Wasn't There" [*Rananim* vol 10, no 2 (May 2002)].
[149] eg, the Cape York tiger-cat story [*K* 116, extracted from *The Bulletin* 8/6/22] & much of chapter 14 "Bits" [*K* pp 269-272], extracted from *The Bulletin* 22/6/22

out to be its unexpected political, or secret-army, "plot"[150]. Up to this point, Lawrence's "romance" is little more than an upgraded or enhanced travel diary, a fictional development from the diary structure of *Sea and Sardinia*. Lawrence's intention, apparently, was to now go ahead and "slap down" each day's "reality", in concert with the advice he had recently given to "Mollie" Skinner on how to write a novel.[151] His intention, initially, seems to have been to frame his daily doings – where he went; whom he met; what was happening around him; what his impressions of Australia (and latterly Sydney and Thirroul) happened to be; and so on – in an orthodox fictional format, while embellishing it with his own, inimitable points-of-view – his incidental remarks or comments, as it were. Nevertheless, his narrative, if it were to qualify as a novel (he fully intended to send it to his publishers Secker and Seltzer as such), would need a *dramatis personae*...some "fictional characters". So this was what he was now doing: casting around for people whom he might borrow from "reality" and, using his various transformation techniques[152], turn into "characters" – central or otherwise – for his new "romance".[153]

Since he arrived in Perth, now several weeks ago, he had come across a variety of local Australians whom he might appropriate for this purpose. "Maudie" Cohen from Darlington, when conflated with "Fanny" Friend in Sydney, was to provide him with his leading Australian female character, Victoria Callcott. Hum, whom he had first met on the boat to Ceylon, was to supply another character, "Jaz"

---

[150] Yet "plot" implies overt or intentional plotting. It is my conviction, however, that the secret-army element in Lawrence's "romance" is incidental, or additional to the storyline, something that he "picked up", in passing as it were, while he was recording daily reality. (*Kangaroo* has no orthodox plot in the traditional fictional sense – the Diggers & Maggies theme being, essentially, montage, or "background" to the slapped-down main narrative [this is further explained below]).
[151] see above & *Fifth Sparrow*, pp 115-116
[152] for a survey of these complex transposition techniques, see my three articles in *Rananim* viz: vol 5, no 1; vol 5, no 2; & vol 5, no 3 (beginning with "Mining Lawrence's Nomenclature" *Rananim* vol 5, no 1 [pp 10-16 (April 1997)], where I discuss George Neville's insight into Lawrence's inability to invent fictional characters & places)
[153] providing "major" characters, rather than the "bit-players", such as the rapacious cabbie

Trewhella, when suitably reprocessed. However, since they first met at Narrabeen on his second day in Sydney, Jack Scott evinced particular narrative potential.[154] Yet Scott, as mentioned above, had his own reason[155] to pursue what he might have thought was a promising relationship with Lawrence. So as the two men sat on the bench opposite Mosman wharf that Thursday morning, June 1, each had interests in the other that they wanted to explore further, and which they would follow up, with far-reaching consequences, in the days to come.

Fortuitously, in *Kangaroo* Lawrence has left a detailed account of what subsequently transpired.[156] The account starts with the opening of chapter 3, "Larboard Watch Ahoy!"

> *"What do you think of things in general?" Callcott asked of Somers one evening, a fortnight or so*[157] *after their first encounter.* [K p39]

In the text, Lawrence locates this conversation, not at Mosman, but fictionally earlier in the cottage ("Torestin") to where Somers and Harriett supposedly went by hansom cab on their arrival in Sydney.[158] The several meetings Scott and Lawrence have together over the next three days (Thursday, Friday and Saturday June 1-3) are conflated and redeployed in various parts of the text, but can be reconstructed as they develop after Scott starts to question Lawrence about his

---

[154] Already Lawrence may have sensed hidden depths in him. When, during their Sunday afternoon encounter at Narrabeen, Somers remarked that Callcott hadn't "*anything risky*" to trust "*his chaps*" with, Callcott – Scott – had replied: "*I don't know so much about that.*" [K p55].
[155] filling the gap in the King & Empire Alliance left by the departure of George Augustine Taylor
[156] so detailed that it is possible to trace the course their developing relationship week-to-week, day-to-day, & sometimes even hour-by-hour (via an analysis of his individual writing sessions)
[157] One of Lawrence's primary transformation (or "fictionalising") techniques was to change the dates of the reality he was slapping down. He says the ferry collision happened the previous Sunday, rather than as it did that Thursday morning. The "*things in general*" conversation was not "*one evening, a fortnight or so*", but on Thursday, June 1, five days after he arrived in Sydney. Similar "time switches" or date transformations are in evidence throughout the text.
[158] as we shall soon see, Lawrence is storing up a lot of trouble for himself by having two (rented) residences in NSW – "Torestin" in Sydney & "Coo-ee" in Thirroul ("Mullumbimby").

political beliefs, prior to making him an offer to join, what will turn out to be, their secret-army organisation.

With his questions to Lawrence ("...*what do you consider...is the bogey of tomorrow?*" [*K* p41]) Scott is "feeling him out" before committing himself further. Callcott [*ie*, Scott] continues: "*If you* [were to] *ask me...I should say that Labour*[159] *is the bogey* [of tomorrow]" [*K ibid*]. In this exchange, Lawrence/Somers declines to be drawn into the turbid pond of local politicking, and consequently this exploratory Mosman Bay conversation apparently peters out, and he and Scott walk back across to the wharf and go by ferry to Circular Quay, where they temporarily part company, to meet up again later in the day. Nevertheless, Scott's interest in Lawrence as a possible recruit for the King and Empire Alliance has been enhanced considerably by their harbourside chat, and he prevails on Lawrence[160] to remain in Sydney and spend the next few days with him at 112 Wycombe Road, where their mutual interest in each other might be further explored.

There is good reason to believe that in the files of Australia's internal security organisation, ASIO (Australia's equivalent of the FBI and MI5), there is, or was, a file that tells the story of Jack Scott's encounters with Lawrence in Sydney between May and August, 1922. A former head of ASIO, Colonel Charles Spry, revealed[161] in 1977 that "a man answering the description of Scott" had met Lawrence "on the wharf and had taken him to stay on the North Shore for <u>three days</u>"[162]. ASIO today denies it has or ever had such a file,

---

[159] Lawrence uses the spelling of the UK Labour Party (not the Australian Labor Party, which had adopted the American spelling)
[160] though he would not have needed much persuading
[161] to my correspondent Ernest Whiting (see *Research-Diary* 14/9/77 & 16/4/98 entries below re Spry & the encounter at "the wharf")
[162] [my emphasis] see Whiting's letter [*Research-Diary* entry 16/4/98 below] (& note there the "three days" that Lawrence also refers to [*K* p103] – a period that Spry could not possibly have known known about from any other source than what was then Australia's internal security service: the Investigation Bureau, which later in the early 1950s morphed into the Australian Security & Intelligence Organisation [ASIO])

while Military Intelligence, for which Scott worked for most of the 1930s, says that their file on him "no longer exists" – both of which assertions are difficult to believe.

The wharf in question we now believe was Mosman wharf, from where it was a walk of a few blocks (uphill) to Scott's flat at 112-114 Wycombe Road[163], Neutral Bay. That morning, however, Lawrence probably accompanies Scott by ferry back to Circular Quay, and may have walked with him to Scott's office at 93b Pitt Street. (Scott is an insurance broker, a partner in the firm of Scott and Broad, insurance agents.) There they part company, no doubt to meet up again in the late afternoon to take a return ferry back to the North Shore.[164]

Lawrence had quite a bit he could do that Thursday in Sydney. First, he intended to go to the shipping agents and arrange for his non-cabin luggage to be sent down to Thirroul and delivered to Craig Street. Then he probably goes to Cooks in Martin Place to collect any forwarded mail waiting for him. He might have cashed some travellers-cheques there, or done some other "banking".[165] He may have also visited some shipping offices to inquire about onward travel (as mentioned above, he is already thinking about which boat he might take on to America). Almost certainly he would have gone to see Gerald Hum again, and may have had lunch in town with him. Lawrence could also have gone to one of the libraries in town to begin preliminary research for his new novel, for later in *Kangaroo* he remarks about the origin of the name "Pommy" – an Australianism for someone from England[166] – which he apparently looked up, probably in a local library, and which later furnishes him with a paragraph in the novel.

---

[163] Scott's address in Wycombe Road comes from an entry in the State Electoral Roll for 1922 (see *Introduction* above & *Research-Diary* 6/2/79 entry below)

[164] the term "North Shore" (see above & below) owed its origin to a sign at the ferry wharves at Circular Quay, from where ferries departed to the northern side of the Harbour & other parts of Port Jackson (which is the correct name for "Sydney Harbour")

[165] Lawrence had a bank account in America, at the Charleroi Bank, into which his American royalty income was deposited by his American agent Mountsier

[166] supposedly because of their "apple cheeks"

> *Pommy is supposed to be short for pomegranate. Pomegranate, pronounced invariably pommygranate, is a near enough rhyme to immigrant, in a naturally rhyming country. Furthermore, immigrants are known in their first months, before their blood "thins down," by their round and ruddy cheeks. So we are told. Hence again, pomegranate, and hence Pommy. Let etymologists be appeased: it is the authorised derivation.* [K p147]

(Indicatively, Lawrence is already undertaking extra research [*cf*, "*it is the authorised derivation*"] for his new "romance".) He hadn't brought any writing materials up to town, as he had not intended, prior to meeting Scott at Mosman, to be in Sydney for more than a day. He must therefore have sent a message, probably via the Friends or Mrs Callcott (*Wyewurk* does not have a telephone), to Frieda informing her of his change of plans, and of his intention to bring Scott down with him on Saturday. So he could not go on with the novel he had just started, except to garner further ingredients for it.

He and Scott probably meet up again later in the day and catch a ferry, this time to Cremorne, a neighbouring suburb to Mosman and Neutral Bay, there to board the tram waiting at the wharf for the short trip up Murdoch Street, where they get out opposite number 51 (the Canberra Flats) and walk up Bennett Street to Scott's accommodation in nearby Wycombe Road.[167] The coincidence that Scott's residence is one street away from Bert Toy's address at 51 Murdoch Street is not lost on Lawrence, and he remarks about it in the text, calling it "*fate*"[168].

Lawrence's subsequent account in *Kangaroo* of his three-day stay – Thursday, Friday and Saturday (*ie*, two nights and

---

[167] Scott rented a flat (or apartment) in the establishment at 112-114 Wycombe Road, Neutral Bay, run by the Misses Tinson (see *Research-Diary* 5/2/79 & 28/3/91 entries below)
[168] "*It's fate that brings you to this house*" (*ie*, 51 Murdoch Street) [K p56]

three days[169]) – with Scott, though "fictionalised" through his various transformation techniques, is comprehensive, and can be reconstructed, given an insight into those techniques. Apparently 112-114 Wycombe Road comprised four large flats or apartments, one of which Scott rented. Scott and Lawrence have dinner there on Thursday evening, and afterwards play chess and chat. Before dinner, however, Lawrence goes out into the small backyard garden where there is a summer-house (actually it was a fern-house[170]) with a "tub-top" lookout on top of it, built so that residents and guests might view the Harbour over the house next door, and which Lawrence describes in *Kangaroo*.

> ...*he went into the garden, even climbed the tub-like summer house, to have a last look at the world. There was a big slip of very bright moon risen, and the harbour was faintly distinct.*
> [K p56]

We do not know what they talked about before or after dinner, but the name of George Augustine Taylor almost certainly came up, and the journalistic gap he had left on Scott and Rosenthal's *King and Empire* journal. It is highly likely that Scott showed Lawrence a book that Taylor had written, called *The Sequel*.[171] We have very good reason to believe that Lawrence read it, for some of Taylor's strident right-wing ideology in it is reflected throughout the text of *Kangaroo*. More significantly, Lawrence derives the name of his other main Australian character in *Kangaroo* – the secret-army leader Benjamin Cooley – from Taylor's *The Sequel*, for the distinctive name "Cooley" appears twice in its text (once as a pseudonym for Taylor).[172] The character Cooley, it will turn

---

[169] see *K* p103 for Lawrence's account of this

[170] see *Research-Diary* 5/2/79 entry below for Norm Dunn's description (signed & witnessed) of the fern-house lookout at 112-114 Wycombe Road

[171] for more about *The Sequel*, see *Research-Diary* 4/4/02 & 11/4/02 entries below

[172] Bruce Steele, recognising that the provenance of the name "Cooley" was important, put forward several possible origins. He suggested it might be a pun on the word "coolie" (*ie*, "In so

out, is an amalgam of Taylor and Rosenthal – the face and figure being Rosenthal's, and the ideas and ideology largely those of George Augustine Taylor, as seen through Lawrence's eyes.[173]

We do not know how Lawrence filled in the following day, Friday. He may have done – and probably did – some of the things mentioned above. Both Hum and Scott belong to "gentlemen's clubs" in Sydney – the Commercial Travellers in Martin Place in Hum's case, and the Imperial Service Club ("the officers' club") in O'Connell Street in Scott's. He may have lunched with one or other of them on Friday in town. In any case, Lawrence later returns – no doubt accompanied by Scott – to 112 Wycombe Road for another evening of chess and chatting, and continuing to read *The Sequel* (ie, further research).

On Saturday morning, around 11am, Scott and Lawrence stroll down from Wycombe Road to the Mosman wharf[174] to catch a ferry into town, and then a tram across the city to Central Railway Station. In *K* chapter 4 "Jack & Jaz", Lawrence describes this walk down to the wharf, embellishing it with some typical Australian blokey banter.

> *Callcott met quite a number of people he knew, and greeted them all heartily. "Hello Bill, old man, how's things?" "New boots pinchin' yet, Ant'ny? Hoppy sort of look about you this morning. Right'o! So long, Ant'ny!" "Different girl again, boy! go on, Sydney's full of yer sisters. All right, goodbye, old chap." The same breezy intimacy with all of them, and the moment they had passed by, they didn't exist*

---

far as Kangaroo represents the Christian 'love ethic', he could in neo-Nietzschean terms be considered a 'slave' & so a 'coolie'." [*Steele* Explanatory Note p374]).

[173] in the same way that Trewhella is largely the face & figure of Gerald Hum – "stuggy", etc – tacked on to the anti-Labor beliefs of Jack Scott & those of Scott's fellow militia officer George Augustine Taylor

[174] this is deduction combined with the logistical "reality" that the easiest way to get to the Mosman ferry from Wycombe Road (by foot) is via Bennett, Florence & Spofforth streets, then Fleet Lane, Royalist Road, & a pathway with steps that lead down to Mosman Bay, opposite the ferry wharf

THE HORRIBLE PAWS

for him any more than the gull that had curved across in the air. They seemed to appear like phantoms, and disappear in the same instant, like phantoms. Like so many Flying Dutchmen the Australian's acquaintances seemed to steer slap through his consciousness, and were gone on the wind.
[K p59]

At Central Station the two of them board the afternoon train for Thirroul, arriving there around 4.30 pm. As they walk together from the station towards the sea and *Wyewurk*, they pause to watch a Saturday afternoon Rugby League football game being played on Thirroul oval, across from the station.[175] This provides Lawrence with another vignette in *Kangaroo*.

Just outside the station was the football field, and Mullumbimby was playing Wollondindy[176]...*This scene was too much for Jack Callcott. Somers or no Somers, he must be there. So there he stood, in his best clothes and a cream velour hat and a short pipe, staring with his long, naked, Australian face, impassive. On the field the blues and the reds darted madly about, like strange bird-creatures rather than men. They were mostly blond, with hefty legs, and with prominent round buttocks that worked madly inside the little white cotton shorts. And Jack, with his dark eyes, watched as if it was Doomsday. Occasionally the tail-end of a smile would cross his face, occasionally he would take his pipe-stem from his mouth and give a bright look into vacancy and say, "See that!" Heaven knows what it was that he saw. The game, the skill? Yes. But more, the motion,*

---

[175] The code of football played on the South Coast of NSW was Rugby League, the working-class version of the more middle-class game of Rugby Union. Thirroul's Rugby League team's nickname was "The Butchers", named after the team's symbol, a magpie, also known as the butcher bird. Lawrence adopted the name of his secret army in *Kangaroo* – "the Maggies" – from this local symbol, investing them with the team's black-and-white "strip" (see *K* p184), *ie*, they had black shirts – the uniform, perhaps not totally coincidentally – of Mussolini's *fascisti*.
[176] In *Kangaroo*, Lawrence called Thirroul "Mullumbimby" (a town in northern NSW). "Wollondindy" is a made-up name, no doubt a corruption (or fictionalisation) of Wollondilly, the name of the local-government area in which Thirroul is situated (itself named after a local river).

> *the wild combative motion...Towards the close one of the chaps got a kick on the jaw, and was knocked out. They couldn't finish the game. Hard lines.* [K p189]

Lawrence in fact describes this Saturday afternoon football game later in chapter 10, "Diggers" when, starved for material, he reprises Jack's arrival that Saturday in Thirroul.[177]

Scott and Lawrence continue on to Craig Street and *Wyewurk*, where Scott stays overnight on Saturday and Sunday (the following Monday is not a working day for Scott, it being the three-day King's Birthday holiday weekend). *Wyewurk*, built as a "weekender", has ample guest accommodation. Apparently, there is no chess-set in the holiday house, so Lawrence and Scott instead play draughts, as Lawrence relates in *Kangaroo*.

> *To give Callcott justice, he was more accustomed to draughts than to chess, and Somers had never played draughts, not to remember. So Jack played a draughts game, aiming at seizing odd pieces. It wasn't Somers' idea of chess, so he wouldn't take the trouble to defend himself. His men fell to this ambush, and he lost the game. Because at the end, when he had only one or two pieces to attack, Jack was very clever at cornering, having the draughts moves off by heart.*
> [K p81]

Over the three-day holiday-weekend many houses (or "holiday places") in Thirroul would have been occupied by people down from Sydney and elsewhere. *Wyewurrie*, the house next door to *Wyewurk*, may have had a piano (there is no evidence that *Wyewurk* had one), and there might have been a "singalong" there on one of the evenings (as described

---

[177] it turns out that there is a lot of repetition or "double-use" in the novel

in the *K* chapter 3 "Larboard Watch Ahoy!") and which may have ended with the first "sex-scene" passage in the novel.[178]

> *"Well," said Harriet, as they closed the door of Torestin. "I think they might have waited just TWO minutes before they started their love making. After all, one doesn't want to be implicated, does one?"* [K p48]

Lawrence and Scott are spending a lot of time in each other's company – up in Sydney, on the train down to Thirroul, and during the three days[179] Scott stays at *Wyewurk*. There are numerous opportunities for discussion and chats. Scott, apparently, is still trying to find out whether Lawrence really is "one of them", and so can be presumed to share their conservative/imperialist beliefs. For he has something he wants to talk to Lawrence about. Indeed, he intends to speak to him about it during his stay there.[180] Meanwhile, if the text is to be believed, he continues to probe Lawrence's attitudes and beliefs, "feeling him out" as it were. It is almost as if he were circling Lawrence, letting drop titbits of his great secret, like burley, to see if he rises to the bait.

He starts, probably on Saturday evening or Sunday morning, with a general observation: *"'There's some of us here that feels things are pretty shaky, you know.'"*[181] There could be a financial smash, he says, adding: *"'... and then hell to pay all round. Maybe, you know. We've got to think about it.'"* Lawrence refuses to take the bait, saying instead that the next thing *"'to come a cropper'"* would be capital and the middle classes (which is not what Scott wants to hear). However, he

---

[178] this "sex-scene was to take on added import, as the people it depicted are Adrian and "Fanny" Friend, which may have given the Friend family an added reason – "delicacy" – to subsequently deny, indeed lie about, their role in the provenance of *Kangaroo* (see the Yeend letters in my *Introduction* above)

[179] Saturday, Sunday & part of Monday

[180] & for which he may have got clearance to do so from his superior, Charles Rosenthal – in fact, this is the purpose of his visit to *Wyewurk*

[181] this & the following quotations are taken from *K* chapter 5, p92 (here I have abandoned the linked Callcott/"Jaz"/Scott nomenclature, as this is clearly Jack Scott speaking)

perseveres, observing that if a financial *"smash"* were to come, *"'there'd be no holding New South Wales in.'"* What Lawrence writes next is a foretaste of what will prove to be his complete lack of comprehension about what he was, apparently, being drawn into by Scott.[182] He has the deeply-conservative Scott also wanting – counter-intuitively – to see *"'the power of money, the power of capital BROKE'"*. Lawrence, apparently, gives Scott to believe he agrees with this paradoxical assertion. He portrays Somers' supposed agreement thus:

> *"Shake," cried Jack, stretching over. And he took Somers' small hand between both his own. "I knew," he said in a broken voice, "that we was mates."*

This is a crucial moment in the novel, for it introduces into the text the Australian concept of "mateship", which is to play a significant role in what ensues (and will be discussed more fully in my chapter 19, "Postscript", below). The main point here, however, is that Scott seems to have got it into his head, early into that King's Birthday weekend, that he had with Lawrence some emerging or developing form of masculine friendship, or bond (indeed, mateship[183]).

For his part, Somers feels *"rather bewildered"* about what Scott/Callcott is talking about. He tells him – and this is no doubt true of Lawrence – that he doesn't have any interest in politics. *"'They aren't my affair,'"* he says. Moreover, he goes on to tell Scott that he's got him wrong, socially and class-wise, and that he isn't his sort of person at all. He tells him: *"'My father was a working-man. I come from the working people. My sympathy is with them, when it's with anybody, I assure you.'"* That is also not what Scott wants to hear – and Lawrence may not in fact have said it, though it probably reflects his own

---

[182] it is probably more accurate to say "a limited lack of interest" (because, for Lawrence & his "Romance", this was at this stage largely-inconsequential "montage")

[183] mateship is regarded by Australian historians & sociologists as a fundamental characteristic of Australia & Australians – for an elaboration of this, see my chapter 19 "Postscript"

hazy political attitude.[184] Nevertheless Scott, according to the text, isn't to be put off. Again, Lawrence gets his politics and social-class ideas in a tangle, as he quotes Callcott/Scott:

> *"Your father was a working-man, was he? Is that really so? Well, that IS a surprise! And yet," he changed his tone, "no, it isn't. I might have known. Of course I might. How should I have felt for you as I did, the very first minute I saw you, if it hadn't been so. Of course you're one of us: same flesh and blood, same clay...Well, well, and your father was a working man! And you now being as you are! Wonderful what we may be, isn't it? Well, well, that brings us a great deal nearer than ever, that does," said Callcott, looking at Somers with glowing smiling eyes which the other man could not quite understand, eyes with something desirous, and something perhaps fanatical in them. Somers could not understand. As for the being brought nearer to Callcott, that was apparently entirely a matter of Jack's own feeling. Somers himself had never felt more alone and far off. Yet he trembled at the other man's strange fervour. He vibrated helplessly in some sort of troubled response.* [K p92]

Indeed, Lawrence does not understand. He hasn't a clue what Jack is talking about, nor getting at, especially this strange idea of "mateship", a concept that Lawrence has probably never come across before (despite having read Henry Lawson's poetry, which has various references to mateship). This lack of understanding will haunt him, almost literally – in his dreams, for example – for the remainder of his "romance".

---

[184] I have asked several Lawrence scholars for an opinion on what they thought Lawrence's "politics" were (as well as being familiar myself with his letters & other works). There seems to be a *de facto* consensus that Lawrence did not take much of an interest in political ideology or party politics. The word apolitical might be an apt term to describe him – certainly "left-wing" or "right-wing" are not (see my comment below on his Eastwood working-class background).

CHAPTER 6

The Diggers and the Maggies

SCOTT'S big revelation (we can take it here that "Jack Callcott" is Jack Scott[185] – for only he would be in a position to tell Lawrence what follows) came later on Sunday, probably in the early evening. So that they could be alone, he asks Lawrence to accompany him down to McCauley's Beach, below *Wyewurk*. There they stand together on the rocks in front of the breaking waves. Scott (as Callcott) opens the conversation. *"'I say,'* he says, *'I shan't be making a mistake if I tell you a few things in confidence, shall I?'"* [K p88] Lawrence – who had half-expected something like this (*"Somers wondered whether Jack was going to say anything to him or not."* [K ibid]) – reassures him: *"'I hope not. But judge for yourself.'"* Scott goes on: *"'Now, look here. This is absolutely between ourselves, now, isn't it?'"* [K ibid] When Lawrence replies yes, he gets to the point.

> *"Well now, there's quite a number of us in Sydney – and in the other towns as well – we're mostly diggers back from the war – we've joined up into a kind of club – and we're sworn in – and we're sworn to OBEY the leaders, no matter what the command, when the time is ready – and we're sworn to keep silent till then. We don't let out much, nothing of any consequence, to the general run of the members."* [K ibid]

There are two accounts in the novel of this crucial conversation, or revelation, regarding the nature, purpose, and background of the secret army that lurks behind the

---

[185] *ie*, Callcott [mark #2]

public façade of the King and Empire Alliance [KEA]. This first account comes in *K* chapter 5 "Coo-ee" and the second in *K* chapter 10 "Diggers" (as mentioned above, chapter 10 is a reprise and elaboration of chapter 5, inserted into the text when Lawrence runs out of new narrative material). Scott's *"general run of the members"* are the ordinary, non-secret-army "civilian" members of the Alliance, which has about 30 local branches and more than 10,000 members spread across Sydney and NSW.[186] The *"kind of club"* is the Alliance's secret inner-core, which Lawrence later calls in chapter 10 "the Maggies"[187]. In reality the KEA's secret army had no "official" name, but was known to its secret soldiers as "the movement" or, colloquially, as "The Garage"[188], it being primarily a mobilisation plan based on car ownership – hence Callcott/Scott's "profession" in the novel: *"a partner in the motor-works place where he works"* (and note in particular the word *"partner"*[189]).

The organisational structure that Lawrence outlines in chapter 5, and more extensively in chapter 10, is highly detailed. In fact, it turns out – astonishingly – that *Kangaroo* is the most comprehensive record we have of secret-army activity in Australia between the wars (and what is known about such activity from other sources[190] confirms the gravamen of Lawrence's account in the novel). At that time,

---

[186] in 34 branches, according to the first issue of the KEA journal *King & Empire* [vol 1, no 1 (January 1921)], implying that there had been a lot of pre-plotting before the KEA emerged from the shadows

[187] as Bruce Steele pointed out [*Steele* p389], Lawrence originally called the Diggers secret army squads "the Dingoes" [*holograph* p325] but later changed this in chapter 10 to "the Maggies" to reflect the black-&-white strip of the local football team, nicknamed "the Butchers" (after the butcher bird, or magpie, which was common to the Thirroul area – see above)

[188] The name "The Garage" is mentioned in a letter from *Bulletin* journalist Malcolm Ellis to Jack Scott (see *Research-Diary* 17/9/77 below) where Ellis said he trusted that Scott's forthcoming trip to Japan was being paid for by "The Garage" (it probably was being paid for by Military Intelligence, *ie* the Army). Ellis, who wrote under the name "Ek Dum", later became assistant editor of *The Bulletin*.

[189] In fact, Lawrence gives Scott [Callcott mark #2] two positions in the *"motor-works place"*. In *K* chapter 2 "Neighbours" Callcott is a *"foreman in a motor-works place"* [*K* p24] & in *K* chapter 5 "Coo-ee" he is *"a sort of partner in the motor-works where he was employed"* [*K* p75] – no doubt "The Garage", in which his other "partner" was, in real-life, Sir Charles Rosenthal.

[190] such as, in particular, Andrew Moore's *The Secret Army & the Premier* [*op cit*]

however, information about the make-up and activities – potential and actual – of the Scott-Rosenthal operation was highly confidential, and not known to the public, nor to what was then "the Media". Indeed, it remains still largely unknown, both to the general public and among much of today's academic community in Australia. Thus it is extremely unlikely, verging on the impossible, that Lawrence could have learnt about the extensive secret-army infrastructure he describes in *K* chapter 5 and *K* chapter 10 from some casual source he happened upon, in the street as it were, in Sydney or Thirroul.[191] Only Jack Scott could have told him.

By now Lawrence must have thought that the material he was deriving from Scott – *"drawing him out"*[K p291] – might provide him with some ingredients for his projected Australian "romance". So he had good reason to continue to *"draw him out"*. (This *"drawing out"* will take on a far more serious connotation in the future *K* "Jack Slaps Back" chapter.) More of a mystery, or puzzle, is why Scott – *"'the indiscreet Callcott'"*[K p110] – chose to divulge so much to him. But I will offer an answer to that important question in my chapter 19 "Postscript" below.

Down on the rock-shelf, Scott tells Lawrence about the structure of "the Maggie" squads – the KEA's secret army – which consists of cells or an inner-core within the "Diggers Clubs". (In *Kangaroo* the "public", non-secret-army side of the KEA is portrayed as the "Diggers Clubs", which is at odds with its name, for Lawrence's choice of the word "Diggers" invests it with a more overtly military connotation than the KEA, which was ostensibly a civilian association, in reality had.[192]) In the text of *Kangaroo* Lawrence reveals how long the

---

[191] Which was until recently the explanation in Lawrence circles for the secret army content in *Kangaroo*. Yet it is now fairly widely accepted that the secret army plot is (despite Bruce Steele's 1994 CUP assertion that "this has now been shown to be without foundation" [*Steele Introduction* p xxviii]), based on *some* reality – see, for example, *Ellis* p45 & *Davis* p8.

[192] The term "Diggers" refers to the WW1 Australian troops, & originated in France in 1916 (though the term "diggers" probably goes back to the goldfield "diggings" of the 1850s). When

KEA cover organisation had been going – "'*18 months, almost two years altogether'*"[K p93] – a period almost to the exact June 1920 date when the King and Empire Alliance had been formed after the election in March 1920 of the Storey Labor Government.

Lawrence, who is understandably confused, tries to make sense of what Scott is telling him.

> *He tried to piece together all that Jack had been letting off at him. Returned soldiers' clubs, chiefly athletics, with a more or less secret core to each club, and all the secret cores working together secretly in all the state under one chief head, and apparently with military penalties for any transgression. It was not a bad idea.*[193]

...which is a pretty good description of the actuality of the dual public/secret structure of the KEA organisation (the "two-tier" operation originally outlined in the Herbert Brookes Papers[194] in Australia's National Archives). Scott appreciates that Lawrence won't understand much of what he is telling him. *"I tell it you just in rough, you know,'"* he says. And indeed, the detail in the two accounts – first in chapter 5, and the second in chapter 10 – differ considerably, although its subsequent repetition, when Lawrence is in dire need of new narrative material, is more extensive. In the first (chapter 5) version Lawrence asks Scott/Callcott what the purpose of all this secret plotting is. The aim, Scott/Callcott tells him, is

---

Lawrence in *Kangaroo* refers to "the Diggers clubs" he is referring to the KEA. (However, in a letter he sent Seltzer in October 1922 [*Letters* #2623], asking ingenuously: "Do you think the Australian Govt. or the Diggers might resent anything? Let me know this as soon as possible", he was probably referring to WW1 ex-servicemen ["the Diggers"] in general.)

[193] this quote & the following exchange come from *K* pp 93-94

[194] Herbert & Ivy Brookes papers [*NLA MS* 1924]. Herbert Brookes, a Melbourne businessman & conservative *eminence grise*, was the organising-mind behind Australia's secret armies between the wars. Among the strongest evidence we have of Lawrence's encounter with a secret army in Sydney in 1922 is the correlation between the dual arrangement of the APL organisation outlined in the Brookes Papers (a public facade & a secret inner-core [see *Research-Diary* 15/3/78 below]) & the twin Diggers & Maggies organisational structure Lawrence describes "fictionally" in *Kangaroo*.

"'*a sort of <u>revolution</u> and a seizing of political power*'"[195]. That must have sounded of interest to Lawrence, poised to splash down more of his new "romance", set in Australia.

Lawrence, at this point in his life, is aware of what fascism is. Until recently he was living in Italy, where Mussolini was much in the news. Like a lot of middle-class Englishmen of his time – and after – the concept of authoritarianism and dictators held a siren attraction. He no doubt shared a general post-war disenchantment with parliamentary democracy, a disillusionment that later led on to appeasement, Mosley and Munich. He is initially attracted by what Scott was telling him. "*Somers at once felt the idea was a good one*," he writes in chapter 5. Yet, to give him credit, he has his reservations, even at this early stage ("*The only thing he mistrusted was the dryness in Jack's voice: a sort of that's-how-it's-got-to-be dryness, sharp and authoritative.*"[196]).

If the storyline reflects reality – as I believe in *Kangaroo* it does – Scott wanted Lawrence to join the KEA's secret army, the Maggies. "'*Feel like joining in?*'" he asks. In the text, Lawrence appears ambivalent, or wary. "*Let me think about it a bit, will you?*'" he replies. However, if he did have any caveats, he must have kept them from Scott, whom he now has to "string along" or "draw out" to obtain more material for the novel he will resume splashing down as soon as Scott is out of the way. Scott has, of course, no idea – and Lawrence certainly isn't going to tell him – that his new chum's interest is entirely literary. Its politics (left, right or centre) are of no interest to him outside his fictional framework.

It is of interest that Scott wanted, apparently, Lawrence to join the secret-army side of the KEA: in other words, its clandestine inner-core. If all he had wanted Lawrence to do was contribute some articles for their magazine, there would

---

[195] note the term "revolution" [my emphasis], for we will return to that – see chapter 19, "Postscript"
[196] these & the following quotes are from *K* pp 92-94

have been no need to tell him about the secret paramilitary side of the two-tier, Janus-faced organisation. Yet if Lawrence were being potentially recruited to perform, in the longer term, the same role and function as George Augustine Taylor[197] (who certainly was part of the secret side of things, as well as being the effective editor of their journal), he would have to be told about "The Garage". At this point Scott would have assumed that Lawrence was going to be in Australia for some time, and was not just "passing through". Lawrence would not have let on that he was only waiting for money from America to arrive – a matter of weeks – before continuing his onward journey to Taos, and was merely biding his time in the interim dashing off a quick piece of ostensible fiction. For Lawrence, Scott was little more than a casual, passing acquaintance; a potential source of narrative material, and half a character[198] for his new "romance".

This first disclosure of secret-army information ends with Scott and Lawrence returning to *Wyewurk*, where "*the women*" [K p95] ask them what they were talking about down on the beach. In the novel Callcott/Scott replies: "'*Politics and red-hot treason.*'"[K ibid] In the second disclosure, five chapters later, the secret-army conversation again starts on the beach below *Wyewurk*. This time, however, Lawrence recalls more of what Scott had told him in Thirroul almost two weeks earlier. I quote the text:

> *He heard again*[199] *all about the Diggers' Clubs: nearly all soldiers and sailors who had been in the war, but not restricted to these. They had started like any other social club: games, athletics, lectures, readings, discussions, debates. No gambling, no drink, no class or party distinction. The clubs*

---

[197] see "The Man Who Wasn't There" [*Rananim op cit*]. Taylor, a civilian-Army intelligence officer, attended the Sydney Town Hall meeting at which the KEA was formed in June 1920 (no doubt at Rosenthal's invitation)
[198] the other half being Adrian Friend [ie, Callcott mark #1] (see above & below)
[199] note the word "again" (confirming it is a reprise of the earlier chapter 5 "Coo-ee" revelations)

were still chiefly athletics, but not SPORTING. They went in for boxing, wrestling, fencing, and knife-+throwing, and revolver practice. But they had swimming and rowing squads, and rifle-ranges for rifle practice, and they had regular military training. The colonel who planned out the military training was a clever chap. The men were grouped in little squads of twenty, <u>each</u> with sergeant and corporal. Each of these twenty was trained to act like a scout, independently, though the squad worked in absolute unison among themselves, and were pledged to absolute obedience of higher commands. These commands, however, left most of the devising and method of execution of the job in hand to the squad itself. In New South Wales the Maggies, as these private squads[200] *were called, numbered already about <u>fourteen hundred,</u> all perfectly trained and equipped.* [K pp 185-186, my emphasis]

In "real life" the KEA's shadow secret-army units were organised into "squads" of five – that being the number who would fit into a car.[201] However, the figure 1400 (which Lawrence could not possibly have invented) is of particular interest, for it gives a unique insight into the size and extent of the secret-core – the "Maggie" squads – of Scott and Rosenthal's KEA organisation (so about one in 10 members of the overall organisation was made up of its secret soldiers). It constituted a formidable State-wide paramilitary force.

"*The colonel*" whom Lawrence in this text refers to as "*Colonel Ennis*" (the name of a judge he met in Ceylon[202]) was in real-life Brigadier-General George Macarthur-Onslow, who had been a general in the Australian Light Horse during WW1, and who was no doubt the military head of the KEA's secret army (Major Jack Scott being the senior "staff officer"

---

[200] the "*private squads*" were of course the KEA's secret army, "The Garage"
[201] the figure of 20 cited here by Lawrence was made up of four "squads" of five (in four cars)
[202] Lawrence & Frieda spent their last two nights in Colombo at the Ennis's bungalow *Braemore* (Lawrence is recycling here the names of people he previously met)

of the metropolitan section of the "army", as well as its overall co-founder). Scott's role is mainly admin. He is what Lawrence refers to as a *"teller"*, or secretary. In fact, he is chief of all the tellers, as the text in chapter 10 makes out:

> ...*in the person of the chief, and interpreted by him unquestioned save by his lieutenant, the chief of all the secretaries, or tellers.* [K p168]

...confirming that Scott, *"the chief of all the secretaries or tellers"*, was the joint leader of the KEA (of which he was, officially, its treasurer – its "teller" – and Rosenthal's 2–i–c, as he had been in England in 1918-19). Initially, in chapter 5, Lawrence makes some effort to keep the assurance or pledge he made to Scott to be discreet, and doesn't divulge too much structural detail, first time round. But this promise will fall by the wayside in chapter 10, when, as we shall see, his need for further narrative material becomes pressing. Then his revelation about *"Colonel Ennis"* carries very little disguise with it. He portrays *"Colonel Ennis"* as wearing white riding-breeches and the distinctive white plume of the Australian Light Horse cavalry division. (In the original text – the first, Thirroul, *holograph* version of the novel – Lawrence gave the Colonel Ennis's secret soldiers black shirts: the uniform of Mussolini's *Fascisti*.[203])

Secret-army revelations aside, much of Sunday and Monday of the holiday weekend is spent preparing a big "thank-you" lunch Frieda and Lawrence are hosting to express their gratitude for the help they have been given by Scott and the Friends, in which task Frieda may have been assisted by "Fanny" Friend, Lawrence saying in the text that *"the two women"* were baking while *"the men"* were down on

---

[203] [*holograph* p325] hence also their fictional name, "The Maggies" (see above re the Thirroul football team's black & white "strip")

the beach.[204] In chapter 2 Lawrence describes their "party" preparations in some detail.[205]

> *Somers knew why Harriet had launched this invitation. It was because she had had a wonderfully successful cooking morning. Like plenty of other women Harriet had learned to cook during war-time, and now she loved it, once in a while. This had been one of the whiles. Somers had stoked the excellent little stove, and peeled the apples and potatoes and onions and pumpkin, and looked after the meat and the sauces, while Harriet had lashed out in pies and tarts and little cakes and baked custard. She now surveyed her prize Beeton shelf with love, and began to whisk up a mayonnaise for potato salad.* [K p34]

In reality, Frieda as a Richthofen was not very domesticated, and she would have needed some help, probably from her now neighbour "Fanny", to prepare a lunch for perhaps seven or eight people, especially using the rather primitive catering facilities (fuel stove, a motley collection of cutlery and crockery, etc) of the holiday cottage.[206] However, they could have used the facilities of both kitchens – *Wyewurk* and *Wyewurrie* – if necessary.

Scott left late on Monday afternoon to return to Sydney, joining the many holiday-makers who had to be back at work on Tuesday. Before he went, however, he apparently

---

[204] the lunch was probably held on the Monday, marking the King's birthday, which was a significant imperialist anniversary for the King & Empire Alliance

[205] The "thank you" lunch is portrayed in chapter 2 "Neighbours" as ostensibly taking place before they went down to Thirroul [see *K* p34]. However, it actually happened a week later on the King's Birthday weekend, probably on Sunday June 4. This is averred to at *K* p86: "*Victoria & Harriet were cooking roast pork & apple sauce, & baking little cakes.*" Lawrence had used the same "*little cakes*" in the previous [*K* p34] passage. This is yet another example of Lawrence's resourceful "double-use" repetition & transformation techniques.

[206] We do not know how *Wyewurk* was furnished & equipped, so this is assumption from experience of such holiday places in NSW resort towns & holiday venues. Lawrence does, however, describe some of the kitchen items they found in the cottage: "*There were eleven white breakfast cups, of which nine had smashed handles & broad tin substitutes quite cannily put on. There were two saucers only. & all the rest to match: seven large brown teapots, of which five had broken spouts: not one whole dish or basin of any sort, except a sauce boat.*" [*K* p84].

arranged with Lawrence for him to come up to town two days later to meet, for the first time, the titular and organisational head of the King and Empire Alliance, Sir Charles Rosenthal, who is to become "Kangaroo", and the title character of Lawrence's new Australian "romance".[207]

---

[207] thus delivering to a grateful Lawrence a larger-than-life (see below) character to help populate his new Australian novel

CHAPTER 7

Getting Down to Business

A LOT has happened to Lawrence since he and Frieda arrived in Sydney over a week ago. He has plenty to write about. But he is determined that Scott won't know that he has started writing a novel in which he, Scott, is to play a leading role. For that would remove any "spontaneity", and put people such as Scott on their guard – and, no doubt, deprive him of further information from them, and about their doings.[208] So, although he was no doubt impatient to put pen to paper as soon as he returned to *Wyewurk* that Saturday, he would not have wanted Scott to see him actually writing, as Scott, no doubt, would ask what he was writing about (Scott having already asked him about his writing intentions in Australia). The Friends next door might have seen Lawrence writing – he tended to write outdoors if possible – but they would not have realised, nor been interested in, what it was. (Lawrence saying that he was translating something would have been accepted without question.[209]) Nevertheless, he is likely to have been making some progress with his new

---

[208] Lawrence in Sydney & Thirroul (in contrast to what he did in Western Australia) made considerable efforts to keep his writing persona in mufti (note Somers' reluctance in *Kangaroo* to talk about what he does [*K* pp 30-31] & the absence throughout the otherwise autobiographical text of any reference to what he was actually doing, almost every day, in Thirroul – writing a novel of Australia). This, added to the insistence in both his & Frieda's correspondence that they "met no one" in Sydney & Thirroul [*Letters* #2528, 2535, 2537, 2541, 2542, 2544, 2546, 2552 & 2557 & Frieda's autobiography [*Frieda*, p120 : "we had no human contacts"] has led many critics & readers of *Kangaroo* grievously astray (*eg*, Steele [generally] & *Davis* p71, *Ellis* p70 [specifically]). To his credit, however, Bruce Steele conceded that the "met no one" terminology does not refer to casual acquaintances [see *Steele* p xxxii]. For further about the repeated "met no one" references, again see "Letters of Introduction" [*Rananim* vol 1, no 1 (October 1993)].

[209] Lawrence had been translating the works of the Sicilian author Giovanni Verga since leaving Taormina in February 1922. He continued his translating after he finished *Kangaroo* in July (the snapshot of Lawrence – see *photo-insert* – sitting in front of *Wyewurk*, taken by Denis Forrester during the weekend of July 29-30, shows Lawrence apparently writing something, probably continuing his translation of Verga's *Cavalleria Rusticana*).

"romance" during the King's Birthday weekend (he would have at least been composing some text in his mind[210]).

The first session, which he wrote the previous Wednesday, consisted of nine manuscript pages, ending this first section, as mentioned above, with Somers and Harriett jogging in a hansom-cab through Sydney on their way to *"51 Murdoch Street"*. The second session, perhaps composed and written on Sunday June 4 – while Scott may have been away visiting the Friends – consisted of about 3050 words [section #2 MS pp 9b-26], recording the arrival at *Torestin* in Sydney and the conversation in the garden there with Jack[211] and Victoria Callcott. The third session [section #3 pp 26-33 c2460 words] – possibly written on Monday afternoon or evening – consisted of his first impressions or comments about Australia and Australians. The apparent absence of class and authority worried him.

> *Somers for the first time felt himself immersed in real democracy…There was no giving of orders here; or, if orders were given, they would not be received as such. A man in one position might make a suggestion to a man in another position, and this latter might or might not accept the suggestion, according to his disposition…Was all that stood between Australia and anarchy just a name? – the name of England, Britain, Empire, Viceroy, or Governor General, or Governor? The shadow of the old sceptre, the mere sounding of a name? Was it just the hollow word "Authority", sounding across seven thousand miles of sea, that kept Australia from Anarchy?* [K pp 20-21]

His fourth writing session, committed to paper on Tuesday June 6, took him from the end of chapter 1, where he decided

---

[210] as explained above & below, Lawrence composed or perhaps collated his text before writing it down ("as if by dictation" [see the *Preface* in volume 2 of my *99 Days*] re this)
[211] Jack Callcott mark #1 [*ie* Adrian Friend]

that *"Given a good temper and a genuinely tolerant nature – both of which the Australians seem to have in a high degree – you can get on for quite a long time without 'rule'."*K pp 22-23 to the trip to Narrabeen on that first Sunday in Sydney [section #4 MS pp 34-51 c3010 words].

The King's Birthday holiday weekend had provided Lawrence with a promising vein of material to go on with. Again, the question must be asked: how much of this – particularly its secret-army material – is "slapping down reality", and how much orthodox fiction (*ie* "creative" writing). Before he came to Australia – in the initial text of his previous book *Fantasia of the Unconscious* – Lawrence praised a Whitmanesque "League of Comrades", intended to foster manly comradeship across America. This bears some similarity to Lawrence's "fictional" secret army in Australia – and indeed Lawrence specifically mentions Whitman's League of Comrades in his "Willie Struthers and Kangaroo" chapter[212]). In *Fantasia* Lawrence had suggested that the League of Comrades could be made up of cells of 10, each with an elected leader. This is uncannily, if not suspiciously, similar to Cooley/Callcott's "fictional" secret army, made up – according to the text cited above – of units of 20, each electing a leader. Yet in reality the actual KEA secret army was <u>not</u> organised that way. Its leaders were <u>not</u> elected, but appointed. This is Lawrentian invention, or rather Lawrentian disguise.[213] The Maggies (as mentioned above) were organised around car-ownership within local branches of the K&E Alliance, and consisted of car-borne units of five secret soldiers. As also mentioned above, Scott and Rosenthal's secret army was essentially a mobilisation plan, made up of middle-class "loyalists" who had agreed to be

---

[212] see *K* p197
[213] &/or a "carry-over" from *Fantasia*. However, Steele is right to emphasise the probable connection between *Fantasia's* League of Comrades and *Kangaroo's* Diggers & Maggies. The similarities are striking. I have little doubt that in attempting to put into words what Scott had told him about the Diggers & Maggies, Lawrence was incorporating some of *Fantasia's* League of Comrades fictional structure.

ready to go into action when called upon and to rendezvous at the garage of a neighbour who owned a car. It now seems that the connection between *Fantasia's* League of Comrades and Scott's secret army was Lawrence's transformation techniques. Apparently, he conflated the two – Whitman's League of Comrades and Scott's "The Garage" – and came up with *Kangaroo's* Maggie squads of 20.[214]

It was his habit, as he indicates in *Kangaroo*, to write in the morning, after finishing his breakfast chores. Indeed, he was following the advice he had given to "Mollie" Skinner[215] in the backyard of *Leithdale* several weeks ago. He now elaborates:

> *He always got up in the morning, made the fire, swept the room, and tidied roughly. Then he brought in coal and wood, made the breakfast, and did any little out-door job. After breakfast he helped to wash up, and settled the fire. Then he considered himself free to his own devices* [K pp 162-163]

If the weather[216] were propitious, this usually meant going out into the front garden of *Wyewurk*, sitting against the wall of the verandah (see the snapshot of Lawrence in the *photo-insert*) and filling one of the exercise-books he had bought in Ceylon with his easy, fluent "as if by dictation" script.[217] There is no hint yet in chapter 2 of any secret-army content, though this narrative-ingredient must have already been simmering in his mind. However, he has plenty earlier to write about before he catches up with Jack Scott's secret-army

---

[214] *ie*, 4x5=20 (a single car-load of five secret soldiers would not have been much of a threat, while four car-loads of mobilised secret soldiers could have delivered a force to be reckoned with)

[215] *cf*: "take an hour – the same hour – that's very important – daily. Write bit by bit of the scenes you have witnessed, the people you know, describing their reactions as you know they do react" [*Fifth Sparrow*, pp 115-116]

[216] the contemporary weather conditions are derived from the daily weather reports in the *SMH* (where it recorded that Tuesday June 6 was "unsettled" [*SMH* p13])

[217] see *Research-Diary* entry 9/1/93 below re Witter Bynner's remarks on Lawrence "writing as if by dictation"

revelations divulged during the recent holiday weekend.

Wednesday is another busy writing day. In the morning between 9am and noon he writes section #5 of his text [MS pp 51-66 c3300 words], from the car-trip back to town in chapter 2, to the start of *K* chapter 3, "Larboard Watch Ahoy!". He has written about 12,000 words in three, or more probably four, days. He has a lot of "catching up" ahead of him, for he is still some distance "behind the action". After lunch he may have spent the rest of the day pottering around the house, and perhaps going for a walk along McCauley's Beach, below *Wyewurk*, with Frieda.

On Thursday Lawrence probably spends some of the morning writing section #6 [pp 67-86 c3950 words] before going, as planned, up to Sydney by the late-morning train to rendezvous with Jack Scott at his Pitt Street office, and accompany him up Hoskins Place[218] to Mendes Chambers at 8 Castlereagh Street, on the third floor of which[219] is the private accommodation of Sir Charles Rosenthal, the head of the King and Empire Alliance, and Scott's immediate superior in the KEA. Lawrence will write a full account of the lunch which will supply the bulk of his later chapter 6, "Kangaroo". Importantly, he will begin that future section with a major clue about how all this came about. (For it is well-nigh incredible that Lawrence, a complete stranger to Australia, could have, on his second day in Sydney, stumbled on an organisation so secret that even today it is known to only a select few.) On the King's Birthday Monday, when Jack had invited him to come up to Sydney later in the week, Callcott/Scott told Somers/Lawrence that he had already mentioned him to his superior, whom he calls Benjamin Cooley, or "Kangaroo".

---

[218] in the text, Lawrence, applying his transformation techniques – this time a geographical switch – converts Pitt Street into the parallel George Street, viz: *"Somers went down to George Street to find Jack and to be taken by him to luncheon with the Kangaroo".*[K p107]
[219] According to the *Sands Directory* for 1922, Rosenthal's architectural practice was on the second floor. However, the *Kangaroo* text implies he also had residential accommodation on the third floor (see my chapter 9 *Betwixt & Between* & my chapter 11 *The Horrible Paws* below).

> *"He'd like to see you. Should you care to have lunch with him and me in town to-morrow?"*
>
> *"Have you told him you've talked to me?"*
>
> *"Oh yes – told him before I did it.*[220] *He knows your writings – read all you've written, apparently. He'd heard about you too from a chap on the Naldera.*[221] *That's the boat you came by, isn't it?"* [K p104]

Many years later, in the late 1930s, a literary soiree in Melbourne was told by a leading Australian business figure[222] that *Kangaroo* had been based on fact, and that Lawrence had indeed run across a secret army in Sydney in 1922. When asked how such an extraordinary event could have occurred, he replied, according to one of those present

> To know the answer to that question, you must look at the passenger list of the boat that brought Lawrence to Sydney. [223]

That passenger was, of course, Gerald Hum, who had met and befriended Lawrence on the *Osterley* between Naples and Colombo, and who introduced him to Jack Scott at the tea-party at Narrabeen on that first Sunday in Sydney. Hum, being a middle-class car-owning conservative, would almost certainly have been involved with the KEA and "The Garage". (In fact, as a supplier of hats, he may have provided them with their makeshift "helmets", which were bowler-hats stuffed with newspaper.[224])

---

[220] *ie*, before he had got his permission to talk to Lawrence
[221] the boat Lawrence is disguising (or "transforming") here as "*the Naldera*" was the *Malwa*, which brought him & Frieda to Sydney
[222] it is my belief that the business figure was probably Sir Philip Goldfinch, titular head of the 1930-32 Old Guard & CEO of Burns Philp, then Australia's second-biggest public company (also see my *Introduction* above)
[223] personal letter from Ernest Whiting {23/5/76] (see *Research-Diary* 8/8/77 entry below)
[224] as mentioned by Andrew Moore [*Moore* p69]

CHAPTER 8

Kangaroo

SIR CHARLES ROSENTHAL was not your ordinary Australian. Nor for that matter was Jack Scott. Yet so taken was Lawrence with them both that he put each of them into two of his later works – Jack Scott becoming Jack Strangeways in *John Thomas and Lady Jane*, and Rosenthal being Major Charles Eastwood in *The Virgin and the Gypsy*. (Neither of which was published in Lawrence's lifetime – so he had no opportunity to revise their text, and thus remove anything defamatory or "sensitive". They are today as he originally wrote them).[225]

Rosenthal, like Major Charles Eastwood, was of Danish ancestry. He had been a major-general in WW1, and had been knighted on the battlefield, where he distinguished himself both as a military leader and through acts of personal bravery.[226] In 1918-19, as mentioned above, he and Scott were put in charge of the repatriation of the Australian troops from Europe, the then Captain Scott being Rosenthal's deputy. Rosenthal was also remarkable physically. He was a very large man[227] (again, like Major Charles Eastwood) and renowned for his strength. He used to take on tug-o'-war teams single-handedly (well, double-handedly). He had trained as an architect, and was now, in 1922, a leader in his profession. In his younger days he had worked as a draftsman in Western Australia, after which he rode back to

---

[225] see "A Roo by Any Other Name" [*Rananim* vol 5, no 3 (August 1997) pp 24-26] for the parallels between Charles Eastwood & Charles Rosenthal on the one hand, & Jack Strangeways & Jack Scott on the other (also see *Research-Diary* 8/8/94 entry below for the original insight)
[226] see my "The Man Who Was Kangaroo" [*Quadrant*, Sydney (September 1987)]
[227] in *Kangaroo* Lawrence describes Cooley as "*bear-like*" [K p136]

Melbourne on a bicycle across the Nullarbor Plain – alone, when the road was little more than a dirt-track in the desert. He was a committed protestant (he was born a Congregationalist) and was avowedly anti-Catholic. He had been recently elected, not only an alderman on the Sydney Municipal Council, but also a member of the NSW State Parliament. He was one of the leading citizens in the State.[228] In mid-1920 he had teamed up with Scott again to form the King and Empire Alliance, the "front organisation" for a shadow APL-style[229] secret army. While he left the running of its "Maggie squads" to Scott and Macarthur-Onslow, he (as Lawrence relates) *"slaved at the other half of the business"*[K p183], the public side. He was also the titular editor of its monthly journal, *King and Empire*. Despite his various achievements and impressive war record, he was comparatively young, still in his 40s (as was Major Charles Eastwood in *The Virgin and the Gypsy*).[230]

The purpose of the lunch in his rooms in Castlereagh Street was apparently to meet Lawrence and see if he might come in useful for their journal *King and Empire*.[231] One of the first questions Cooley asks Somers is: *"'I hope you are going to write something for us?'"*[K p109] Though we should assume that Lawrence's account of the lunch in *Kangaroo* is reasonably accurate, the ideology Cooley espouses at the lunch is mainly that of George Augustine Taylor and *The Sequel*, put into the

---

[228] & the voice of the returned servicemen in Sydney – see the *SMH* report [*SMH* 31/5/20] of the 1920 Moore Park Father Jerger incident (cited above) where he was the principal speaker from the "loyalist"/protestant platform

[229] The Australian Protective League (APL) was the original name of what became Lawrence's Diggers & Maggies organisation, as revealed in the Brookes Papers mentioned above (also see Joan Jenson's *The Price of Vigilance* [Rand McNally Chicago (1968) at p234] confirming that c.1918 the American Protective League precedent/model was brought to Australia)

[230] Lawrence may have derived the surname "Eastwood" from a village in the Black Forest to the east of where he was staying in Germany in 1912. The village was named Rosenthal. It has been speculated that Lawrence's use of the name "Eastwood" could be a reference to "the squire of [his home village] Eastwood", Thomas Barber, who was a captain in the Boer War. However, Major Charles Eastwood in Lawrence's novella bears no similarity to Captain Thomas Barber (apart from the name "Eastwood"). Barber was not particularly large and robust (like Rosenthal), nor did he have any Jewish connection, & and, unlike Rosenthal, his parent were not Danish.

[231] Somers is later offered the job of editor of a new socialist newspaper [*K* pp 200-202], but that is almost certainly a switch or transposition of the offer Rosenthal presumably made during this lunch in his apartment.

mouth of Cooley as part of Lawrence's transposition/amalgamation techniques.

> *They arrived at Mr. Cooley's chambers punctually. It was a handsome apartment with handsome jarrah furniture, dark and suave, and some very beautiful rugs. Mr. Cooley came at once: and he WAS a kangaroo. His face was long and lean and pendulous, with eyes set close together behind his pince-nez: and his body was stout but firm. He was a man of forty or so, hard to tell, swarthy, with short-cropped dark hair and a smallish head carried rather forward on his large but sensitive, almost shy body.* [K p107]

Before arriving at Cooley's apartment, Jack Callcott[232] explains why Cooley is called "Kangaroo"– he "'*Looks like one*'"[K p104]. But his name is also intended to be a reference to the Australian coat-of-arms, which features as heraldic supporters a kangaroo and an emu. Indeed, "Emu" is said in the novel to be the name of Cooley's secret-army equivalent in Victoria (actually Sir John Monash – who is the choice in the current CUP edition of *Kangaroo* as the inspiration or model for Cooley[233]).

One of the most controversial aspects of the novel is Lawrence's portrayal of Cooley as being Jewish. He introduces Cooley's pseudo-Jewishness at the lunch in Castlereagh Street.

> *...there came an exceedingly sweet charm into his face, for a moment his face was like a flower. Yet he was quite ugly. And surely, thought Somers, it is Jewish blood. The very best that*

---

[232] [mark #2] *ie* Scott
[233] A choice (see *Steele* p xxix) somewhat undermined by Lawrence's description in this chapter of Cooley as someone "*they like on The Bulletin*" [K p104], there being no sign of anything Lawrence could have read in any current *Bulletin* issue praising of Monash. Yet on page 7 of *The Bulletin* of Thursday June 8 – the issue from which Lawrence extracted the Cape York tiger-cat story – there is an article that specifically praised Rosenthal, his name heading a list of five NSW MPs who were "one of a whole herd of highly qualified business & commercial [parliamentarians] with bright records as fighting soldiers".

> *is in the Jewish blood: a faculty for pure disinterestedness, and warm, physically warm love, that seems to make the corpuscles of the blood glow. And after the smile his face went stupid and kangaroo-like, pendulous, with the eyes close together above the long, drooping nose. But the shape of the head was very beautiful, small, light, and fine. The man had surely Jewish blood.* [K p110]

Rosenthal – partly because Rosenthal is a common Jewish name, and partly because of his Levantine appearance – was often mistaken for being Jewish. (Later, in the 1930s, when Rosenthal was appointed the Administrator of Norfolk Island, *The Bulletin* felt constrained to point out that he was not, contrary to popular perception, Jewish.[234]) Cooley's supposed, or apparent Jewishness has caused much comment down the years, particularly in the light of the Holocaust. It was the main reason why two of Lawrence's Jewish acquaintances, Koteliansky and Dr David Eder, were subsequently[235] put forward as the inspiration for Cooley in *Kangaroo*. (We will return to Cooley's Jewishness, and its possible fascist ramifications, in my final chapter "Postscript".) However, it is worth pointing out here that Lawrence's portrayal of Cooley being "possibly" or ambivalently Jewish would argue against the CUP's choice of Sir John Monash as the inspiration or model for the character Benjamin Cooley. For there was no doubt about Monash's Jewishness, as that was clearly what he unashamedly was, while there *was* doubt about Rosenthal, who was of the protestant faith.)

In the text, after the lunch table is cleared and they move

---

[234] See *Research-Diary* 27/1/77 & 20/12/82 below re my early mistake about Rosenthal being Jewish (& while in corrective mode, I have to confess I have mislaid *The Bulletin* reference above about Rosenthal & "popular perception". But having had staff-access to *The Bulletin's* archives [subsequently destroyed] for many years, my assurance that it was there can be taken as reliable).

[235] by a wide range of people, including Bruce Steele [see *Steele* p xxix]

"into the study"[236] for coffee, Cooley comes to the purpose of the meeting. He begins:

> *"The indiscreet Callcott told you about our Kangaroo clubs"* [K p110]

Here Lawrence is referring to the "Maggies" secret inner-core – "The Garage" – not its ostensibly innocuous "Diggers Clubs" civilian cover-organisation. (In fact, he does not actually introduce the name "Maggies" until chapter 10 – see below.)

> *"He gave me a very sketchy outline"* [Somers/Lawrence replies].
> *"It interested you?"* [Cooley/Rosenthal asks]
> *"Exceedingly."* [K ibid]

The conversation turns to politics, and Cooley/Rosenthal begins to advance authoritarian and anti-democratic ideas. There is nothing in newspaper or other reports that Rosenthal ever said any of these things. However, Taylor did, having laid them out in *The Sequel*, which Lawrence almost certainly read while staying in Jack Scott's accommodation in Sydney[237]. Cooley goes on:

> *"I want to keep ORDER...I want to remove physical misery as far as possible. That I am sure of. And that you can only do by exerting strong, just POWER from above.* [K p111]

---

[236] Note the word "study", indicating residential/domestic accommodation (see *K* p107 above & *Appendix 1* below re Rosenthal's Castlereagh Street living quarters). It had long been a puzzle how a busy architect's office in Sydney's CBD could have had such lavish fittings & décor as Lawrence describes in *Kangaroo* – "a queer old copper bowl, Queen Anne silver, a tablecloth with heavy point edging, Venetian wine-glasses, red and white wine in Venetian wine-jugs, a Chinaman waiting at table, offering first a silver dish..." [K p108]. The explanation is that Rosenthal maintained an apartment on the third floor above his architects' office, which was a not-uncommon practice in Sydney at that time.

[237] on Thursday, Friday & Saturday June 1-3 (& from where, as outlined above, Lawrence derived the name "Cooley" – *ie*, off a shelf in Scott's bookcase)

In the text, Somers agrees with this. Yet we cannot tell how much of what Cooley espouses in this chapter – rank authoritarianism, drifting towards fascism – is Rosenthal, or Taylor, or Lawrence. In fact, a lot of it must surely be Lawrence himself, and what he then believed in, or was sympathetic to. (This and other similar passages in *Kangaroo* have done almost as much damage to Lawrence's reputation in progressive circles as all his alleged misogamy and male chauvinism in works like *Women in Love* and *Lady Chatterley's Lover*.) In this account in *K* chapter 6 Cooley goes on to advocate a dictatorship in Australia, with himself as the *Führer*. Man needs, he says…

> …*to be relieved from this terrible responsibility of governing himself when he doesn't know what he wants, and has no aim towards which to govern himself. Man again needs a father – not a friend or a brother sufferer, a suffering Saviour. Man needs a quiet, gentle father…I offer myself* [K p113]

Somers almost physically warms to Cooley…"*this man's warm, wise heart was too much for him*".[K ibid] Lawrence is on the verge of hero-worship, if not something more serious ("'*Why, the man is like a god, I love him,*' he thought to himself."[K ibid]). These and similar proto-fascist (and homoerotic) passages in this chapter should be kept in mind when we come to *K* chapter 11, and the climactic Saturday evening confrontation with Cooley in his apartment in town (the homoerotic element will be discussed more fully in *Appendix 1*).

After the lunch is over, Somers and Callcott – according to the text – walk back together to Callcott's (*ie*, Scott's[238]) office in Pitt Street, from where Lawrence can take his leave

---

[238] Callcott mark #2 is Scott. I shall replace the name "Callcott" with Scott's name when I am sure it is Scott whom Lawrence is referring to (as mentioned above, Callcott can be either Scott [Callcott mark #2] or Adrian Friend [Callcott mark #1]).

to return to *Wyewurk*. According to the text Callcott[239] asks Somers:

> "'What do you think of Kangaroo?'"
> "'He's certainly a wonder,'" (replies Somers [K p116])

On the way back to Thirroul, Lawrence buys a current issue of *The Bulletin* to take back to *Wyewurk*. For when he comes to write up the meeting with Cooley he inserts, immediately after his account of the lunch, an extract from its June 8 issue, describing a (fictional) fight at *"Cape York"* between a kangaroo and a *"tiger-cat"*.[240] This is the first of what will become a number of "extracts" he inserts into the text of *Kangaroo* (unkind souls might call it plagiarism – although to most of the extracts he gives scrupulous attribution).

Lawrence arrives back in Thirroul in the early evening by the late afternoon train (no doubt after collecting any new mail from Cooks in Martin Place). By now – just over a week since he started writing, and three chapters already written – Lawrence decides to call the novel *Kangaroo*, and for its principal Australian protagonist to be Benjamin Cooley, based primarily on Charles Rosenthal, with a strong injection of the absent Taylor's ideology added to the brew, reproduced from Lawrence's recall of his reading Taylor's *The Sequel*.[241]

As will soon become clear, it is my strong belief that some sort of homoerotic event occurred at this crucial Thursday June 8 meeting in Rosenthal's apartment in town. I believe that Rosenthal asked Lawrence to stay behind after Scott left to return to his office. Then, Rosenthal – having discerning what he thought were homosexual indications in Lawrence – made some homoerotic overtures, which I believe

---

[239] *ie* Scott [Callcott mark #2]
[240] see *K* pp 116-117 & *The Bulletin* 8/6/22 re the (borrowed) *"tiger cat"* extract
[241] see footnote below

are reflected (obliquely) in the text:

> *...I'm very glad you came. You understand what I mean, I know, when I say we are <u>birds of the same feather</u>. Aren't we?"*
> *"In some ways I think we are."*
> *"Yes. <u>In the feathery line</u>. When shall I see you again?"*
> [K p115, my emphases]

It is my contention that the phrases *"birds of the same feather"* and *"in the feathery line"* imply homosexuality.[242] (This contention will be will be followed up following chapters, and most especially in *Appendix 1*, "The Curious Incident of the Red Wooden Heart".)

---

[242] Today, the phrase "birds of a feather" carries overt homosexual connotations. It is in use across the gay community. There is, for instance, a gated gay retirement community in New Mexico of that name. The title of the 1978 film *La Cage au Folles*, about two gay men living in St. Tropez, can be rendered in English as "birds of a feather". This was the name of a 2002 play about two gay penguins in New York's Central Park Zoo & the title of a 2012 book of short stories "inspired by gay life". It is the name of a company in Chicago that organises LGBT weddings & of a gay speed-dating service in Vancouver. Whether the expression was in use in a homosexual context in 1922 is problematical. Yet in an era when homosexual practice had to be clothed in code & euphemism, Lawrence's use of the words *"the feathery line"* could be interpreted as carrying a homoerotic connotation. (What else could he have meant by *"feathery"*?) In any case, the ordinary meaning of Rosenthal's question carries an intimation of a shared covert interest. (Even in our more liberated world of sexual relationships, the question implied by the question *"are we birds of the same feather?"* could be seen as the equivalent to today's more common homosexual approach: "Are you a friend of Dorothy, too?")

CHAPTER 9

Betwixt and Between

A CONSIDERABLE gap is opening up between what is happening from day to day in Sydney and Thirroul, and what Lawrence is writing about. He is now more than a week "behind the action". The "singalong" – the "Larboard Watch Ahoy!" chapter 3 episode – happened the previous Saturday, and the chess game which starts that chapter, two days earlier. He spends Friday June 9 writing most of chapter 3 "Larboard Watch Ahoy!" [section #7 MS pp 86-104 c3960 words]. This goes back even further, to the meeting with Jack Scott opposite Mosman wharf on Thursday June 1.[243] But not much else is happening down at *Wyewurk*, so he has plenty of opportunity to "catch up", writing his daily "quota" of around 4000 words a session.

Lawrence spends some time on Friday replying to the mail he picked up at Cooks in Sydney on Thursday. (He apparently writes his letters in the afternoon or evening.) He tells his agent Mountsier that his new novel is going well ("at a great rate") and will be finished by August (he informs him, however, that he has only £31 left[244]). He tells his mother-in-law that he's writing "a weird novel of Australia".[245] He tells his U.S. publisher Seltzer that it's going well ("but no sex").[246] He tells his future hostess in Taos, Mable Dodge

---

[243] It is important to note here that Lawrence's account of that Mosman Bay meeting was written *after* his meeting with Rosenthal, described above. The gravamen of the exchange at Mosman between "Jaz" & Somers (where Somers is interrogated about his political beliefs & his attitude to "the Empire", etc) is in fact a transfer from what probably occurred in Rosenthal's Castlereagh Street apartment, when Lawrence was (in reality) questioned about such "ideological" matters, so important to the KEA (& as a possible future contributor, or interim editor, for their journal).

[244] *Letters* #2535 [to Mountsier] (Lawrence is keeping to his writing schedule)

[245] *Letters* #2534 [mother-in-law]

[246] *Letters* #2536 [to Seltzer]

[Stern/Luhan], that it's "a queer novel", and that he might do something similar in America.[247]

Saturday is mostly spent writing section #8 [MS pp 104-126 c5040 words]. He is keen to "catch up", with plenty of narrative material already mentally processed and waiting to be written down. In his next session, committed to paper on Sunday June 11 [section #9 MS pp 127-148 c4800 words], he goes even further back, to the trip down to Thirroul and moving into *Wyewurk* almost two weeks ago. In fact, he is reprising their earlier move into *Torestin/Wyewurk*[248] – a "double-use" or repetition stratagem he will make increasing use of in future chapters.[249]

Monday June 12 is another busy writing-day. (He is now writing almost a chapter – and around 5000 words – a day.) He writes section #10 [MS pp 148-159 c4950 words], from the clean-up of *Coo-ee* and a dip in the sea, to the end of chapter 5, with Harriett lying in bed and watching the sea and sky through their bedroom window ("...*she liked to lie luxuriously in bed and watch the lovely, broken colours of the Australian dawn*"[K p101]).

On Tuesday June 13 he writes section #11, consisting of about 5700 words[250] [MS pp 160-186], from the start of the "Kangaroo" chapter and the lunch in Cooley's chambers, to the Cape York tiger-cat story. Lawrence is still catching up – although the lunch with Rosenthal is now less than a week ago. It may be that he is also reassessing where he is going with the text.[251] He starts a second notebook about here. He may also have written something about which he had second

---

[247] *Letters* #2537 [to Mabel Dodge]
[248] *Torestin* fictionally; *Wyewurk* actually
[249] as intimated above, a great deal of *Kangaroo* is made up of repetition & reprise – for example, the two (separate) arrivals at *Torestin* & *Coo-ee*; the two meetings with Struthers/Garden (when there was only one); various meetings with Cooley/Rosenthal; two trips to the Palace Gardens "*aviaries*"; two sets of Jack Callcott/Scott secret army revelations (in "Coo-ee" & "Diggers"); & even-more-manifestly the two repetitious "*granulated silver*" paragraphs in chapter 17 [K p340]
[250] probably in two "sittings", morning & afternoon
[251] for example, how his "splashing-down" technique might accommodate the new more substantive ("thicker") political material he is beginning to get from Scott & Rosenthal

thoughts, for around this time some pages were cut out of the *holograph* MS.

On Wednesday Lawrence posts two letters, one to Frieda's sister Else ("We don't know a soul here"[252]) and one to his erstwhile Ceylon host, Earl Brewster ("I am writing a novel...queer show"[253]). He writes section #12 [MS pp 187-213 c6240 words[254]], from the Cape York tiger-cat story to the supposed second meeting with Cooley. However, the text of this second meeting appears very artificial, and is probably an imaginative (*ie* fictional) continuation of the meeting with Rosenthal in his Castlereagh Street chambers, rather than anything "fresh", or splashed down from reality.[255]

On Thursday June 15 he writes section #13 [pp 214-228 c4140 words] from Cooley's supposed – entirely factitious – visit to see Harriett, to Lawrence (in real life) going for a walk on the rocks below *Wyewurk,* and musing about abandoning the world of social activity (*ie,* mixing with people like Scott and Rosenthal) and retreating into the realm of nature and associating himself with the unruly sea, where he would be free of *"the cloy of human life"* and could take on *"that icily self-sufficient vigour of a fish"*[K p125].

It is in this introspective mood that he apparently has some contact with the local coal-mine, the Excellsior Colliery, and its Welsh manager, or some other mine employee. On the same Thursday, probably in the afternoon, he strolls along McCauley's Beach to the mine's coal-jetty, which juts out into the sea between *Wyewurk* and Sandon Point. Given Lawrence's Eastwood mining background – and his daily need for narrative material – it would be unusual if he did not take advantage of the proximity of the nearby mine to explore extra story elements.

---

[252] *Letters* #2541 [to Else Jaffe]
[253] *Letters* #2542 [to Brewster] (just how queer a show it will prove to be will soon become apparent)
[254] again, probably morning & afternoon
[255] he is starting to invent things

Lawrence probably spends Friday morning writing his brief section #14 [MS pp 229-236 c1680 words (a scant seven *holograph* pages)], from the start of chapter 7 "The Battle of Tongues" and the jetty-meeting with "Jaz", up to – but not including – a fictional third meeting (though actual second meeting) with Rosenthal in Sydney, which is yet to take place, and which he will not record until the following Monday – four days hence. Because Thursday, and more particularly Friday of this week mark the beginning of another significant turning point in the novel. At the start of the week he is still in full flight. The previous Friday he told Mountsier that the novel was progressing satisfactorily.[256] On the same day he also told his American publisher Seltzer that the novel "is going well".[257] In fact on the following Wednesday [June 21] Frieda will tell Mabel Dodge in Taos that Lawrence "has gone at his new novel full tilt".[258] Yet, ominously, Lawrence is beginning to write about recent happenings, having at last caught up with (or used up) earlier events.

Over the next two days Lawrence writes nothing. It seems that he is in the throes of some form of "writer's block" (or, more likely, he has run out of the more-substantive secret-army plot-material to splash down). We do not know if the jetty incident happened or not, or whether it was concocted. It is highly unlikely that he could have encountered "Jaz" – in the person of either Hum or Scott – at the coal-jetty. It is much more likely that, if he did meet anyone, it was someone connected with the colliery. Now Lawrence is, seemingly, creating a third manifestation of the ubiquitous Cornishman Trewhella – Hum, Scott, and now someone involved with the mine (probably the mine manager, Jacob Carlos Jones[259]).

---

[256] *Letters* #2535 [to Mountsier, where he wrote: "If the novel...keeps on at the rate it is going at, it should be ready by August."] (my emphases - the August "deadline" is probably the product of how many days' daily-writing he estimated he would have before he boarded the boat to America [but he's sticking to his writing schedule])

[257] *Letters* #2536 [to Seltzer]

[258] *Letters* #2546 [to Mabel Dodge]

[259] I have Joe Davis to thank for his name

Clearly, Lawrence's diary ingredients are wearing thin: indeed, petering out. So, having nothing fresh to splash down, he decides to travel up to Sydney once more to try to obtain some fresh political material from Scott or Rosenthal, or both. The text – both published and the *holograph* – indicates a trip up to town on Saturday morning June 17. (It is quite likely, however – in fact almost certain – that this trip up to Sydney was also the result of an invitation from Rosenthal to renew, or rather pursue, their recent "feathery" acquaintanceship.) This time, however, Frieda goes with him. Lawrence and Frieda catch the mid-morning train – Frieda is not an early riser – and arrive at Central Station before midday. They then go down to Circular Quay and board a ferry across to Neutral Bay to stay with Scott. Then, late in the afternoon, Lawrence catches the ferry back into town to have his second meeting with Rosenthal in his office-cum-apartment in Castlereagh Street.[260]

There are a number of accounts of what transpired, for Lawrence was to have considerable difficulty putting this homoerotic encounter into words.[261] Their exchange begins (in the published version) with Somers telling Cooley, in *"a hard, cutting voice"*, that he would be unwise to rely on the men he was recruiting, adding:

> *"Look at these Australians – they're awfully nice, but they've got no inside to them. They're hollow. How are you going to build on such hollow stalks? They may well call them corn-stalks. They're marvellous and manly and independent and all that, outside. But inside, they are not. When they're QUITE alone, they don't exist.'"* [K pp 130-131]

---

[260] it is significant – & highly so – that Frieda was not invited to the dinner in Rosenthal's city apartment that night, even though she had come up to Sydney with her husband (obviously because it was not to be "a mixed event")

[261] viz, chapters 10 and 11 of the *holograph*; the Taos typescripts (the published text); the false start to the "At Sea in Matrimony" chapter (*"Somers went back chasten to Kangaroo"*); & possibly the "missing" original chapter 10 (which Lawrence excised from the *holograph* text – see below) [also see the page-reference numbers cited below]

In the original *holograph* text Cooley demurs, strongly. He tells Somers that they may well be "cornstalks" but they bear corn, and are generous people, to the point of recklessness. Cooley goes on:

> "*I love them. I love them. Don't you come here carping to me about them. They are my children, I love them. If I'm not to believe in their generosity, am I to believe in your cautious, old-world carping, do you think, I WON'T!" he shouted fiercely. "I WON'T. Do you hear that!" And he sat hulked in his chair glowering like* <u>some queer dark god</u>[262] *at bay.* [holograph p245, my emphasis]

The published text then switches from politics to a new theme, "*Love*". This is, if the text is to be believed, to be of greater interest to Lawrence than politics (he is, after all, "The Priest of Love"[263]). But Rosenthal's idea of "*Love*" is not Lawrence's, apparently. He (as Cooley) tells Somers:

> "*I trust myself entirely to the fire of love. This I do with my reason also. I don't discard my reason. I use it at the service of love, like a sharp weapon. I try to keep it very sharp – and very dangerous. Where I don't love, I use only my will and my wits. Where I love, I trust to love alone." The voice came cold and static.*
>
> *Somers sat rather blank. The change frightened him almost as something obscene. This was the reverse to* [his] *passionate thunder-god.* [K p131]

---

[262] Take particular note of those three words "*queer dark god*", for I believe they are highly significant. The term "dark god" appears in only one Lawrence novel, & that novel is *Kangaroo*, where it occurs no less than 25 times (see footnote over-page).

[263] *The Priest of Love* was the title of Harry T Moore's biography of Lawrence [Heinemann, London, 1974]

In fact, there are three gods in this exchange. According to the published text, Cooley's god is, ostensibly, the god of power (which later turns out to be proto-fascism[264]). Here, his idea of love is pretty close to Lawrence's and Whitman's "love of comrades".[265] He tells Somers: "'*But I have power – through love.*'" [K ibid]. The second god is the traditional or orthodox form of love, which at first Lawrence espouses and stands up for. "'*I live by the sway of love*'"[K p133] he says, apparently implying heterosexual love. However, it is another god that raises its head in the remainder of the conversation. In the *holograph* text Lawrence introduces this god to an apparently uncomprehending Cooley, initially in terms of "'*…the divine unknown; God who can never be known; God who has at least one <u>name that can never be uttered</u>*[266]'".[K p137] Now it is Cooley who, fictionally, does not know what Somers is talking about. ("*The frown of impatience gathered on the brow of Kangaroo.*"[K ibid]). In the revised, Taos-version Lawrence is even more explicit.

> "*You see,*" *said Somers, trying hard to be fair,* "*what you call my demon is what I identify myself with. It's my best me, and I stick to it. I think love, all this love of ours, is a devilish thing now: a slow poison. Really, I know the dark god at the lower threshold – even if I have to repeat it like a phrase. And in the sacred dark men meet and touch, and it is a great communion. But it isn't this love. There's no love in it. But something deeper. Love seems to me somehow trivial: and the spirit seems like something that belongs to paper. I can't help it – I know another God.*" [K p137]

Indeed he does. From this point in the novel his "*Dark God*

---

[264] see my chapter 19, "Postscript", below re Lawrence & fascism
[265] see *Steele Introduction* p xxx re *Fantasia*, Lawrence, Whitman, & "the love of comrades"
[266] [my emphasis] it may be that the "*at least one name* [or word] *that never be uttered*" is "homosexual"

that Enters from Below" [267] will become an increasingly significant facet of the narrative. Lawrence goes on to talk about a number of other *"dark gods"*.[268] On the surface, these various *"dark god"* manifestations have no obvious homoerotic connotations, or implications. Yet the fact that they seem to have been sparked by, initially, the first lunch in Rosenthal's apartment (where the *"feathery"* incident occurs), and then more substantively after the subsequent *à deux* dinner in on Saturday June 17, could give his *"dark god"* at least an attendant homoerotic implication.[269]

At this June 17 assignation, some sort of homosexual encounter probably[270] took place (possibly in Rosenthal's bedroom, rather than *"the study"*). The relevant accounts, cited in my footnote above, bristle with homoerotic innuendo and homosexual implication, *viz:* "*many* [men] *have been alone a long time*" [K p131]; "*Should not a man know the whole range* [of love]*?*" [K p143]; "*in the sacred dark men meet and touch, and it is a great communion*" [K p137]; "*Somers would have given him heart and soul and body, for the asking, and damn all consequences. He longed to do it.*" [K p132]; "*I love you so. I love you so.*" [K p208]; "*Richard's hand was almost drawn…to touch the other man's body. He had deliberately to refrain because automatically his hand would have lifted*" [K p136]; "*he was helplessly attracted to him*" [K p205]; "*Suddenly, with a great massive movement* [he] *caught the other man to his breast.*" [K p208]; "*you have the most loveable eyes I have ever known…I have never loved a man as I love you*" [holograph

---

[267] as I take pains to emphasise from now on, this "*dark god*" is eroticism in general – what Lawrence later refers to as "*the dark threshold of the phallic me*" [K p135] – & not necessarily homosexuality. However, Lawrence's "*phallic me*" may have included – as many have speculated [see *Appendix 1*] – some element or ingredient of a homoerotic nature, & indeed, this is what Rosenthal's homosexual antenna may have already picked up in him.

[268] including "*The great dark God outside the gate*" [K p285]; "*the dark god he had sensed outside the door*" [K p176]; "*the dark god knocking afresh at the door"* [K p297]; "*The dark God, the forever unrevealed*" [K p266]; "*the dark god at the lower threshold*" [K p137]; "*the dark God he declared he served*" [K p154]; & "*the men in whom the dark God is manifest*" [K p283].

[269] This possibility is perhaps reinforced by the final mention of the "*dark god*" in chapter 17, where Lawrence writes of "*the greater mystery of the dark God*", and then goes on: "*To meet another dark worshipper, that would be the best of human meetings.*" [K p328].

[270] I would argue, obviously

text]; and *"In those few moments when he was clasped to the warm, passionate body of Kangaroo, Somers' mind flew with swift thought. 'Damn his love. He wants to FORCE [271] me.'"* [K p208].

After leaving Rosenthal's "rooms", Lawrence describes his early-evening return to Wycombe Road:

> *He was spending the night at the Callcotts. Harriet, too, was there. But he was in no hurry to get back there. It was a clear and very starry night. He took the tram-car away from the centre of the town, then walked.* [K p137]

He must have arrived by ferry at the Cremorne wharf, probably around 8.30-9.00 pm; caught the waiting tram up Murdoch Street (as he had done previously with Jack Scott); alighted opposite 51 Murdoch Street on the corner of Florence Street; then walked the several hundred yards up Bennett Street to 112 Wycombe Road, where a small group – he called it "a party" – was waiting for him.

> *He arrived at Wyewurk at last, and found a little party. William James was there, and Victoria had made, by coincidence[272], a Welsh rarebit. The beer was on the table.*
>
> *"Just in time," said Jack. "As well you're not half an hour later, or there might a' been no booze. How did you come —tram?"*
>
> *"Yes – and walked part of the way."*
>
> *"What kind of an evening did you have?" said Harriet.*
>
> *He looked at her. A chill fell upon the little gathering,*

---

[271] Written not immediately after the June 17 "dinner date" in Rosenthal's apartment, but later when Lawrence was reprising the occasion the following Saturday, June 24, recalling what had happened a week earlier, & possibly implying that Rosenthal had forced his attentions on him (which may explain, for example, the "curious *seashell-like* look" [K p138] on Lawrence's face when he arrived at 112 Wycombe Road). So take particular note of Lawrence's word, in upper-case, "FORCE", which implies some unwillingness or reluctance on Lawrence's part in whatever transpired that night in Rosenthal's apartment.

[272] the "coincidence" is the fact that "Fanny" Friend's maiden name is Owen, & her family is (like the rarebit) Welsh – a coincidence, however, that would be lost on the reader, for Lawrence has situated Victoria's family background not in Wales but in Somerset (when she was based on "Maudie" Cohen, whose family indeed came from Somerset)

from his presence.
   "We didn't agree," he replied. [K pp 138-139]

Precisely who made up *"the party"* that night at Scott's place in Wycombe Road is not clear. Clearly Scott was there, and Frieda and Lawrence. "Jaz" in his guise of Hum was certainly not there, for he was no doubt snugly at home with his family up in his house *Casita* further north in Chatswood. However, "Jaz" was almost certainly present in his secondary, or alternate, guise as Scott. It seems, however, that at least two other people were there too – Adrian Friend and his pretty, flirtatious 25-year-old wife, "Fanny" (*née* Owen).

What happens next is not clear. According to the text, Somers and Victoria are left alone after Harriett retires to bed and while Callcott[273] accompanies someone down Bennett Street to the tram-stop in Florence Street. If that person was (as is likely) Adrian Friend, then "Fanny" would have gone with them. Perhaps Lawrence was just imagining that she stayed behind to flirt with him (or else it occurred the following day, Sunday, when there was, it seems, a lunch-party at 112 Wycombe Road[274]). Whenever it happened, one would like to think that this episode had some reality in it, as it provides a rare glimpse into Lawrence's enigmatic sexuality, or libido. The ensuing flirting appears mutual.

> *The two men went. Somers still sat in his chair. He was truly in a devil of a temper, with everybody and everything: a wicked, fiendish mood that made him LOOK quite handsome, as fate would have it. He had heard Jack's hint. He knew Victoria was attracted to him* [K p142]

"Jack's hint" appears to be a reference to the end of the previous paragraph, where Jack Callcott says: *"'I'll step along*

---

[273] *ie* Scott [Callcott mark #2]
[274] see below

as far as the tram with you, Jaz, I feel like walking the Welsh rabbit down into his burrow. Vicky prefers Mr. Somers to me pro tem. – And I don't begrudge her. Why should I?'"[K p142] Lawrence describes what (apparently) happened next.

> *She looked at him with her dark eyes dilated into a glow, a glow of offering. He smiled faintly, rising to his feet, and desire in all his limbs like a power. The moment – and the power of the moment. Again he felt his limbs full of desire, like a power. And his days of anger seemed to culminate now in this moment, like bitter smouldering that at last leaps into flame. Not love – just weapon-like desire. He knew it. The god Bacchus. Iacchos! Iacchos! Bacchanals with weapon hands. She had the sacred glow in her eyes. Bacchus, the true Bacchus. Jack would not begrudge the god. And the fire was very clean and steely, after the smoke. And he felt the velvety fire from her face in his finger-tips.* [K p143]

Hot stuff, yet they no doubt go off separately, at least in Lawrence's mind, to their virtuous beds – assuming that this incarnation of "Victoria Callcott" is indeed "Fanny" Friend.[275]

Later on this June 17 Saturday night in Sydney at 112 Wycombe Road (or perhaps the next night), Lawrence experiences a dream – or rather a nightmare. Given what is to happen a week later, this dream takes on some significance. In fact, it is a foretaste of the "nightmare" that will overwhelm him the following Saturday, and which provides the watershed episode in the novel: the famous "The Nightmare" chapter. As Lawrence will relate in that chapter, he had for some weeks, soon after he arrived in Sydney, been having

---

[275] The character Victoria Callcott has a number of manifestations in *Kangaroo*. She starts off in Western Australia being based on "Maudie" Cohen (*father a surveyor*, etc). In NSW she comes to be based on "Fanny" Friend (*née* Owen), & is in the car taking Lawrence back to town on that first Sunday at Narrabeen. Then she is the next-door neighbour in Thirroul who chats with Lawrence & flirts with her husband Adrian (Callcott mark #1). Finally, she is the *coquette* with the "*sacred glow in her eyes*" at 112 Wycombe Road (before she later departs with her husband to return to their country property, less than half-way through the novel).

unsettling dreams. This dream at 112 Wycombe Road on June 17 is one such proto-nightmare.

> ...*the dream had been just this. He was standing in the living room at Coo-ee, bending forward doing some little thing by the couch, perhaps folding the newspaper, making the room tidy at the last moment before going to bed, when suddenly a violent darkness came over him, he felt his arms pinned, and he heard a man's voice speaking mockingly behind him, with a laugh. It was as if he saw the man's face too – a stranger, a rough, strong sort of Australian. And he realised with horror: "Now they have put a sack over my head, and fastened my arms, and I am in the dark, and they are going to steal my little brown handbag from the bedroom, which contains all the money we have." The shock of intense reality made him fight his way out of the depths of the first sleep, but it was some time before he could really lay hold of facts, like: "I am not at Coo-ee. I am not at Mullumbimby. I am in Sydney at Wyewurk, and the Callcotts are in the next room." So he came really awake. But if the thing had really happened, it could hardly have happened to him more than in this dream.* [K p144]

As we shall see when we come to "The Nightmare" chapter itself, that later episode – experienced in the Carlton Hotel in Castlereagh Street on Saturday June 24 – was not a "real" dream, but a period of nightmarish recall, prior to him lapsing into sleep. This dream the previous Saturday in Scott's flat in Neutral Bay is, seemingly, an actual nightmare. It is tempting to assume that, although his waking-self still does not comprehend the reality of the Diggers and the Maggies (and never will, for he has no conception of what a secret army is), his subconscious or unconscious mind is becoming concerned about the murky waters he is venturing, perilously, into.[276] (Lawrence's non-waking mind plays an inordinate role in his life and literature, as evinced for example in such works as *Fantasia of the Unconscious*.)

On the following day, Sunday June 18, there may have been a luncheon party at 112 Wycombe Road. If so, "Fanny" and Adrian Friend may again have been present (and it is possible, as mentioned above, that the "flirting" incident happened then, rather than the – logistically improbable – previous evening). In any case, either after lunch or in the evening, Scott and Lawrence have another talk about Rosenthal and the secret army. At last he is getting what he has at least partly come up for (having failed to get any more out of Rosenthal the previous evening). Again, his interlocutor – Scott – appears in his alternate persona of "Jaz".[277] Clearly Lawrence (if we rely on what the text says) is questioning Scott, once again, about the King and Empire organisation, seeking further information.

> "I was wondering," said Somers [ie Lawrence], "whom Kangaroo depends on mostly for his following."
> William James [ie Scott] looked back at him, with quiet, steady eyes.
> "On the diggers – the returned soldiers chiefly: and the sailors."
> "Of what class?"
> "Of any class. But there aren't many rich ones. Mostly like me and Jack, not quite simple working men. A few doctors and architects and that sort." [K p156]

Lawrence next asks Scott about the purpose of it all. What are

---

[276] indeed, that earlier dream might have been prescient, for the "*rough, strong sort of Australian*" is a good description of Jack Callcott when he reappears in the "Jack Slaps Back" chapter later in the text
[277] whenever Scott is telling Lawrence about "The Garage" & his involvement in it, Lawrence usually endeavours to disguise this source by obliging Scott to put on his Hum hat (as "Jaz")

they – these doctors and architects and so on – trying to do? Is it just "excitement" that they want? He puts the question to Scott (still wearing his "Jaz" hat):

> "Do you think it IS the excitement they care about chiefly?"
> "I should say so. You can die in Australia if you don't get a bit of excitement." There was silence for a minute or two.
> "In my opinion," said Somers, "it has to go deeper than excitement." Again Jaz shifted uneasily in his chair.
> "Oh, well – they don't set much store on deepness over here. It's easy come, easy go, as a rule. Yet they're staunch chaps while the job lasts, you know. They are true to their <u>mates</u>, as a rule." [K p157, my emphasis]

Once again, the Australian concept of <u>mateship</u> is raised[278], and left hanging.

The conversation apparently then turns to *"the First"* – Benjamin Cooley (aka Charles Rosenthal). Lawrence wants to know more about him. Can he carry it through? (whatever "it" might be). But it is Scott (still wearing his "Jaz" hat) who poses the question.

> "You think Kangaroo would get them over the fence?" said Jaz carefully, looking up at Somers.
> "He seems as if he would. He's a wonderful person. And there seems no alternative to him."
> "Oh yes, he's a wonderful person. Perhaps a bit too much of a wonder. A hatchet doesn't look anything like so spanking as a lawn-mower, does it now, but it'll make a sight bigger clearing."
> "That's true," said Somers, laughing. "But Kangaroo isn't a lawn-mower."

---

[278] this will be explored in my chapter 19, "Postscript"

> *"Oh, I don't say so,"* smiled Jaz fidgeting on his chair. *"I should like to hear your rock-bottom opinion of him though."*
>
> *"I should like to hear yours,"* said Somers, *"You know him much better than I do. I haven't got a rock-bottom opinion of him yet."*
>
> *"It's not a matter of the time you've known him,"* said Jaz. *He was manifestly hedging, and trying to get at something.* [K ibid]

That *"something"* turns out to be – and this is initially very hard to take seriously – *"Jaz"*/Scott's idea that the way forward is to let *"the Reds"* have their revolution, and in the ensuing chaos for the Diggers and Maggies to step in and *"make the revolution"* their own. He elaborates:

> *"Well now, my idea's this. Couldn't we get Kangaroo – to join the Reds – the I.W.W.'s*[279] *and all? Couldn't we get him to use all his men to back Red Labour in this country, and blow a cleavage through the old system. Because, you know he's got the trump cards in his hands. These Diggers' Clubs, they've got all the army men, dying for another scrap. And then a sort of secret organisation has ten times the hold over men than just a Labour Party, or a Trades Union. He's damned clever, he's got a wonderful scheme ready."* [K p160]

To anyone who knows anything about revolutions – or politics for that matter – this is a pretty silly idea, and it would be easy to treat such nonsense in terms of Lawrence's naivety, or ignorance about practical politics. Yet there is good reason to believe that either Scott did say something like this, or else Lawrence picked it up from another, nearby,

---

[279] Note Lawrence's mention of the IWW – the Industrial Workers of the World (the IWW, or the "Wobblies"). See my chapter 16 *"The Row in Town"* re "Jock" Garden & the IWW.

source. Because this is precisely the scenario George Augustine Taylor envisaged in *The Sequel* – the book that almost certainly had been on Scott's bookshelf at 112 Wycombe Road (and within Lawrence's reach when he stayed there for two nights).

The trip up to Sydney had been useful for Lawrence. Although he didn't, as far as we know, obtain any further secret-army information from Rosenthal, he did manage to come away from that meeting with some more "montage" or "colour" that helps him to develop his character Cooley further.[280] Moreover, he now has the "romantic" (heterosexual) episodes of the weekend to bolster his narrative. Also his later conversation with Scott on Sunday afternoon or evening will provide him with more details about the King and Empire Alliance and its secret army. In all probability, what he learnt from Scott that Sunday would help him compose *K* chapter 10 "Diggers" later this week.

It is highly-significant that, from this moment onwards, Adrian and "Fanny" Friend (Victoria Callcott and Callcott mark #1) disappear from the narrative, presumably because they go back, after the school-holiday period is over, to their rural property at Galong, south-west of Sydney.[281] Their unexplained, indeed enigmatic, disappearance from the storyline – less than halfway through the text – indicates that Lawrence's connection with the Friend family also ends here, with this departure of his hitherto-helpful (though randy) next-door neighbours, Adrian and "Fanny" Friend.[282]

The train trip back to Thirroul on Monday provides Lawrence with some additional narrative material. We know this return-trip occurred that day because the weather on Monday was particularly nippy, as the daily weather-reports

---

[280] leaving behind a trail of homoerotic references & implications (I resisted to use the expression "flesh out")
[281] this is where Callcott [mark #1] vanishes from the scene & the pages of Lawrence's "romance"
[282] leaving *Wyewurrie*, the house next door to *Wyewurk*, empty for the rest of the novel

in Tuesday's newspapers were to confirm.[283] A day or so later Lawrence wrote:

> *This was the first wintry day they had really had. There was a cold fog in Sydney in the morning, and rain in the fog. In the hills it would be snow – away in the Blue Mountains. But the fog lifted, and the rain held off, and there was a wash of yellowish sunshine.* [K p144]

(A "southerly change" had struck the NSW coast, and the temperature dropped to 51 degrees, which is chilly for Sydney.) In the train back to Thirroul Frieda strikes up a conversation with a fellow-commuter.

> *Harriet of course had to talk to a fellow-passenger in the train, because Lovat was his glummest. It was a red-moustached Welshman with a slightly injured look in his pale blue eyes, as if everything hadn't been as good to him as he thought it ought, considering his merit.* [K pp 144-145]

Lawrence has not committed any text to paper since last Friday, when he wrote about the meeting on the jetty with whomever this "Jaz" was (and after his "writer's block" set in). Now the weekend up in Sydney has furnished him with some (in fact, ample) new material, and so when he gets back to *Wyewurk* he is ready to resume his narrative and continue with the second part of "The Battle of Tongues" – his account of the meeting with Rosenthal on Saturday evening, June 17. He probably wrote section #14 [MS pp 214-228 c4140 words] on that Monday evening after he returned to Thirroul. But before that, he also wrote a letter (in time to catch the mail-train up to Sydney) which proves to be a significant communication in our effort to piece together the story of the

---

[283] [SMH 20/6/22 p11]

composition and writing of *Kangaroo*. In a postcard to his future hostess in Taos, Mabel Dodge[284], he tells her that he had just received a letter from her (his postcard reply was postmarked Thirroul [Monday] June 19) and thanked her for a book she had sent and which he received "two days ago" (*ie* on Saturday). More to the point, he also told her: "Am stuck in my novel".[285]

There is something (indeed, more than something) of a puzzle here. In subsequent days he and Frieda will repeat this "am stuck" mantra several times, to different correspondents. The problem is that he was <u>not</u> stuck, not on Monday, nor at any time during the remainder of what will prove to be a busy writing week. Between Monday afternoon and Friday evening he will write half of one chapter, three new chapters, and part or whole of another chapter which has not survived.[286] Composition-wise, something is very wrong here. He is by no means stuck – at least not in the normal meaning of that word. The explanation might lie, however, in what he actually implied by the word "stuck".

We know he was "stuck" the previous Thursday – that was why he went up to Sydney – so this second "stuck" wording is probably a reference to that earlier hiatus, and not to anything on Monday June 19, when his impatient pen would have been poised to slap down the events of the previous few days. In fact, the "stuck" reference almost certainly refers, not to his narrative in general, but to the political or secret-army element of it. It was not that he had nothing to write about – quite the contrary, particularly given the multiplicity of the events of the weekend. His problem, however, is that since the first meeting with Rosenthal in his rooms in town, now more than a week ago, he has no further

---

[284] still Stern at this point
[285] *Letters* #2543 [to Mabel Dodge] Lawrence wrote this letter up in Sydney or in the train down to Thirroul, for he posted it at the post office next to the station after he arrived back
[286] plus the false start to the "At Sea at Marriage" chapter which he later cancelled & over-wrote [see below]

secret-army information (certainly from Rosenthal) that he can use to write about the Diggers and the Maggies, which is, by now, a central element of his narrative. (Yet, as we shall see, he will eke out some of what he managed on Sunday to obtain from Jack Scott over the next five days.)

After putting down on paper the final part of K chapter 7 "The Battle of Tongues" (describing his meeting with Rosenthal; the Saturday evening "party" at 112 Wycombe Road; his dalliance – real or imaginary – with "Fanny" Friend; and the train ride back to Thirroul), he goes on to describe his return to *Wyewurk*, where, quite unexpectedly, he goes for a "dip" in the ocean…and then has sex with Frieda.

> *Somers turned indoors, and suddenly began taking off his clothes. In a minute he was running naked in the rain which fell with lovely freshness on his skin. Ah, he felt so stuffy after that sort of emotional heat in town.* [K p146]

What he describes as *"that sort of emotional heat in town"* could be a reference to his unrequited encounter with "Fanny" Friend, and feeling a bit frisky when he got back to *Wyewurk*. On the other hand, this rather melodramatic plunge into the briny– that late in the day, and in those inclement, mid-winter conditions – can be better explained in terms of wanting to wash something off, or cleanse himself of something he had encountered up in Sydney. In any case, Frieda came out to see what he was up to.

> *Harriet in amazement saw him whitely disappearing over the edge of the low cliff-bank, and came to the edge to look.* [K p146]

Then she went back into the bungalow and returned with a towel.

> *But he ignored the towel, and went into the little wash-place and under the shower, to wash off the sticky, strong Pacific. Harriet came along with the towel, and he put his hand to her face and nodded to her. She knew what he meant, and went wondering, and when he had rubbed the wet off himself he came to her.*
>
> *To the end she was more wondering than anything.*[287] *But when it was the end, and the night was falling outside, she laughed and said to him: "That was done in style. That was chic. Straight from the sea, like another creature."* [K p147]

This romantic episode[288] was followed by a rather cosy, and somewhat uncharacteristic, interlude of domestic bliss on Monday evening inside *Wyewurk* ...although Lawrence didn't quite see it that way – "cosy" – in the text:

> *Style and chic seemed to him somewhat ill suited to the occasion, but he brought her a bowl of warm water and went and made the tea. The wind was getting noisier, and the sea was shut out but still calling outside the house. They had tea and toast and quince jam, and one of the seven brown teapots with a bit off the spout shone quite nicely and brightly at a corner of the little red-and-white check teacloth, which itself occupied a corner of the big, polished jarrah table. But, thank God, he felt cool and fresh and detached, not cosy and domestic. He was so thankful not to be feeling cosy and "homely". The room felt as penetrable to the outside influence as if it were a sea-shell lying on the beach, cool with the freshness and insistence of the sea, not a snug, cosy box to be secured inside.* [K ibid]

---

[287] well may she have wondered, as she was yet to learn why Lawrence was in such an emotive state following his trip up to Sydney

[288] When Australian artist Sidney Nolan came to paint his 1981 *Kangaroo* series (see "Claws in the Arse" *Appendix 2* below) he devoted one canvas to this sex-scene between Lawrence & Frieda, entitling that painting "Chic" – a delightful use of the term (originally on Frieda's part) which Lawrence himself described in the text as "*ill suited*" to the occasion. His original *holograph* term, which he replaced on the typescripts, was "*incongruous*".

The chapter ends with Lawrence musing about what Jack had told him up in Sydney, to be recorded in the next chapter, "Volcanic Evidence"…that he is "a *Pommy*". And it is now that he inserts into the text what he calls the *"authorised derivation"* of the term "Pommy"[289] (as someone from England) *"and a fool"* for taking things too seriously, rather than taking…

> *…things as they come, as Jack says. Isn't that the sanest way to take them, instead of trying to drive them through the exact hole in the hedge that you've managed to poke your head through?* [K p148]

That – *"poking your head through the hole in the hedge"* – sums up what Lawrence has been trying to do since the lunch in Rosenthal's rooms on Thursday June 8…the *"hedge"* being the King and Empire Alliance and its secret army. In this passage, at the end of "The Battle of Tongues" chapter, he acknowledges that he is poking, not his head, but his nose in where it is no longer welcome. Moreover, to continue his imagery, he is not seeing what he wants to see when his head or nose protrudes through the hedge. He realises that his poking around – his questioning of Rosenthal and Scott – has been obtrusive, as well as unrewarding. He ends this section of the text confessing (in the *holograph* version[290]) that *"in this business he had made a fool of himself"*.

---

[289] the expression "a Pom" or "Pommie" is still used among some older Australians for someone from England ("a £10 Pom" referred to a UK immigrant brought out to Australia on a post-WW2 assisted-passage [*ie* a £10 fare] programme)
[290] [*holograph* p268]

CHAPTER 10

Stuck, Unstuck, and Stuck Again

ON TUESDAY morning June 20 Lawrence starts a new chapter, "Volcanic Evidence". This is the beginning of a three-day period when he is casting around to find new ingredients to advance his narrative. At the moment, however, he has nothing he can add to his secret-army sub-plot. At the start of this chapter he describes this deprivation (through the voice of Somers) as *"coming to the end of his tether"*.^{K p149} But he is not giving up. According to the text, Somers decides to send Cooley a memento-cum-souvenir, apparently intended to indicate his continuing interest in their activities. The memento is a red wooden heart on which is inscribed a German adage, *"Dem Mutigen gehort die Welt"*, which Lawrence translates as *"The World Belongs to the Manly Brave"*.^{K p150} There is a strong likelihood that Lawrence sent such a memento to Rosenthal, for the name on the reverse side of the heart was almost certainly "Rosenthal", after the Black Forest village where it was made, and where in the Rhineland in 1912 Lawrence bought it as a "love token" for Frieda.[291] According to the text, Somers enclosed a letter with the red wooden heart, telling Cooley: *"I send you my red motto-heart...I will be your follower, in reverence for your virtue – Virtus. And you may command me."*^{K ibid}

By now Scott and Rosenthal would have known that Lawrence wasn't going to contribute to their journal. We can

---

[291] see my article "In the Valley of the Roses" [*Rananim* vol 4, no 2-3 (December 1996) pp 14-17]. (On Sunday May 12, 1912, Lawrence went to a village fair in Waldbröl, where his cousin Hannah Krenkow lived, where he probably bought the wooden heart souvenir [or else at a later fair nearby]. At the time he was trying to prove to Frieda that he was "manlier" than a German officer she had led him to believe she was flirting with [for an extended explanation of this, see *Appendix 1* & "The Curious Incident of the Red Wooden Heart"].)

probably deduce when Lawrence said what follows (which is taken from the later "Row in Town" chapter, when the union leader Struthers offers Somers the job of editor of a new socialist newspaper). It is no doubt a Lawrentian transformation from an offer probably made by Rosenthal at their first meeting in his rooms on June 8.

> *"I won't promise at this minute,"* said Richard, rising to escape. *"I want to go now. I will tell you within a week. You might send me details of your scheme for the paper. Will you? And I'll think about it hard."* [K p202]

Of course, Lawrence ceased long ago to be in the market for paid writing-work, for he now had other fish to fry: his new "splash-down-reality" novel (which, alas, was no longer "going well"). In any case, Rosenthal and Scott had no further use for, nor need of him. Lawrence, however, had a considerable and ongoing interest in them, for he is looking to them to provide him with a continuation of his secret-army sub-plot. So he has to do his best to keep in touch with them.

In fact, Lawrence – even if he had agreed to write for them – would have found a journalistic career a brief one, for the King and Empire Alliance was, as mentioned above, about to go out of business (and any offer they might have made in this regard may already have been withdrawn). At a series of meetings in Sydney in mid-to-late June, Scott and Rosenthal, together with their accomplices, had decided to close down or mothball the KEA organisation[292], whose only reason for existence had been to confront the State Labor Government

---

[292] the final decision was probably taken at an "inner-circle" meeting prior to the KEA's second annual conference, which was held in Sydney the day before Lawrence came up to Sydney on June 17 to see Rosenthal. The *SMH* reported [*SMH*, 17/6/22, p15] that the conference had agreed with a leadership motion to merge the KEA with another local patriotic body. Although the conference re-elected Rosenthal as President, Scott did not stand for Treasurer (but was nevertheless elected to the executive committee). His position as *"chief of all the tellers, or secretaries"* (& Rosenthal's 2-i-c) was apparently no longer needed, the political crisis (that had originally led to the creation of the secret army in mid-1920) having passed. The KEA – Lawrence's "Digger Clubs" – struggled on for another six months or more, then disappeared from the scene.

and their Catholic-Irish and trade-union supporters. Now, since the election in March, New South Wales has been returned to safe conservative hands. The red bogey was back in its box. A red wooden heart – even with the inscription "Rosenthal" on it – would now have fallen on unresponsive ground. Yet Lawrence wasn't to know this, and Scott and Rosenthal weren't likely to tell him. He was still hoping – indeed expecting – that there was more to be drawn from that well.[293]

The first part of "Volcanic Evidence" takes the narrative from the red-wooden-heart episode and Lawrence being *"at the end of his tether"* to the end of his account of his conversation with Scott the previous Sunday. However, prior to that, he injects some more "montage" – or "padding" – into his text, starting with his current reading of the local Sydney newspapers (for he is still very much in the throes of being "stuck", and in need of fresh material to advance his narrative).

> *The newspapers were at this time full of the pending strike of coal-miners and shearers: that is, the Australian papers. The European papers were in a terrific stew about finance, and the German debt, and the more imposing Allied debt to America.* [K p151]

On Wednesday June 21 the *Sydney Morning Herald* carried a "cable" story from London[294] about "the German debt" – which would tend to confirm that Lawrence wrote the first part of "Volcanic Evidence" that morning, following his perusal of the morning paper, delivered as usual to his front-door.

Yet it is of more than passing interest that Lawrence,

---

[293] it was around this time, midway through writing *Kangaroo*, that he wrote to his fellow-novelist Catherine Carswell telling her: "Myself I like that letters-diary form." [*Letters* #2548 (22/06/22)]
[294] [*SMH* 21/6/22 p11]

hitherto stuck in his novel, has let several days pass before putting down on paper what he learned from Scott the previous Sunday. One would have thought it would be one of the first things to be recorded on his return to Thirroul. Seemingly, his questioning of Scott had provided him with some additional political information (cf. *"'I was wondering,' said Somers, 'whom Kangaroo depends on mostly for his following.'...'A few doctors and architects and that sort.'"*[K p156] [responded Callcott[295]]). Yet there may have been one caveat that inhibited Lawrence from saying much more at this stage. This was his pledge, made more than a week ago on the rocks below *Wyewurk* (with Scott's matey arm draped around his shoulder), that he would keep what he was being vouchsafed in the strictest confidence (cf. *"'Now, look here. This is absolutely between ourselves, now, isn't it?'"*[K p91]). So it is possible, indeed probable, that what he wrote on Tuesday morning about his talk on Sunday with Scott was not the whole story of that conversation.[296]

On Tuesday Lawrence received a considerable amount of mail from England, and he devoted part of his Wednesday "Volcanic Evidence" writing-sessions[297] to commenting on the content of the letters.

> *There came dreary and fatuous letters from friends in England...Somers had fourteen letters by this mail. He read them with a sort of loathing, one after the other, piling them up on his left hand for Harriet, and throwing the envelopes in the fire. By the time he had done he wished that every mail-boat would go down that was bringing any letter to him, that a flood would rise and cover Europe entirely, that*

---

[295] [mark #2] *ie* Scott
[296] In fact, there are two accounts of that Sunday meeting. On the *holograph* pp 284-290 Lawrence wrote one version first, then crossed it all out & replaced it with the published text. There seems no reason for the changed text – which has no secret-army content – except perhaps that he might have regretted some hurtful things he had said about Richard Aldington's wife, the poet Hilda Doolittle ("HD") (see *Steele* pp 383-386 for the cancelled text).
[297] morning & afternoon/evening

> *he could have a little operation performed that would remove from him for ever his memory of Europe and everything in it – and so on. Then he went out and looked at the Pacific. He hadn't even the heart to bathe, and he felt so trite, with all those letters; he felt quite capable of saying "Good dog" to the sea: to quote one of the quips from the Bulletin.*[298] *The sea that had been so full of potency, before the postman rode up on his pony and whistled with his policeman's whistle for Somers to come to the gate for that mass of letters.* [K p152]

It is not easy to deduce when Lawrence composed and wrote what in the "Volcanic Evidence" chapter. While it seems that all of *K* chapter 8 was written on Tuesday [section #16 pp 249-270 c5480 words] and Wednesday [section #17 pp 270-290 c4140 words], there are no obvious "breaks" in his handwriting to help us differentiate what must have been a number of mini-sessions that made up his daily writing quota.[299]

"Volcanic Evidence" consists of several makeshift elements, "cobbled together", and ending with a blatant (and rather clumsy[300]) "pinch", from a May 11 copy of the Sydney *Daily Telegraph,* of an article about volcanoes[301]. This "old" copy of the *Daily Telegraph* had probably been kept and stored in or under *Wyewurk* for kindling purposes. For a Lawrence deprived[302] of political information, they were a handy source of auxiliary narrative input. Yet following the substantive "Jaz"/Scott material at the start of the chapter, most of this "portmanteau" material is barefaced padding, and does little

---

[298] Neither Bruce Steele nor I could find any contemporary reference in *The Bulletin* to this "*quip*" [*Steele* p38]. It must have come from a "back-issue" that I also have been unable to track down, even in my *Bulletin*-office library in Sydney.
[299] Lawrence was in the habit of taking "breaks" when writing text (note the several breaks in his May 25 letter to Mountsier mentioned above)
[300] he left in the headings & cross-heads!
[301] transcribed into the text word-for-word (including headings & cross-heads!)
[302] following the closing down of the KEA

to advance the storyline (though the volcanoes article does presage the "volcanic" outburst of the coming "The Nightmare" chapter). "Volcanic Evidence" ends with Lawrence wondering when events will provide him with "*a leg up into affairs*" K p168 (*ie*, further ingredients for his frozen secret-army sub-plot).[303]

On Wednesday, probably after lunch, Lawrence replies to the mail he received the day before, and posts off his replies (the letters are postmarked Wednesday June 21). They furnish us with a useful insight into his state of mind as he flounders about trying to find a way forward, now that Scott and Rosenthal have deprived him of any further information about "*their affairs*". He tells William Siebenhaar in Perth that he and Frieda "take excursions around".[304] He tells his U.S. agent Mountsier that he's done more than half of *Kangaroo*, but is now "slightly stuck".[305] Meanwhile, Frieda, writing herself to Mabel Dodge in Taos, says that Lawrence "has written a novel, gone it full tilt at page 305, but has come to a stop and kicks".[306] He tells his American publisher Thomas Seltzer, who is keen to see his new novel, that he has done more than half of *Kangaroo*, adding "the Lord alone knows what anybody will think of it: no love at all, and attempt at revolution".[307] In the Seltzer letter he goes on to confess that he is having problems with his new Australian novel. "I hope I shall be able to finish it: not like Aaron, who stuck for two years, and Mr Noon, who has been now nearly two years at a full stop". He adds that he has hopes of completing it. "I

---

[303] it is worth noting that the actual quote in the text is "*when his own devil would get a leg up into affairs*", implying that "*his own devil*" may have been beginning to take a more active role in the composition of the novel *(cf. Fantasia)*

[304] *Letters* #2547 [to Siebenhaar] (where the Lawrences may have gone on such local outings is not known)

[305] *Letters* #2545 [to Mountsier]

[306] *Letters* #2546 [to Mabel Dodge (Stern)]. It appears that Lawrence numbered each page of the manuscript as he went along (but see below for more about "page 305").

[307] *Letters* #2544 [to Seltzer]. Lawrence apparently continues to believe that what he has run into in Australia is some sort of revolutionary activity (when, ironically, it's actually anti-revolutionary activity, the exact opposite to what he thinks it is) [see chapter 19, "Postscript" below]

think I see my way." This optimism might merely have been bravado, or he may have decided to give affairs *"a leg up"* by writing to Rosenthal[308], seeking another meeting, and planning another visit up to Sydney (for the dramatic consequences of this trip, see below).

On Thursday Lawrence starts a new chapter, "Harriett and Lovatt at Sea in Marriage" [section #18 MS pp 290-309]. This is a "philosophical" (or sociological) chapter about the state of the relationship between Somers and Harriett,[309] and it opens with some general remarks about marriage.

> *When a sincere man marries a wife, he has one or two courses open to him, which he can pursue with that wife. He can propose to himself to be (a) the lord and master who is honoured and obeyed, (b) the perfect lover, (c) the true friend and companion* [K p179]

But these words were written over some earlier, cancelled text, which had nothing to do with matrimony. Originally, on the *holograph*, the chapter began:

> *Somers went chastened back to Kangaroo, realising that if one was given a real thing in this life one should not carp at it. <u>He wanted to feel absolutely at one with the other man</u>.*
> [*holograph* p299, my emphasis] [310]

The cancelled text goes on to relate a conversation – lasting a hundred or so words – supposedly with Cooley, and presumably up in Sydney. The deleted text is too brief to draw any inferences about when or where such an incident might have occurred, nor what he might have gone on to say. It is presumably a reprise or elaboration of his meeting with

---

[308] enclosing a red wooden heart
[309] *ie* himself & Frieda
[310] given what Rosenthal's sexual proclivities turned out to be, this was a dangerous frame of mind to have when spending an evening alone with him

Rosenthal the previous Saturday June 17 (described above) in his apartment in Castlereagh Street. He apparently stopped half-way down MS p299 – the opening page of the new chapter – unsure of where to go next. The conclusion has to be that, here, he was once more "stuck", or at least in two minds.[311] The cancelled and overwritten text points to two writing sessions, though the rest of the chapter seems, by contrast, to have been written quickly, in one "sitting".

Yet there is a curious anomaly here. One of the letters written the previous day, Wednesday, was in fact a joint letter to Mabel Dodge [Stern/Luhan]. Frieda started the letter, and Lawrence added two postscripts. It was in this June 21 letter that Frieda wrote those (above-quoted) words: "L has written a novel, gone it full tilt at page 305 – but has come to a stop and kicks". In the numbering sequence of the *holograph* text, p305 falls half way through the "Harriett and Lovatt at Sea in Marriage" chapter. Lawrence does not appear to be stuck here. On the contrary, there is no sign hereabouts of a "break" in his handwriting that would indicate a pause or problem. Rather he is going full-steam-ahead with an uxorial disquisition about being *"Lord and Master"* of the *"good ship Harriett and Lovatt"* [K p169 *et seq*]. The "page 305" Frieda is referring to could not have been the extant p305 in the *holograph* manuscript, because when Frieda wrote those words, *holograph*-page 305 had yet to be written. It did not exist. (Lawrence did not start "Harriett and Lovatt at Sea in Marriage" until the next day, Thursday.) Moreover, there is no evidence of Lawrence being "stuck" at that point in the text. The probability is that Frieda's "stuck" comment referred to the start of the original chapter 9, which Lawrence deleted and began again on page 299 with the published chapter "Harriett and Lovatt at Sea in Marriage". We can assume from the cancelled and over-written text that he was

---

[311] possibly about the advisability of saying any more about the confrontation in Rosenthal's apartment on Saturday June 17 [see *Appendix 1*]. To be frank, he was dithering.

stuck there, and so *that* (not p305) must have been the page Frieda was referring to. Frieda, who tended to be vague about such matters, had simply got the page-number wrong.[312]

In the two other letters Lawrence wrote that same Wednesday – one to Mountsier and the other to Seltzer – he also referred to "being stuck". As well, we have Lawrence's postcard two days previously to Mabel Dodge saying he was "stuck in my novel". Yet, as intimated above, he was anything but stuck, writing this week two full chapters, one half-chapter, and one lost chapter. He was still stuck on Monday because he had apparently obtained nothing substantive from Rosenthal, and if he did get something from Scott, he was reluctant at this point to break his secrecy-oath and make use of it. He was still "stuck" on Wednesday, when he and Frieda wrote their joint letter to Mabel Dodge, for at this stage there was nothing new he could say about his secret-army storyline. Instead, he inserted his new discursive chapter, "Harriett and Lovatt at Sea in Marriage". Yet that did not, by no means, solve his "being stuck" problem. It merely put it off. So on Thursday evening he was again *"at the end of his tether"*. On the following day, however, in an act of frustration verging on desperation (or else resourcefulness), he will decide to violate his oath of secrecy to Scott. But we will come to that in a moment. First, we have to explain why the good ship *Harriett and Lovatt* has suddenly hove into view.

It is not hard to find what inspired this new "Harriett and Lovatt" chapter. Some time on Wednesday, probably in the afternoon, the domestic bliss of Monday is shattered when Lawrence and Frieda have a blazing row. He refers to this mega-row at the start of the following *K* chapter 10, "Diggers".

---

[312] In footnote #53 of his CUP *Introduction*, Bruce Steele also remarked on this "page 305" reference in Frieda's 21/6/22 letter #2546, saying that it was "perhaps a characteristic imprecision". For more about Frieda's "imprecision", see Richard Aldington's comments, when writing to the Australian literary figure Adrian Lawlor [Aldington-Lawlor correspondence, 20/11/48 (cited above)]: "It is useless to ask Frieda [anything], she has the memory, not like a sieve, but a bottomless bucket."

> *They had another ferocious battle, Somers and Harriet; they stood opposite to one another in such a fury one against the other that they nearly annihilated one another. He couldn't stay near her, so started walking off into the country.* [K p177]

After the altercation, Lawrence stomped out, and proceeded to hike up the steep incline of Bulli Pass to Sublime Point, the escarpment high above Thirroul. At the opening of the next chapter, "Diggers", Lawrence describes the view to be had from this famous lookout.

> *There was the scalloped sea-shore, for miles, and the strip of flat coast-land, sometimes a mile wide, sprinkled as far as the eye could reach with the pale-grey zinc roofs of the bungalows: all scattered like crystals in the loose cells of the dark tree-tissue of the shore. It was suggestive of Japanese landscape, dark scattered toy houses. Then the bays of the shore, the coal-jetty, far off rocks down the coast, and long white lines of breakers.* [K ibid]

(Lawrence is to re-use this "hike-up-the-mountain" episode later in his penultimate K chapter 17.)

After an absence of more than an hour or more, Lawrence returns to *Wyewurk*. The *"ferocious battle"* is forgotten, and he finds at *Wyewurk* a now-conciliatory Frieda. He too had worked off any angst, for the climb had been strenuous, and we now find him in a more amenable – indeed amorous – frame of mind. For they have sex again. [313]

> *He went home again, and had forgotten the quarrel and forgotten marriage or revolutions or anything...Harriet*

---

[313] At this stage of their married life, sex twice in three days (*ie*, Monday & Wednesday) was extremely unusual. For an explanation of this extraordinary behaviour, again see *Appendix 1* & "The Curious Incident of the Red Wooden Heart"

> was waiting for him rather wistful, and <u>loving him rather quiveringly.</u> And yet even in <u>the quiver of her passion</u> was some of this indifference, this twilight indifference of the fern-world[314]. [K p179, my emphases]

He ends the "Harriett and Lovatt at Sea in Marriage" chapter conceding that he had made a spectacle of himself as a *"lord and master"* and that *"He had nothing but her, absolutely"*[K ibid]. Then he brings in his Dark God again:

> But he kicked against the pricks. He did not yet submit to the fact which he HALF knew: that before mankind would accept any man for a king, and before Harriet would ever accept him, Richard Lovat, as a lord and master, he, the selfsame Richard who was so strong on kingship, must open the doors of his soul and let in a dark Lord and Master for himself, the dark god he had sensed outside the door. [K pp 175-176]

    Yet if Lawrence is to advance his stalled "romance", he has to find something more substantive than casual plagiarism, or flippant comment about his relationship with Frieda, and communing with his Dark Gods. What he does decide to do, pending another trip up to Sydney, is to reprise part of his earlier *K* chapter "Coo-ee", which told of the meeting with Scott two weeks ago on the rocks below *Wyewurk*, and the details Scott divulged then about "The Garage". This information underpins the novel's political narrative, and is the nub of its secret-army sub-plot, and so on Friday – stuck for anything else substantive – he revisits it for *K* chapter 10, "Diggers" [section #19 MS pp 310-336 c5780

---

[314] "the fern-world" is Lawrence's reference to the ferns & other native "rain-forest" vegetation that grew on either side of Bulli Pass

words].³¹⁵

Before he started "Diggers", however, he wrote something else: the "missing chapter" in *Kangaroo*. In the *holograph* manuscript of *Kangaroo* there is evidence of 10 consecutive pages between the existing K chapters 9 and 10 being excised, probably with a razor blade, and obviously by Lawrence. The surviving stubs give little indication of their possible content³¹⁶, but this no doubt was his original chapter 10, following (not before³¹⁷) "Harriett and Lovatt" – those 10 excised-pages being the missing chapter. The fact that he had second thoughts about what the pages had originally said implies that they might perhaps have been "too sensitive" to leave in, Lawrence having reservations about what he had just put down on paper. It may be germane that both the stubs and the excised start to "Harriett and Lovatt" apparently talked about "Kangaroo" – *ie* Cooley/Rosenthal.³¹⁸ In any case, for one reason or another, they were unsatisfactory, and he had to think of something else.

So, stuck for anything new, he decides on yet another reprise, and proceeds to replay Scott's visit on that King's Birthday holiday weekend, inserting now his description of the football game on the oval across from the station which they had watched almost three weeks earlier. Then he dredges up from his memory more of what Scott had told him about the Diggers and the Maggies.³¹⁹

---

³¹⁵ we cannot be sure when he wrote what in this chapter, as the pauses in his handwriting are again inconclusive

³¹⁶ however, Bruce Steele in his CUP *Kangaroo* says this about the missing chapter: "The contents of the [ten] excised pages can only be guessed at: it is clear from the page stubs that Kangaroo was mentioned several times." [*Steele Introduction* footnote #53 at p xxxvii]

³¹⁷ we know the pages were excised before he wrote "Diggers" – rather than later when he revised the manuscript extensively between July 7 & July 15 (see my chapter 18 "Departure, Taos & Second Thoughts" below) – because of the sequence of page-numbers that he inserted, page-by-page, as he went along (& which he did not alter after the excision)

³¹⁸ see *Steele ibid* above

³¹⁹ In the first iteration of Scott's secret army revelations (in chapter 5, "Coo-ee") only the Diggers side of the two-faced secret army is disclosed. The Maggies only come on the scene in this reprise in chapter 10.

> *After breakfast Somers got Jack to talk about Kangaroo and his plans. He heard <u>again</u>[320] all about the Diggers' Clubs: nearly all soldiers and sailors who had been in the war, but not restricted to these.* [K pp 183-184, my emphasis]

The additional detail he adds here to the secret-army sub-plot is considerable, although it may have also come from his more recent Sunday meeting with Scott, and held back until now (*ie*, not included in his earlier Tuesday account of that meeting in "Volcanic Evidence"). Whatever may be its connection with Scott's earlier *"Coo-ee"* revelations, it is yet another example of Lawrence's complex transformation techniques[321], not to say ingenuity (in making more extended use of what Scott had divulged to him on the rocks below *Wyewurk*). It is in this chapter that Scott divulges significant "new" information about matters that Lawrence three weeks ago had sworn an oath of secrecy never to divulge. So, revealing it now indicates either betrayal, or, more probably, shows – in that he would break his word, pledged to Scott under (to an Australian) the sacred bond of mateship – how crippled he now is for fresh narrative material.[322]

Yet, for Lawrence, what had been vouchsafed him by Scott on the King's Birthday weekend, now several weeks ago, might not have seemed such a big secret at all. It is abundantly clear that he neither comprehends nor understands the significance of what he has been deriving from Scott[323] – that in fact *"the indiscreet Callcott"* had revealed to him what was then Australia's greatest political secret: its hidden secret-army dimension. Surely, had he grasped this,

---

[320] note the word "again"

[321] as described earlier

[322] It is significant that this "Diggers" chapter is about Scott, rather than Rosenthal. It may be that these revelations were also a function of Lawrence's disinclination or reluctance, at this point, to add to what he had already tried to say (up to five times) about his June 17 meeting with Rosenthal (but which he will, perforce, have to return to when he "pads out" his forthcoming confrontation with Rosenthal tomorrow night).

[323] *en passant*, as it were (see my various comments above)

he would never have dared to write about it in a novel he had every intention of seeing published internationally...and, moreover, read in Australia by Scott and Rosenthal and their secret-army cronies.[324] As tomorrow will rather dramatically show, Lawrence has no idea what he has stumbled on, or rather into, in Sydney. At this point his understanding of the reality of "The Garage" is perhaps summed up in the words of Harriett, describing in *K* chapter 5 "Coo-ee" what she thought her husband was getting mixed up in. *("Pah!' she said. 'A bit of little boys' silly showing off.'"*[K p95])

The "Diggers" chapter ends, irrelevantly, with details of their housekeeping budget (cauliflowers a shilling, cabbages 10 pence[325]). Yet Lawrence is now only too aware that he cannot go on like this, and that if he wants to advance his narrative and its secret-army sub-plot, he will need something more substantive to write about soon...starting, hopefully tomorrow.[326]

---

[324] He did not go back & change what he had written – divulged – about Scott & Rosenthal's secret army – a circumstance that caused me a great deal of concern when I first saw the virtually-uncorrected *holograph* text of *Kangaroo* in mid-1977 (how could he left it unchanged? - that was a bad moment in my research: see *Research-Diary* entry 10/6/77 below re this)

[325] see *K* p191 re the cost of living in Thirroul

[326] he will of course have no need to explain to Frieda (who might otherwise have felt left out of things) why he has to go up to Sydney again, for he had already done that when he told her earlier in the week the real reason why he had posted the red wooden heart to Rosenthal (again, see *Appendix 1*)

CHAPTER 11

The Worst Day of his Life

LAWRENCE DECIDED to travel up to Sydney on Saturday June 24 to *"get a leg up into affairs"*[K p168]. On the previous Tuesday he probably sent Rosenthal a letter[327] proposing a meeting, and Rosenthal apparently replied (presumably via the telegram the messenger boy was trying to deliver), saying he could spare him some time late on the Saturday.[328] Given the lateness of today's Saturday meeting, Lawrence has arranged (possibly by telephone) to stay that night with Jack Scott again at 112 Wycombe Road (where, as we shall see, there is a telephone: a rare facility in the Sydney of 1922). Nonetheless, Lawrence by now is determined not to return to Thirroul empty-handed. So he decides – quixotically – to also go and see "Jock" Garden (whom in the novel he calls "Willie" Struthers) at his office in the Sydney Trades Hall, and to whom he no doubt still has the letter of introduction provided by William Siebenhaar in Perth.[329]

This Saturday in Sydney in June 1922 will turn out to be one of the most traumatic days in Lawrence's entire life, and will give him ample material – much more than he bargained for – to move his stalled narrative forward. We are fortunate to have a detailed record of what happened up in town *"this*

---

[327] containing the red wooden heart
[328] It would have to be a dinner engagement, for Rosenthal was obliged to spend much of the day up in the Blue Mountains, where he had to attend a Chamber of Commerce lunch at Katoomba [*SMH* p1 26/6/22]. Yet Lawrence is playing with fire here in going to see Rosenthal again, for the leader of the KEA may – & indeed will (see below) – misinterpret why he has come up to see him again, especially after his eyes alighted on the red wooden heart & its accompanying *Mut* note (intended by Lawrence, ingenuously, to affirm his heterosexuality – see Appendix 1).
[329] see chapter 2 above about the two letters-of-introduction Lawrence was furnished with in Perth, one of which was no doubt addressed to "Jock" Garden at the Sydney Trades Hall in the Haymarket – which was why Somers & Harriett had walked in that direction on their first day in Sydney (to see where that address was)

memorable day" (Lawrence's own description of it[K p205]) from the several versions of events in *Kangaroo* and from various other sources. So comprehensive is this record that we can use it to retrace Lawrence's movements this dramatic Saturday, hour-by-hour.[330]

6am – Lawrence rises about 5am and catches the early morning train up to Sydney (*"Richard got up in the dark, to catch the six o'clock train"*[K p304]), arriving at Central Station about 8.30 am. There is some early morning rain, but it clears before midday. He leaves Central Station via Eddy Avenue (*"In Sydney it was raining, but Richard did not notice. He hurried to the Hall"*[K ibid]) and crosses Castlereagh, Pitt and George Streets to Ultimo Road, where he notices the recently-opened Kuo Min Tang building at 75 Ultimo Road, which he tucks away in his mind as a possible story ingredient. He turns right into Thomas Street, crosses Hay Street, and walks up Dixon Street, where he buys a custard apple at one of the Chinese stores, arriving at the Trades Hall (*"where the Socialists and Labour people had their premises: offices, meeting-rooms, club-rooms, quite an establishment"*[K p139]) on the corner of Goulburn and Dixon Streets shortly after 9am.

c9.30am – He sees Garden in his office (he presents him with his letter-of-introduction) and they talk about local politics. (*"He was very dark, red-faced, and thin, with deep lines in his face, a tight shut, receding mouth, and black, burning eyes. He reminded Somers of the portraits of Abraham Lincoln"*.[K p193]) Lawrence questions him about the current political situation and the role of the returned servicemen (as Garden later recalled to fellow Communist Frank Hardy – a meeting also confirmed

---

[330] Lawrence's movements "*this* "*memorable day*" – the worst day in his life – are a reconstruction derived from various sources, primarily the "splash down reality" text of *Kangaroo* (in particular *K* chapter 11 "Willie Struthers & Kangaroo")

by Garden's biographer Arthur Hoyle[331]). Lawrence will make virtuoso use of this interview with Garden later in chapter 16, "A Row in Town".[332]

c10am – Lawrence leaves the Trades Hall, walks up Goulburn Street and turns left into George Street. ("[He] *went in silence down the crowded, narrow pavement of George Street, towards the Circular Quay*"[K p202]) He strolls along George Street – Sydney's main thoroughfare – no doubt glancing at shop windows, then crosses Liverpool and Bathurst streets into the heart of the city. He has the rest of the day free before his scheduled meeting with Rosenthal in the late afternoon/early evening, though he has probably arranged (no doubt by phone) to see Hum for lunch.

c10.30-11am – He calls into Dymocks bookshop at 428 George Street, where he buys two new notebooks. (The ones he bought in Ceylon are nearly full.[333]) He peruses the shelves, perhaps to see if any of his books are on sale. He is seen, and accosted, by a young shop-assistant, Frank Johnson, who later told his literary friend Jack Lindsay[334] about the encounter (*cf.* Lindsay's memoir, *The Roaring Twenties* – Lindsay later wrote

---

[331] I am indebted to my research-associate John Ruffels for this information. It was John who contacted both Frank Hardy & Arthur Hoyle & received letters from them confirming Garden's recall of his meeting with Lawrence, & moreover Hoyle's belief that such a meeting did take place (see *Research-Diary* 28/4/92 entry below).

[332] Here Lawrence is generating the first of three fictional events derived from this single meeting with "Jock" Garden: first, when "Jaz" takes him to see "Willie" Struthers; second, his report of Rosenthal's reaction to the news that he had been to see Garden; then thirdly the "Canberra House/Hall" Row-in-Town material mentioned above. As we will see when we come to the Row in Town, that third representation of the "actual" June 24 meeting with Garden will also do double-duty: a morning session repeating the material first canvassed in chapter 11 (see my chapter 16 below) & in the evening the "invented" meeting at which Struthers is counted-out, etc. So in fact Lawrence gets <u>four</u> story elements from the one June 24 meeting – a remarkable *tour-de-force* (& only someone of Lawrence's genius could have carried it off).

[333] Lawrence composed the MS of *Kangaroo* (the *holograph*) in four school exercise-books – two apparently bought in Ceylon & two subsequently in Sydney. It is highly likely that these latter two were bought at Dymocks – at that time Sydney's main bookstore, & on Lawrence's route to the GPO.

[334] see *Research-Diary* 1/2/85 entry below re my meeting with Jack Lindsay in Cambridge, when he confirmed the Dymocks non-event

a poem about missing meeting Lawrence[335]). Lawrence may have spent some time in the bookshop, perhaps going up to Dymocks' lending library and second-hand books section on the third floor. He may even have borrowed a book, leaving the store a little after 11am, possibly with a carry-bag containing the two new notebooks, the custard apple, and maybe a volume or two.

c12 noon – He continues his way along George Street, crosses King Street, and arrives at the General Post Office (the GPO) before midday. Either before or after this he may have crossed over Martin Place to the Cooks office, between Pitt and George Streets, to collect mail or make further inquiries about onward travel to America. (He is thinking of leaving on SS *Tahiti* on August 11,[336] and has told his U.S. contacts this.) He buys some stamps at the GPO, emerging at the Pitt Street-end of the building.

c12.30-1pm – He walks back down Martin Place, where he finds a paper-seller on the corner of George Street, and may have bought a copy of *The* [pink covered] *Bulletin* for his future reading. ("*Richard called at the General Post-office in Martin Place…he came out again, and stood on the steps folding the stamps he had bought, seeing the sun down Pitt Street, the people hurrying, the flowers at the corner, the pink spread of Bulletins for sale at the corner of George Street*".[K p202]) He would have crossed George Street, and walked up Wynyard Street to Carrington

---

[335] Lindsay wrote his poem in 1935, 13 years after his failed encounter with Lawrence at Dymocks in Sydney in 1922. It was entitled "To D.H. Lawrence" & comprised 96 lines. Lines 28-42 read: *You were there/only a mile or so away/Well I recall the day/Frank said to me/You've just missed D.H. Lawrence; he came in/to buy some books; he's living down the coast./I simply couldn't believe it, & didn't care;/I talked of other things excitedly – /locked in the dense Shakespearian past,/having no sense,/no window of experience,/to know your pieties & the blood-light that they cast./Lawrence, you were there./Ah, to have met you in Australia/in 1922.* The poem was unpublished in Lindsay's lifetime (he died in 1990 aged 89) & was first published by the Ancora Press in 2012. (Lindsay helped found the Fanfrolico Press in London. It was associated with the Mandrake Press which in 1929 published an edition of Lawrence's paintings.)
[336] his "romance" is taking longer than he thought

Street, where he apparently rendezvous with Gerald Hum in his Carter & Co office there. He may have waited a short time while Hum got ready, and where Hum probably gave him a contact for the Kuo Min Tang, whose name he had seen on a building in the Haymarket earlier in the day.[337] Then they go off together for lunch, hailing a hansom cab outside the GPO and directing the cabbie to take them to the Sydney Domain (aka the Palace Gardens), where they get out near Mrs Macquarie's Chair (a rock-shelf overlooking Farm Cove).

c1pm-2.30pm – On the way they purchase some food (*"Richard bought sandwiches and a piece of apple turnover, and went into the Palace Gardens to eat them."* [K p395]). They sit on the grass-bank above Farm Cove and have their picnic lunch.[338] In front of them are the post-war remnants of the Australian Fleet, at anchor in front of Government House. (*"In front in the small blue bay lay two little war-ships, pale grey, with the white flag having the Union Jack in one corner floating behind. And one boat had the Australian flag, with the five stars on a red field. They lay quite still, and seemed as lost as everything else, rusting into the water.*" [K p395]) Lawrence is in no hurry to go (*"He took himself off to the gardens to eat his custard apple – a pudding inside a knobbly green skin – and to relax into the magic ease of the afternoon"* [339]), but Hum would have wanted to get back to his home and family in Chatswood, so they no doubt walked together

---

[337] On the back-inside-page of one of the exercise-books he had bought at Dymocks, Lawrence wrote a name he was given by Hum, "Chan on Yan", & also Chan's Sydney postal address: "Kuo Min Tang/P.O. box 80/Haymarket". Hum's hat company Carter & Co advertised in various Chinese publications in Sydney, & had business connections with that community (he exported his imported Panama "hat bodies" to China). There is no evidence that Lawrence wrote to Chan, or made any effort to contact the KMT. However, as he did not then know if he was going to obtain anything of interest from Garden at the Trades Hall, where he was headed (or from Rosenthal later in the day), he might have noted the contact as he passed by, should he have need to follow it up.

[338] What they talked about is probably reflected in *K* chapter 11 "Willie Struthers & Kangaroo", where Lawrence said that Somers had been taken to the Trades Hall ("*Canberra House/Hall*") by "Jaz". Lawrence presumably told Hum (who in this guise is "Jaz") about his morning-meeting with "Jock" Garden, calling him "*rather a terror*" but "*shrewd*", though he would want to touch him. "*But he's a force,*" Somers tells "Jaz", "*he's SOMETHING.*" (It is this conversation with "Jaz" that Lawrence subsequently has – transposed from the afternoon lunch with Hum – with Rosenthal later in the day in his apartment in Castlereagh Street.)

[339] the quotations on this page are from *K* p206

through the Botanic Garden and down Macquarie Street to Circular Quay, where Hum probably catches a ferry across to Milson's Point, from where he can get the train to Chatswood.[340]

c2.30-5.30pm – Lawrence now has more than two hours to fill in before his scheduled appointment to see Rosenthal later in the afternoon, prior, as he intends, to then crossing over the Harbour to visit Scott at 112 Wycombe Road, and stay overnight there. He strolls around the streets of Sydney, observing the passing parade. (*"He wandered the hot streets, walked round the circular quay and saw the women going to the ferries"*) This, apparently, is his first opportunity to observe Australian women at close quarters (at least it is his first comment about them, in general). (*"So many women, almost elegant. Yet their elegance provincial, without pride, awful. So many almost beautiful women. When they were in repose, quite beautiful, with pure, wistful faces, and some nobility of expression. Then, see them change countenance, and it seemed almost always a grimace of ugliness. Hear them speak, and it was startling, so ugly. Once in motion they were not beautiful. Still, when their features were immobile, they were lovely."*) He considers their attitude erotic. (*"Almost every one of the younger women walked as if she thought she was sexually trailing every man in the street after her. And that was absurd, too, because the men seemed more often than not to hurry away and leave a blank space between them and these women. But it made no matter: like mad-women the females, in their quasi-elegance, pranced with that prance of crazy triumph in their own sexual powers which left little Richard flabbergasted."*) He also wonders at the pedestrian habits of the locals (the City Council was trying to impose a "keep to the left" regime on

---

[340] See *K* p307 for Lawrence's report of this lunch on the grass. But here Lawrence loses track of what he did that day when he went to the Palace Gardens with Hum. In that text passage he has Somers returning again to where in the p307 text he had already had lunch (see *K* p305) after Somers "*wandered the hot streets…& saw the women going to the ferries."* Yet that is what he did <u>after</u> lunch, before going to Cooley/Rosenthal's apartment at around 5.30 pm (see *K* p306).

the pavements). ("*Hot, big, free-and-easy streets of Sydney: without any sense of an imposition of CONTROL. No control, everybody going his own ways with alert harmlessness. On the pavement the foot-passengers walked in two divided streams, keeping to the left, and by their unanimity made it impossible for you to wander and look at the shops, if the shops happened to be on your right. The stream of foot passengers flowed over you.*" K p209). We do not know how long he walked the city streets. He may have filled in time by going to one of the city libraries, perhaps the School of Arts library in Pitt Street. In any case he arrives at the door to Rosenthal's apartment on the third floor of 8 Mendes Chambers about 6pm for his dinner-date with the leader of the King and Empire Alliance, the "Kangaroo" of his hitherto-stalled novel.

c5.30-7pm – Two days later Lawrence is to write in chapter 11: "*Somers went in the evening of this memorable day to dine*[341] *with Kangaroo. The other man was quiet, and seemed preoccupied.*" K p205 Almost immediately, or perhaps as they sipped aperitifs, Lawrence drops his bombshell. ("*'I went to Willie Struthers this morning,' Somers said.*"[342]) Up to this point Lawrence, as already intimated, has no idea what he is getting mixed up in. He is a political ingénue. For example, he finds it difficult to work out whether the Digger movement is conservative or radical – though his conversation with the local union boss "Jock" Garden that morning should have begun to open his eyes. However, they are not sufficiently open to see how aghast and appalled Rosenthal will be when he learns that this stranger, to whom his deputy Jack Scott may have revealed the innermost details of their illegal secret army, has been talking to, of all people, a founder of the Australian Communist Party, and the leader of the militant union

---

[341] take particular note of the words "*to dine* with Kangaroo", his original intention apparently being to spend some time *à deux* in Rosenthal's apartment that evening – an intention abruptly terminated when he told Rosenthal whom he had been to see that morning

[342] the quotations in this & the following paragraphs are from *K* pp 209-211

movement in New South Wales – the very people the King and Empire Alliance had been, for more than a year, secretly plotting to confront and combat. Little wonder at Rosenthal's hostile – indeed explosive – reaction. This is as bad as whatever his worst nightmare could possibly be, "the sum of all his fears". Rosenthal had just been elected a member of parliament, and is a prominent member of the current NSW government. He is a leading citizen; an alderman on the City Municipal Council; a frequent guest at Government House; a Major-General in the Army; a pillar of his church; a senior Mason; a war hero; a leader in his profession; and a Knight of the Realm.[343] All this and more is in immanent jeopardy from this casual acquaintance whom his deputy Scott had somehow picked up (off the street, as it were) and brought to see him about a possible job with their about-to-be-disbanded organisation, and soon-to-be-defunct journal. As Scott had earlier told Lawrence, running a secret army in Australia is technically treason, and the penalty for that is, by law, death. (In chapter 5 Callcott – *ie* Jack Scott – called what he told Somers/Lawrence on the beach below *Wyewurk* "'*Politics and red-hot treason*'"[K p105].) The seriousness of the situation has to be brought home to this ridiculous little upstart, quick smart. ("*Kangaroo looked at him sharply through his pince-nez*")

In the text, Cooley (*ie* Rosenthal) leaves the room for a considerable interval, no doubt to telephone his deputy Scott in Neutral Bay and apprised him of what he had just been told; and to discuss what to do about it. On Cooley's return the exchange immediately turns hostile. ("'*Why have you deceived me, played with me*' [344], *suddenly roared Kangaroo*.")

---

[343] these various accomplishments & positions are derived from numerous reports in local newspapers & magazines – see *eg* below: *Research-Diary* 8/4/76 (a major-general); 11/4/76 (an MP & alderman); 13/4/76 (re Warren Perry's biography of Rosenthal); 18/11/76 (praised in *The Bulletin*); & also see my *Quadrant* article, "The Man Who was Kangaroo" [*op cit*].

[344] Those words "*Why have you...played with me*" might imply much more than is at first apparent. In fact – as I explain in *Appendix 1* – the virulence, indeed the ferocity, of Rosenthal's reaction to the news that Lawrence had that morning been to see the militant union leader "Jock" Garden might have had as much to do with his sudden apprehension of Lawrence's duplicity, in potentially revealing the KEA's secrets to its sworn enemy, as his concomitant (&

THE HORRIBLE PAWS

Cooley, according to the text, then becomes very nasty indeed. *"'I could have you killed,'"* he says, and goes on: *"'I am sorry I have <u>made a mistake in you</u>*³⁴⁵. *But we had better settle the matter finally here. I think the best thing you can do is to leave Australia. I don't think you can do me any serious damage with your talk. I would ask you – before I warn you – not to try.'"*³⁴⁶ Cooley is no longer the benign, benevolent, Jehovah-like figure [*cf. "there came an exceedingly sweet charm into his face, for a moment his face was like a flower"*] with whom Lawrence had lunch a week or so ago. The secret-army leader has now been transformed – inexplicably to Lawrence – into a monster. (*"He had become again hideous, with a long yellowish face and black eyes close together, and a cold, mindless, dangerous hulk to his shoulders. For a moment Somers was afraid of him, as of some great ugly idol that might strike. He felt the intense hatred of the man coming at him in cold waves. He stood up in a kind of horror, in front of the great, close-eyed horrible thing that was now Kangaroo. Yes, a thing, not a whole man. A great Thing, a horror."*) Fearing for his very life, Lawrence makes for the door. (*"...he kept all his wits about him, and as by inspiration managed the three separate locks of the strong door".*) Rosenthal is close behind him. (*"'Good-night!' said Somers, at the blind, horrible-looking face. And he moved quickly down the stairs and out into the street."*) Lawrence is now a very aware and a very frightened individual. (*"Dark streets, dark, streaming people. And fear. One could feel such fear, in Australia."*) Where is he to go? What is he to do?

c7pm-midnight – He wanders the pavements for a while, rubbing shoulders with the Saturday-night cinema crowds, then goes to the Carlton Hotel, a block down from Mendes Chambers in Castlereagh Street, and books himself a room for

---

more personal) sudden realisation that Lawrence had been "leading him on" to obtain more secret-army information, & had not come to see him, as he had anticipated, to enjoy a pleasant *à deux* dinner, which might have led on to a more intimate occasion.
³⁴⁵ my emphasis – for take particular note of the portentous phrase "*made a mistake in you*" (again, see previous footnote & *Appendix 1*)
³⁴⁶ again, the extracts in this passage are from *K* pp 210-211

the night (despite the expense – it would have cost him perhaps £1 for the overnight stay). He had intended to go across the Harbour to spend the night with Jack Scott at 112 Wycombe Road, but that was out of the question now, given Rosenthal's (presumed) phone call to Scott an hour or so ago telling him what Lawrence had done, and whom Lawrence had been to see that morning. (*"Were you disgusted with Lovatt* [Harriett/Frieda later asks Callcott/Scott in the "Jack Slaps Back" chapter] *when he didn't turn up the other Saturday?' said Harriet. 'I do hope you weren't sitting waiting for him.' 'Well – er – yes, we did wait up a while for him.'"*[347]) So Lawrence has to find somewhere else to sleep that night.

During this Saturday evening in the Carlton Hotel in Sydney, Lawrence experiences what he calls in the novel "The Nightmare", which is to provide the ingredients for the famous chapter – *K* chapter 12 – that he is to write (two days later) after he returns to *Wyewurk* next morning.[348]

---

[347] see *K* p286 (Harriett/Frieda asks this of Jack Callcott/Scott at the start of the *K* "Jack Slaps Back" chapter)

[348] As I explain above & below, this is not an "actual" nightmare, but a period of nightmarish recall, lasting perhaps two or more hours, when Lawrence calls up from his dormant memory what had happened in Cornwall & England during the war. He also on this *"memorable evening"* in the Carlton Hotel (& probably next morning too) starts converting that memory into what will become the text of *K* chapters 11, 12 & 13 ("Willie Struthers & Kangaroo", "The Nightmare" & "'Revenge', Timotheus Cried") & which he will commit to paper in the coming week.

CHAPTER 12

The Nightmare

YET THAT is not the chapter[349] he writes next, after returning to Thirroul, presumably departing from Central Station on Sunday morning. He has the dramatic and traumatic events of yesterday yet to commit to paper. His composition is now, however, very much "up to speed". He is no longer stuck. He probably gets back to *Wyewurk* in the early afternoon, where he would have had a lot to tell Frieda[350]. What he intends to write about is no doubt simmering inside him. The morning drizzle has cleared to a fine, cold day. Perhaps he goes for a late afternoon walk along McCauley's Beach. He has much to mull over.

On Monday June 26 he starts[351] writing chapter 11, "Willie Struthers and Kangaroo" [section #20 MS pp 337-359 over 5000 words[352]], describing Saturday's trip up to town to meet "Jock" Garden; his mid-morning departure from Trades Hall; and his traumatic confrontation in the evening with Rosenthal. This is – not unexpectedly – the start of an intensive writing period, as he now has plenty of material at his disposal. Over the next four days – Monday to Thursday – he writes more than 30,000 words, comprising three chapters: "Willie Struthers and Kangaroo", "The Nightmare", and "'Revenge!' Timotheus Cries". He averages over 6000 words per session, mostly in small, dense script, writing up to

---

[349] Ever since *Kangaroo* was published in October 1923, a question-mark has hung over this famous chapter. His American publisher Thomas Seltzer questioned its appropriateness, & suggested that it might be published separately [*Letters* #2623 & #2628]. But Lawrence demurred [*Letters* #2627].
[350] Who would have wanted to know what happened up in Sydney. He certainly told her about not turning up at Jack Scott's place, as he had intended, & as Harriett/Frieda later mentions the "Jack Slaps Back" chapter below.
[351] however, he may well have written the opening part of chapter 11 the previous day, or night
[352] probably spread over several writing sessions

350 words a page.[353]

He will make two uses of some of this material, both his meeting with Garden (in chapter 11 and later in *K* chapter 16, "A Row in Town") and what happened afterwards. In particular, he will give a longer account of what he did after leaving the Trades Hall on Saturday morning and went to the Domain/Palace Gardens for lunch with Hum. Initially in chapter 11 he merely takes a hansom cab to *"the aviaries"*. (*"'Jaz,' he said, 'I want to drive round the Botanical Gardens and round the spit there – and I want to look at the peacocks and cockatoos.'"*[K p202]), but later embellishes it considerably in "A Row in Town" (*"With mid-day came the sun and the clear sky: a wonderful clear sky and a hot, hot sun. Richard bought sandwiches and a piece of apple turnover, and went into the Palace Gardens to eat them."*[K ibid]). At this point – only three days after the Saturday-evening confrontation with Rosenthal in his apartment – the memory of that scarifying experience is very fresh in his mind, and needs to be converted into text.

On Tuesday he writes section #21 [MS pp 359-381] totalling c7500 words[354], starting with the beginning of "The Nightmare" chapter, recalling the persecution he and Frieda had suffered during the war. His mind goes back to other times of fear in his life. (*"He had known such different deep fears. In Sicily, a sudden fear, in the night of some single murderer, some single thing hovering as it were out of the violent past, with the intent of murder."*[K p212]) Importantly, at the end of this long and famous chapter, he asks himself why it has suddenly all come out.

> *It was like a volcanic eruption in his consciousness. For some weeks he had felt the great uneasiness in his unconscious. For some time he had known spasms of that*

---

[353] He will apparently write 22 pages of text on Monday [pp c337-359]; 21 pages on Tuesday [pp c360-381]; 23 pages on Wednesday [pp c382-405]; & 25 pages on Thursday [pp c405-430].
[354] in two sessions at least

> *same fear that he had known during the war: the fear of the base and malignant power of the mob-like authorities...it had come back in spasms: the dread, almost the horror, of democratic society, the mob...Why? Why, in this free Australia? Why? Why should they both have been feeling this same terror and pressure that they had known during the war, why should it have come on again in Mullumbimby? Perhaps in Mullumbimby they were suspected again, two strangers, so much alone. Perhaps the secret service[355] was making investigations about them.* [K p259]

That unease may well have helped spark the earlier "Volcanic Evidence" chapter (note the words "*For some time*" and his use of the word "*volcanic*"). Indeed, it could be that rising disquiet about Scott and Rosenthal and their sinister organisation had been stirring, as he describes, in his unconscious, or subconscious, for some time – hence perhaps his earlier nightmare on Saturday night at Wycombe Road. Although his conscious, sentient mind still has little or no idea what he has come across in Australia, now it does seemingly suspect that what has been troubling him may have something to do with his encounters with Rosenthal and "Jock" Garden, as he remarks in the text:

> *Perhaps it was this contact with Kangaroo and Willie Struthers, contact with the accumulating forces of social violence* [K p260]

Critics have long been puzzled why Lawrence injected this vivid account of his experiences during the First

---

[355] In 1922 Australia indeed had a "secret service". It was called the Commonwealth Investigation Bureau (see *Moore* p16 *et seq* re Colonel HE Jones & the founding of the Australian Protective League). Although it would not have been interested in Lawrence at that time, it appears it once did have a file about his involvement with Scott & Rosenthal & the KEA (see my reference above to Ernest Whiting & Colonel Spry of the APL/CIB's successor ASIO).

World War, beginning in Cornwall in 1915, into *Kangaroo*, for it seemed out of place – and time – in a novel about Australia. This conclusion to "The Nightmare" chapter (*"perhaps it was this contact"*) supplies at least part of the answer. It is also worth mentioning that Lawrence had not used his wartime experiences in England, substantively, in a work of fiction prior to *Kangaroo*. They may have been "locked away" in his unconscious, or subconscious, mind, waiting to come out. It is also worth noting, as Richard Rees did in *Brave Men*,[356] that *Kangaroo* is the last novel in which Lawrence – an intensely autobiographical author – portrays himself as one of his "fictional" characters. Perhaps, with "The Nightmare", he exhausted his store of autobiographical material (or else had future reservations about using such personal material). After *Kangaroo* he may not have wanted to open that Pandora's Box again (wherein it was not all beer and skittles). Even when he comes to write about "the country of my heart" in and around Nottinghamshire for the *Lady Chatterley* books, he does not, overtly, portray himself as one of the characters (Parkin and Mellors being more in the nature of wishful thinking than *roman à clef*).

On Wednesday[357] he continues recalling his persecution in Cornwall in section #22 [MS pp 381-403 c3800 words] up to his leaving Cornwall, on the orders of the military authorities, and returning to London before moving to Oxfordshire to stay in a friend's cottage (from where he has

---

[356] *Brave Men: A Study of D H Lawrence & Simone Weil* [Victor Gollancz, London, 1958] (Middleton Murry had earlier made the same point, saying that in *Kangaroo* Lawrence "killed off his alter ego")

[357] Although written on Wednesday June 28, the likelihood is that this text, as with the rest of *K* chapters 11 & 12, was probably at least partly drafted in his mind on the night of Saturday June 24 in his room in the Carlton Hotel, before lapsing into sleep (& perhaps next morning, too). Previously (on Monday &/or Tuesday) he had completed – on p359 of section #18 of the holograph – this account of the Saturday meeting, with Somers exiting Rosenthal's third-floor apartment. On Wednesday he continued with a new paragraph beginning: "*He was thankful for the streets*" & ending "*Dark streets, dark, streaming people. & fear. One could feel such fear, in Australia.*" Then, at the bottom of p359, although he had started a new sentence beginning "*There are such different fears. In Europe...*" he changed his mind, deleted this text, & on the next page, p360, decided instead to open a new chapter, inserting over his previous chapter 11 continuation a slightly different sentence: "*He had known such different deep fears. In Sicily...*" (next to the name, also interpolated, of his new chapter-12 heading, "The Nightmare").

to travel up to Derby for his third and final summons to attend a medical examination). On Thursday June 29 Lawrence completes "The Nightmare" chapter and adds the "'Revenge!' Timotheus Cries" chapter [section #22 MS pp 403-430 c7560 words[358]], bringing him back from Cornwall to Sydney and the start of *K* chapter 14, "Bits". The text ends with him finally surrendering to sleep. So it wasn't an actual nightmare, after all, but rather a period of nightmarish recall in his room at the Carlton Hotel the previous Saturday night. (*"After all his terrific upheaval, Richard Loved at last gave it up, and went to sleep. A man must even know how to give up his own earnestness, when its hour is over, and not to bother about anything anymore, when he's bothered enough."*[K p268]) Nevertheless, he has now used up – at least first time round – the material from the previous "memorable" Saturday. He must have realised now that he wasn't getting any more political material from such KEA sources. (Meanwhile, Garden was off to Melbourne to attend a week-long trade-union conference.)

Lawrence was now back where he had been the previous week, with nothing substantive to advance the secret-army sub plot of his "slap-down-reality" novel, and a lot of bridges burnt. He will be obliged to resort to alternative sources – and his dark deities – increasingly from now on.[359]

---

[358] again, in at least two writing sessions

[359] The CUP edition of *Kangaroo* also attempts to explain why Lawrence imposed on a story of Australia an account of what had happened in Cornwall in 1916-17. Bruce Steele says in his relevant Explanatory Note [*Steele* p394] that "'The Nightmare' is closely autobiographical". In his Introduction to the text, Steele expands on this, explaining that "The Nightmare" chapter is connected to Somers's realisation that Kangaroo (Cooley) "wants to impose his will & to enforce the old 'mechanistic' ideal of benevolence", adding: "This realisation revives Somers's fear of evil idealism which motivated the masses in the War & he re-lives his own experience of it in a 'nightmare' (chap. xii)." [*Steele* p xxxi]. Steele argues that what Cooley is saying about "the old 'mechanistic' ideal of benevolence" implies "love by force" which "degenerates into the bloodthirsty violence of fascism". It is perceptive of Steele to link the ideology espoused by Cooley with fascism (see my chapter 19 "Postscript" re *Kangaroo*, Lawrence & fascism). He is also right in associating Lawrence's nightmare-experience in *K* chapter 12 with Lawrence's ultimate realisation that Cooley/Rosenthal's ostensible or surface benevolence has a darker side to it – indeed, some "*Horrible Paws*" (those paws assumed an even-more-sinister implication in the context of the pawing attentions of the "*bear-like*" Rosenthal the previous Saturday June 17 night).

IMAGES OF LAWRENCE'S 99 DAYS IN AUSTRALIA

A studio portrait of Lawrence, possibly taken in Sydney in July 1922 for his US visa application

The battered front gate of Wyewurk (photographed by Fred Esch in 1956)

Billabong, *the "end house" at North Narrabeen, where Lawrence first met Jack Scott on Sunday May 28, 1922*

Charles Rosenthal (foreground) having afternoon tea in the garden of Billabong *c.1908 (Taylor is on the right, partly obscured)*

The beach below Wyewurk, *looking north (c.1910)*

Wyewurk's *living-room (much as when Lawrence and Frieda were staying there in 1922) - photo by Fred Esch c.1956*

(top) The house in Australia Street, Newtown, where Lawrence and Frieda visited their shipboard acquaintances the Forresters and the Marchbanks on July 4-5, 1922

(right) Frieda and Laura Forrester at their needlework on the verandah of 200 Australia Street, Newtown (probably on the morning of July 5, 1922)

Frieda and Laura strolling in the Botanic Garden on July 5 (Lawrence is not in-shot, probably because he was off visiting The Sun *newspaper library in town)*

Frieda and Laura Forrester enjoying a rest at Mrs Macquarie's Chair during their Botanic Garden stroll (two weeks earlier Lawrence and Gerald Hum had had lunch this spot)

The scene switches to Thirroul and Wyewurk *on the weekend of July 29-30, when the Marchbanks and Forresters came down to stay for two days. Denis Forrester (who took this and all but one of the other "Forrester" snaps) probably immediately turned around and caught Lawrence sitting against the verandah of* Wyewurk, *apparently writing something (see last page of this photo-insert). Those depicted in this happy group are (from left) Mrs Marchbanks, Frieda, Mr Marchbanks, and Laura Forrester. They are leaning against the fence that separated* Wyewurk *from the next-door vacant allotment.*

This is obviously an earlier picture, probably taken on the Saturday of the weekend of July 29-30. It shows (from left) Lawrence, Mrs Marchbanks, Frieda, Laura and Denis Forrester (obviously Marchbanks took this snap so Forrester would be in-shot).

Denis Forrester is back behind the camera for this photograph against the side of Wyewurk (from left: Lawrence, Laura Forrester, Freida, and Mr and Mrs Marchbanks)

One of Forrester's Loddon Falls photographs (Lawrence, Mrs Marchbanks and Frieda). The picnic-party was lucky to be at the Falls that weekend, for normally the water over the Falls is little more than a trickle, but the storm of the previous week, which Lawrence described in Kangaroo, *had turned the Falls into a veritable cascade.*

The better-known Loddon Falls photograph showing (from left): the driver Lawrence engaged for the trip to the Falls, Mr Marchbanks, Lawrence, Mrs Marchbanks, Laura Forrester and Frieda

The defining photograph of Lawrence in Australia. He is seated beneath the verandah of Wyewurk, apparently writing in his notebook, possibly - after finishing Kangaroo - *continuing his translation of Verga's* Cavalleria Rusticana.

Major William John Rendall Scott - Jack Scott - who is portrayed in Kangaroo *as Jack Callcott. It was Scott who told Lawrence about the Diggers & Maggies*

A dapper Major George Augustine Taylor (left) - the secret army's eminence grise *- on military manoeuvres*

Sir Charles Rosenthal - the "Kangaroo" of Lawrence's novel (note his close-set eyes)

CHAPTER 13

Bits and Pieces

AFTER THE burst of activity of the previous four days, Lawrence needed a break. So on Friday June 30 he and Frieda go off on a day-trip to Wollongong. It is a typical, sunny Australian winter's day, cold and diamond-sharp.

> *A very strong wind had got up from the west. It blew down from the dark hills in a fury, and was cold as flat ice. It blew the sea back until the great water looked like dark, ruffled molefur. It blew it back till the waves got littler and littler, and could hardly uncurl the least swish of a rat-tail of foam. On such a day his restlessness had driven them on a trip along the coast to Wolloona*[360]... *they got to the lost little town just before mid-day.* [K p272]

This is Lawrence at what he does best – describing, vividly, what happened, and what he saw and did.[361] They catch the train down the coast to Wollongong, a much-larger town than Thirroul, and walk along Main Street towards the sea, noting the shop windows, local hotels, and the steelworks (Lawrence, unfamiliar with local industry, calls it a *"brickworks or something"*[362]) belching smoke further south. They buy some sandwiches at a shop and go down to the ocean beach where they find a sheltered place in the dunes to eat them. Then, as they walk along the water's edge, a rogue

---

[360] "Wolloona" is Lawrence's transformation of the now City of Wollongong, south of Thirroul. Lawrence probably saw the name *Wolloona* on a house in Murdoch Street, Cremorne, which he may have passed on his way to or from Jack Scott's flat in Neutral Bay. (Wollongong has since grown considerably from Lawrence's "lost little town".)
[361] "splashing down reality" in fact
[362] the *"something"* [K p273] was BHP's Port Kembla steelworks

THE HORRIBLE PAWS

wave catches them unawares, and Lawrence's hat falls off into the sea, and he darts in after it. Frieda is convulsed with laughter. (*"His hat! His hat! He wouldn't let it go'*[363] *– shrieks, and her head like a sand-bag flops to the sand – 'no – not if he had to swim' – shrieks – 'swim to Samoa.'"*[K p274]) They miss the train back and have to return to Thirroul via a local bus. Once again, Lawrence observes the ordinary Australian fellow-passengers, and likes what he sees.

> *Real careless Australians, careless of their appearance, careless of their speech, of their money, of everything – except of their happy-go-lucky, democratic friendliness. Really nice, with bright, quick, willing eyes.* [K p275]

The chill westerly wind is almost blowing a gale as they walk from the bus-stop in Station Street the half-dozen blocks or so back to *Wyewurk*.

> *The wind blew them home. He made a big fire, and changed, and they drank coffee made with milk, and ale buns.* [K p277]

Frieda reclines in front of the fire and reads a Nat Gould novel, while Lawrence no doubt ponders about where his "romance" is taking him – or, rather, is not taking him. Where he is going to get the material to finish it now? Certainly not from Scott or Rosenthal. He would have wanted to begin the next chapter the following morning, Saturday July 1.

Nonetheless, the next day Lawrence starts writing chapter 14, describing Friday's trip to Wollongong [section #24 MS pp 431-447 c4000 words]. He calls the chapter "Bits", and it begins with material he extracts from the current issue of *The Bulletin*, which, as mentioned, he probably purchased up in Sydney the previous Saturday, June 24. (Although the

---

[363] see Paul Delprat's illustration of this incident in *Appendix 2* "Claws in the Arse"

"Bully" was a general magazine[364], it also carried some literary content on its Pink Page, which Lawrence put down as "*a dowdy bit of swagger*".[K p269])

> *The following day Somers felt savage with himself again...he looked at the big pink spread of his Sydney Bulletin...he liked the Bulletin better than any paper he knew...So he rushed to read the "bits".* [K p269]

The "*bits*" are taken from the famous Aboriginalities page of *The Bulletin*, which consisted of items sent in by pseudonymous readers (and heavily edited), reflecting "the Australian way of life". Lawrence adds his own comments:

> "'1805': The casual Digger of war-days has carried it into civvies. Sighted one of the original Tenth at the Outer Harbour (Adelaide) wharf last week fishing. His sinker was his 1914 Star." *Yes, couldn't Somers just see that forlorn Outer Harbour at Adelaide, and the digger, like some rag of sea-weed dripping over the edge of the wharf fishing, and using his medal for a weight?* [K ibid]

Lawrence in this chapter quotes no fewer than 12 extracted "*Bits*", almost word-for-word, adding the captions of several *Bulletin* cartoons (all scrupulously attributed). This is another example of how Lawrence, stretched for narrative ingredients, shamelessly plundered whatever printed material he could find at hand.

> *Somers liked the concise, laconic style. It seemed to him*

---

[364] *The Bulletin* recorded not only Lawrence & Frieda's arrival in Sydney, but their departure as well – thanks, no doubt, to Bert Toy's editorial input. (Mrs Jenkins, as well as giving Lawrence a letter-of-introduction to Toy, no doubt also wrote to him herself, alerting him to Lawrence's impending arrival in Sydney.) In a contemporary *Bulletin* issue [July 7, 1922] the Melbourne-based literary critic Adrian Lawlor wrote a piece on current English novelists in which he praised Lawrence as "the hope of the future novel" (see Aldington's *Kangaroo Introduction* cited above & my chapter 19 "Postscript" below re Lawlor & Aldington).

> *manly and without trimmings. Put ship-shape in the office, no doubt. Sometimes the drawings were good, and sometimes they weren't...Bits, bits, bits. Yet Richard Lovat read on. It was not mere anecdotage. It was the sheer momentaneous life of the continent. There was no consecutive thread. Only the laconic courage of experience.*
> [K ibid]

Additionally, he begins introducing a new element into the text, consisting of imaginary conversations between himself and the supposed reader. At first they are substantive...

> *He could have kicked himself for wanting to help mankind, join in revolutions or reforms or any of that stuff. He was a preacher and a blatherer, and he hated himself for it. Damn the "soul", damn the "dark god", damn the "listener" and the "answerer", and above all, damn his own interfering, nosy self. What right had he to go nosing round Kangaroo, and making up to Jaz or to Jack?* [K p272]

...but they soon become more discursive, even frivolous, as his "splashed-down" material draws thin again. However, he is about to get a powerful injection of sub-plot material which will give him the elements – the much-needed elements – of his next chapter. For on Sunday he receives an unexpected visitor to *Wyewurk*, in the person of Jack Scott.

However, it is a very different Jack Scott[365] to the one who featured earlier in the novel.

---

[365] aka Jack Callcott [mark #2]

CHAPTER 14

Jack Slaps Back

JACK SCOTT came down from Sydney on Saturday afternoon July 1, probably staying overnight with the Friend family at their "compound" on the outskirts of Thirroul.[366] This was no doubt the first day Scott could get away from Sydney following Lawrence's failure to show up at 112 Wycombe Road the previous Saturday, and after Rosenthal had telephoned his deputy to inform him[367] that his new mate Lawrence had been "nosing around" the Trades Hall and talking to "Jock" Garden – the *"bête rouge"* of the King and Empire Alliance. When Rosenthal had rung Scott that previous Saturday night, one thing he would have wanted to know – straight away – was how much his deputy had actually divulged to Lawrence about their secret organisation. It is unlikely however that Scott would have confessed just how indiscreet he had been. So what Scott wanted to find out now was how much Lawrence had "taken in" of what he had told him (*cf.* "'I tell it you just in rough, you know.'" [K p93]), and, more importantly, what use he might make of it. This Sunday afternoon confrontation on the verandah at *Wyewurk* will bring home to Lawrence – starkly – the dangerous game he had been playing for the past several weeks.

Jack trotted over to Coo-ee on the Sunday afternoon [K p285]

---

[366] We can assume he was on the best of terms with the Friend family/clan, so that was the obvious place for him to stay (now that *Wyewurk* was out of the question, given the events of the previous weekend). Note below that he "*trotted over*", implying he came from somewhere that had horses, which the Friend edge-of-town "compound" would have had.

[367] see my chapter 10, *The Worst Day of His Life*, above, when Cooley/Rosenthal leaves the room "*for some time*" – no doubt to telephone Jack Scott & inform him of what Lawrence had done, & whom he had been to see that morning

There are several versions of what follows. The *holograph* text – which is not the most accurate – is not as stark as the final version, which was written, interlinear, over the cancelled typed-text several months later, in the comparative safety of Taos.[368] In that ultimate, published, version of "Jack Slaps Back", Jack Callcott[369] oozes suppressed violence and dire menace. (*"...his face looked different...His eyes were dark and inchoate."* [K p286]). Lawrence quickly gathers the purpose of his visit. Jack...

> *...had come like a spy to take soundings...Some of the fear he had felt for Kangaroo he now felt for Jack. Jack was really very malevolent.* [K p287]

Scott gets straight to the point.

> *"You've found out all you wanted to know, I suppose?" said Jack.* [K p291] [370]

The confrontation then turns hostile, and Scott begins making ominous threats.

> *"...we want some sort of security that you'll keep quiet, before we let you leave Australia."* [K p292]

Lawrence apparently tries to reassure Scott that their secrets – whatever they may be – are safe with him.

> *"You need not be afraid," he said. "You've made it all too repulsive to me now, for me ever to want to open my mouth*

---

[368] as Lawrence revises & rewrites the text, he tends to revert, as if released from constraint, towards what is, presumably, "reality" – *ie*, as he revises, he gets more factual
[369] [mark #2], *ie* Scott
[370] There is a curious, almost amusing, irony in this. Lawrence doesn't know what Scott & Rosenthal are doing – organising a secret army – & Scott hasn't any idea what Lawrence is doing – writing a book about them & their organisation. One cannot but wonder what would have happened if either had realised what the other was really up to.

about <u>it all</u>.³⁷¹ *You can be quite assured: nothing will ever come out through me."* [K ibid, my emphasis]

How could Lawrence, with a straight face, have said that – assuming he did say it (with or without a straight face) – with 13 chapters of *Kangaroo* in the next room waiting to be added to? Scott, however, is not satisfied.

> *Jack looked up with a faint, sneering smile. "And you think we shall be satisfied with your bare word?" he said uglily.*
> [K ibid]

On the other hand, it is well within the bounds of possibility that when Lawrence used the words *"nothing will ever come out through me"* he may have thought he was referring to some particular aspect of what Scott had told him, and which to him seemed relatively innocent. Not knowing anything about secret armies, he simply didn't know what Scott was getting so worked up about. Scott of course would have suspected nothing about the manuscript in the next room, which Lawrence had been busy splashing down for the past four weeks or so. Scott's concern was about what he knew to be the highly-sensitive secret-army information he had so recklessly and indiscreetly divulged to his erstwhile mate. Yet as Lawrence did not himself know the significance or implications of any of that information (he did not even know he had been vouchsafed it), he could well have thought that it was indeed *"nothing"*³⁷². That possibility would go some way towards explaining the ingenuousness – indeed, duplicity – of Lawrence's retort.

The confrontation ends, fictionally, with Harriett emerging from the house with a tea-tray and asking what the

---

[371] the brief words "*it all*" is as close as Lawrence ever got to referring to politics & secret armies in *Kangaroo*
[372] or at least nothing of any special import

two men had been arguing about.

> *"It was about time you came to throw cold water over us,"* smiled Jack. [K p293]

Then, apparently, Scott took his leave.

> *"Ah, well!" said Jack. "Cheery-o! We aren't such fools as we seem. The milk's spilt, we won't sulk over it."* [K ibid]

Today we can only assume that Scott and Rosenthal went on to conclude that Lawrence posed no exigent threat to them and their organisation, their minds being at least partly put to rest by his assurance that he was about to leave for America, and consequently would soon be "out of their hair". For they were only concerned about what Lawrence might reveal <u>in Australia.</u> Not only did they not know about the manuscript in the next room, it would never have entered their heads that what they had told him would be turned into a book which would soon be published around the world. Extra reassurance might also have come from Jack's realisation, after questioning Lawrence, that his new-found mate had in fact little or no comprehension about what the KEA and "The Garage" were really doing.[373] Despite what the text says later, this is the last time Lawrence has any direct[374] contact with Scott, Rosenthal and the King and Empire Alliance.

During the confrontation there is an especially menacing moment, which Lawrence records, when Jack suggests to Harriett/Frieda that she should leave Somers and remain in Australia, while Lawrence goes on to America.[375]

---

[373] which must have come as some relief to him, at least
[374] except via Hum, as we shall see below (Hum being almost certainly also a paid-up member of the KEA)
[375] the following exchange rings very true of Scott

Jack Slaps Back

> *"Why don't you stay in Australia?" Jack said to her, with the same quiet, husky note of intimacy, insistency, and the reddish light on his face.*
>
> *She was somewhat startled and offended. Wasn't the man sober, or what?*
>
> *"Oh, he wouldn't give me any money, and I haven't a sou of my own," she said lightly, laughing it off.*
>
> *"You wouldn't be short of money," said Jack. "Plenty of money."*
>
> *"You see I couldn't just live on charity, could I?" she replied, delicately.*
>
> *"It wouldn't be charity."*
>
> *"What then?"*
>
> *There was a very awkward pause. Then a wicked redness came into Jack's face, and a flicker into his voice.*
>
> *"Appreciation. You'd be appreciated." He seemed to speak with muted lips. There was a cold silence. Harriet was offended now.* [K pp 292-293]

Jack Scott had an infamous reputation as a philanderer (remarked on by many[376]). In *Kangaroo* Lawrence refers several times to Callcott's attractiveness to women (once in his alternate guise of "Jaz", *viz*: "'I believe he'd make any woman like him...Got that quiet way with him, you know, and a sly sort of touch-the-harp-gently, that's what they like on the quiet.'"[K p64]). It may be that Scott was deploying his notorious influence over the female sex on Frieda[377], probably to hit back at Lawrence by taunting him in front of Frieda. Still, it's a particularly threatening exchange in the text, and makes Jack's "*Slap back*" even more sinister and intimidating.

Lawrence is yet – as of noon on Sunday – to finish chapter 14 "Bits", and to think about whatever his next

---

[376] A number of people I interviewed during my research used the description "a ladies' man" to describe Scott (see his stepson's use of the term cited in *Research-Diary* 9/6/76 below [& also observe his photograph in the *photo-insert*]).

[377] at one point Somers says that Harriett "*quite liked Jack*" [K p175]

153

chapter might consist of. The likelihood is that he used the morning before Scott turned up to write the remaining words of "Bits" [section #25 MS pp 447-468 c5000 words[378]], consisting of a very discursive exegesis, apparently inspired by another *Bulletin* "Bits" item about the herd instincts of cattle[379], and in which Lawrence imagines himself, like a bullock trapped in a muddy waterhole, struggling to get out of the pot of spikenard[380] (in which he has been stuck, on and off, for several weeks). He also makes a reference to what he calls *"this gramophone of a novel"*[K p280], echoing the "splash-down-realty" nature of the work that he had earlier recommended to "Mollie" Skinner. This, however, is Lawrence at his most discursive, or frivolous – and irritating. He ends the chapter on a note of *"blood consciousness"* and self-sacrifice (*"...to the dark God, and to the men in whom the dark God is manifest..."*[K p283]) – *ie* himself.

On Monday July 3 Lawrence starts converting into text chapter 15 "Jack Slaps Back" [section #25 MS pp 469-486 c3300 words], not with the dramatic events of the previous day, but with a continuation of the discursive, chatty tone of the previous "Bits" chapter. He opens by confessing, frankly, what his major problem is. (*"Chapter follows chapter, and nothing doing..."*[381]) It is possible, indeed probable, that the opening of this chapter was partly written on Sunday (before Jack arrived), and is thus a continuation of that session. He upbraids the reader (*"If you don't like the novel, don't read it."*) reminding him/her what the novel is about (*"To be brief, there was a Harriet, a Kangaroo, a Jack and a Jaz and a Vicky, let alone a number of mere Australians."*), adding some casual domestic detail (*"Harriet is quite happy rubbing her hair with hair-wash and brushing it over her forehead in the sun."*). After bringing in his

---

[378] perhaps with a second session in the afternoon
[379] *The Bulletin* [23/6/22]
[380] ointment
[381] the several quotations in this paragraph are taken from *K* pp 284-285

Dark God again...

> ...*outside the gate it is one dark God, the Unknown. And the Unknown is a terribly jealous God, and vengeful*

...he moves on to convert the confrontational events of the previous day into text (*cf.* "*Jack trotted over to Coo-ee on the Sunday afternoon...etc*"). We are assuming – as mentioned above – that the published version, written later in Taos, is the more accurate. In the first *holograph* version[382], written the day after it happened, there is little threat, and Callcott[383] is sardonic and sarcastic rather than evil and threatening, and it is Somers[384] who speaks sharply, calling Cooley and Callcott "*liars*" because they act like "*he-men*", in contrast to Somers' "*she-man*". Scott comes on much more strongly – indeed, he is portrayed as downright dangerous – in the subsequent Taos revised[385] versions.

---

[382] *holograph* pp 454-468
[383] [mark #2] *ie* Scott
[384] *ie* Lawrence
[385] [TS1a&bR]

CHAPTER 15

Interlude, and a Trip to the Zoo

TUESDAY July 4 is not a writing day, as Lawrence goes up to Sydney to make inquiries about their onward travel arrangements. He intended to go to the American consulate in Martin Place to apply for their U.S. visas. But he doesn't realise that July 4 is American Independence Day, and the consulate is closed. So he will have to go back there tomorrow. Nevertheless, as Somers later does in *K* chapter 17, he probably goes to the Union Line shipping office[386] to inquire about onward travel.

> *Richard spent the afternoon going round to the Customs House and to the American Consulate with his passport, and visiting the shipping office to get a plan of the boat. He went swiftly from place to place.* [K p293]

He decides to remain in Sydney that night so that he can go to the consulate when it reopens tomorrow. The probability is that he stays the night with the Hums in Chatswood, for in the morning he goes, according to the text, to Taronga Park Zoo in the company of Hum's young daughter Enid[387]. (As we will see in a moment, it seems very likely that Lawrence and Hum spent some time the previous evening discussing the political situation in Sydney – a topic that Lawrence was still very much interested in.)

---

[386] the New Zealand Union Line company operated RMS *Tahiti*, the boat Lawrence intended to take on to America
[387] whom he calls in the text "Gladys", a name he could have derived from a *Bulletin* advertisement for Hillier's chocolates, viz [K p54]: "*Madge: I can't think what you see in Jack. He is so unintellectual. Gladys: Oh, but he always brings a pound of Billyer's chocolates.*" (Lawrence changed Hillier's to Billyer's – a typical Lawrence initial-letter/rhyme switch.)

Interlude, and a Trip to the Zoo

> *And yet, when he went over to the Zoo, on the other side of the harbour – and the warm sun shone on the rocks and the mimosa bloom, and he saw the animals, the tenderness came back. A girl he had met, a steamer-acquaintance, had given him a packet of little extra-strong peppermint sweets. The animals liked them.* [K ibid]

He is particularly taken with the kangaroos.

> *The female wouldn't come near to eat. She only sat up and watched, and her little one hung its tiny fawn's head and one long ear and one fore-leg out of her pouch, in the middle of her soft, big, grey body.* [K ibid]

He will make use of this image when later in America he writes his only poem about Australia[388], entitled "Kangaroo", whose opening lines read:

> *Delicate mother Kangaroo*
>
> *Sitting up there rabbit-wise, but huge, plump-weighted,*
>
> *And lifting her beautiful slender face, oh! so much more gently and finely*

But when he gets to the consulate in Martin Place, there are problems. He is told that both he and Frieda must have photographs taken for their visas, and that Frieda will have to come up from Thirroul and go to the consulate in person. ("*…both the Customs House and the Consulate wanted photographs and Harriet's own signature. She would have to come up personally.*"[K p339]) Thus Lawrence is obliged to catch the

---
[388] first published in *Birds, Beasts & Flowers* [Martin Secker (London) 1923]

2pm train back to Thirroul to fetch Frieda (there was no other way of contacting her, as there is no telephone at *Wyewurk*). In the evening there is a full moon, and Lawrence goes for a walk along the moonlit beach, before retiring.

> *It was a time of full moon. The moon rose about eight. She was so strong, so exciting, that Richard went out at nine o'clock down to the shore. The night was full of moonlight as a mother-of-pearl. He imagined it had a warmth in it towards the moon, a moon-heat. The light on the waves was like liquid radium swinging and slipping.* [K p340]

Lawrence will make telling use of this *"liquid radium"* image when he comes to write his second-last chapter the following weekend. He is probably also giving some considerable thought to where he is going with his novel, now that his first-hand access to KEA information has been terminated.

Next day Lawrence and Frieda travel up to town, probably by a mid-morning train. They get their photographs taken and processed (Lawrence's is, possibly, still extant, for he may have kept a copy of it for future use[389]), then take them to the American Consulate, where everything is, this time, routine. (*"There were no difficulties."*) Yet they don't go back to Thirroul that day, but remain in Sydney, where they pay a visit to one of the couples they had met earlier on the voyage from Perth to Sydney, Denis and Laura Forrester.[390] Lawrence needs to spend more time in Sydney, as he now has an idea where his next chapter might come from.

In the Forrester family album[391] there is a photograph of

---

[389] I am indebted to the late Keith Sagar for information about this photograph. In a letter to the publishers of my first [1981] book on Lawrence, enclosing a copy of this photograph, Sagar said: "There is just a chance that the enclosed studio portrait, obviously of about that period, may have been the one Lawrence had taken in Sydney".

[390] Lawrence & Frieda had met the Forresters & the Marchbanks, on *Malwa* between Perth & Sydney [see *Nehls* vol 2 (1919-25) pp 157-158].

[391] see *Research-Diary* 22/2/76 below re our discovery of the "missing" Forrester photographs (after the indefatigable John Ruffels had tracked down the Forresters' address in Strathfield)

Interlude, and a Trip to the Zoo

Frieda and Laura Forrester sitting on the verandah of the house the Forresters were renting in Australia Street, Camperdown, knitting or sewing together (Lawrence mentions in a later letter[392] that Frieda had been doing some embroidery). There are also several snaps in the album of Frieda and Laura Forrester strolling in the Botanic Garden in town – almost certainly taken by Denis Forrester, and no doubt during the same two-day visit.[393] Notably absent from these photographs is Lawrence himself. The assumption must be that he was engaged elsewhere, at least when the Botanic Garden snaps were taken (otherwise he would surely have been in-shot). The strong probability is that he is, today or tomorrow, undertaking some local research (see next chapter) for his "romance", which is once more stuck – as far as the political sub-plot is concerned – following Jack Scott's "*slap back*" visit the previous Sunday.

Later in the afternoon he and Frieda go back to stay the night with the Forresters in Camperdown. There they have dinner, together with their other *Malwa* acquaintances, Mr and Mrs Marchbanks, who are staying in the same rented premises in Australia Street, and who are also English immigrants – machinery mechanics – brought out to Australia to work in a nearby clothing factory. In 1958 Denis Forrester recorded the occasion for Edward Nehls (as Forrester told Nehls's Australian operative, the Sydney journalist Fred Esch[394]).

> ...he came to look us up...his royalties check had not arrived and he was short of cash. Marchbanks had more money than we at the time, and he willingly did what he could to help Lawrence. It was not a large

---

[392] *Letters* #2542 [to Koteliansky]
[393] some of the Forrester photographs, courtesy of the Forrester family & our co-publisher Tom Thompson, are reproduced in this volume's *photo-insert*
[394] Nehls had commissioned Esch, who worked for the *SMH*, to undertake some research about Lawrence's time in Australia on his behalf. Esch subsequently interviewed Denis Forrester (see *Nehls* below about Forrester's later visit to Thirroul & *Wyewurk*).

amount anyhow...As a result of this contact, D.H. invited the four of us to "Wyewurk" for a week end.³⁹⁵

Next day Lawrence and Frieda return to Thirroul and *Wyewurk*, probably by the late afternoon train.³⁹⁶ Lawrence now has some writing to do.³⁹⁷

---

³⁹⁵ *Nehls* pp 157-158 [see *Research-Diary* 22/2/76, 4/3/76 & 7/3/76 below re this visit]
³⁹⁶ he possibly spent part of that day in *The Sun's* newspaper library – see next chapter
³⁹⁷ the text of which was no doubt already beginning to hatch in his mind

CHAPTER 16

The Row in Town

LAWRENCE'S next chapter, "A Row in Town", is the climax of the novel, even though it is two chapters from the end. It is, by any measure, a literary *tour de force*, and how he put it together – its provenance – show him at his creative and resourceful best (in his "slap-down-reality" mode). His exigent problem, and it was an acute one, was that his only source of information for his secret-army sub-plot – the activities of the Diggers and Maggies – was now, with the severing of contact with Scott and Rosenthal, ended. Consequently his narrative is not only stuck, but in limbo, with no apparent prospect of a credible or logical conclusion.[398] However, while up in Sydney he apparently undertook some research into some May Day disturbances[399] – riots in fact – that had occurred in Sydney over a year before. This will provide him with the ingredients he so desperately needs to continue his narrative.

The most likely (initial) origin of information about these riotous events was Gerald Hum, who is now Lawrence's only first-hand source for information about what is happening in Sydney, at least on the conservative side of things.[400] We have of course no reason to know for certain, but it is likely that, while staying with Hum at his home in Chatswood on

---

[398] Just how hamstrung he now is for substantive plot material is reflected in the 17 *holograph* pages of discursive text with which he starts the "Row in Town" chapter (& which have nothing to do with the riot in "Canberra Hall/House").

[399] Australian historian Don Rawson, as mentioned in my *Introduction* above, was the first to link these May 1921 incidents with *Kangaroo*. He suggested in his 1968 article [Rawson *op cit*] that Lawrence might have derived his fictional secret army from the King & Empire Alliance, & the "Row in Town" from these Domain riots. He even suggested that Lawrence might have based his character Benjamin Cooley on the KEA leader, Charles Rosenthal [*ibid*].

[400] Garden could have mentioned the Domain riots to him, but that is unlikely, as they did not show the union movement in a particularly advantageous light

Wednesday night, a frustrated Lawrence, seeking to learn more about the Diggers and politics in Sydney and NSW, heard from Hum about the violent May Day clashes – there were more than one – that had occurred in the Domain (Sydney's "Speakers Corner") the previous year, when conservative elements harassed, indeed assaulted, Labor and unionist May Day speakers' platforms.[401] It is likely that when Lawrence evinced interest in this event, Hum suggested that, should Lawrence want to know more about this major confrontation between left and right (in which the King and Empire Alliance played a prominent role), he might consult the newspapers on file at *The Sun* newspaper office, where Hum's journalist cousin, Howard Ashton, worked. The reports in *The Sun's* newspaper library (either from back-issues or from newspaper cuttings filed there) would have told Lawrence that at the May Day clashes "Jock" Garden was counted out by groups of ex-soldiers – no doubt elements of Scott's "The Garage" – just as "Willie" Struthers is in the text of *Kangaroo*. Added credence to such a possibility is given by the fact that Lawrence cites *The Sun* as a source of information in the eventual "A Row in Town" text [K p320]. Even more indicative is the fact that Lawrence makes some effort to

---

[401] The initial May Day incident occurred on Sunday May 1, 1921, & was reported in the *SMH* the following day [*SMH* 2/5/21 p8] in the following gaudy terms: "A disgraceful scene marked the celebration of May Day in the Domain yesterday afternoon, when a portion of a Union Jack was placed on the end of a pole & burnt; the rest of it was torn to shreds, strewn on the ground, & trampled upon. Another incident deeply resented by the patriotic section of the crowd was the hoisting of a large red flag on a lorry:" (note that, according to the conservative *SMH*, there were two sections in the crowd, the "patriotic" one &, presumably, the "unpatriotic" one, or the working-class rabble). The *SMH* report went on: "The feeling of the soldiers present found expression...A riot almost ensued." The following Sunday May 9 there was a "loyalist" counter-demonstration in the Domain, attended, according to Monday's *SMH* report (under the headings "PATRIOTIC RALLY/HUNDRED THOUSAND PEOPLE IN THE DOMAIN/AVENGE THE INSULT TO THE FLAG/UNPRECEDENTED SCENES") by 100,000 people – an exceptionally large crowd in Sydney in 1921 (one suspects, given the *SMH*'s right-wing bias, that the figure was grossly exaggerated). Despite the presence of 500 police, not only did "disgraceful & unprecedented scenes" ensue, but "ugly" ones too, with Labor platforms being charged by wedges of ex-servicemen, & several speakers, including "Jock" Garden, being counted out. (An echo or replay of the riotous events in Moore Park almost exactly a year before - see the Father Jerger incident mentioned above.) Similar reports appeared in the other Sydney newspapers, including, significantly, *The Sun* (see next three footnotes below re this). It is worth noting that the various reports in the Sydney newspapers the following day made a particular point of Garden's IWW rhetoric, intending to highlight the extreme left-wing nature of the May Day riot (& which Lawrence repeated in his fictional portrayal of the incident in the Row in Town).

"disguise" this source, deliberately altering the politics of the paper from conservative (in reality) to socialist, calling it *"the Radical paper"* [K ibid] (which it most certainly was not). Lawrence does not change things (deviating from "reality") unless he has a good reason for doing so – and that is almost always for reasons of disguise or transformation. The fact that he specifically quotes *The Sun*[402] makes it very likely that its office in Castlereagh Street, which was a short walk from the Botanic Garden[403], was the primary source of his "A Row in Town" information. But wherever he got the information – most probably from the newspaper Howard Ashton worked for[404] (who could have arranged access to *The Sun's* cuttings-library) – it allowed him to move his story forward. (It should be no surprise that Lawrence was using published sources to advance the plot of *Kangaroo*. He had been using newspaper and magazine content as source material ever since he began writing his novel of Australia, now more than a month ago.)

There is another significant ingredient in what went to make up the "A Row in Town" chapter: repetition. As he had several weeks previously, with his arrival at *Wyewurk* and Jack Scott's visit to Thirroul on the King's Birthday weekend, he now reprises his more-recent Saturday June 24 visit to the Trades Hall, and his interview there with "Jock" Garden,

---

[402] *The Sun* office was at 32 Castlereagh Street – a block away from Rosenthal's office/apartment at 8 Castlereagh Street. *The Sun* was owned by Sydney businessman Hugh Denison, & was a conservative broadsheet (though it was radical in the sense that it was the first such paper in Sydney to put news on its front page). This is an example of one of Lawrence's transformation techniques – in this case, the opposites-switch.

[403] ...where, that day, Frieda & Mrs Forrester were strolling around the Garden's flower-beds while being photographed (presumably) by Denis Forrester (see *photo-insert*). It will be noted, as remarked above, that Lawrence is not in-shot. It is unlikely Forrester handed the camera to Lawrence to take the pictures, so we may assume he was elsewhere (for otherwise he would surely have also been in the picture). My assumption is that he was off visiting *The Sun* newspaper office in nearby Castlereagh Street (see above). He may, however, have made two visits to *The Sun* cuttings library - the first one that day to see what was there, & a second & longer one the following morning for further research (while Frieda was at Australia Street Camperdown engaged in needlework with Laura Forrester – also see picture in the *photo-insert* [when Lawrence is again not in-shot]).

[404] Howard Ashton – who also reviewed books for *The Sun*, & was to become the paper's editor – later made a habit of calling his cousin Hum "a typical Cornishman" – possibly a sly reference to the novel's character "Jaz" Trewhella. (However, although Hum was born in Cornwall, he was of German not Cornish stock. It was, according to Paul Delprat & the Ashton family, "Howard's little joke" [presumably about his portrayal in *Kangaroo*]).

while also elaborating on what he and Hum did between the meeting with Garden in the morning and his confrontation with Rosenthal around 5.30-6.00 pm that afternoon/evening.

However, the "A Row in Town" chapter again begins in a discursive mode, with Lawrence discoursing about herd-instincts and *"the mob-spirit"*.

> *Why does a flock of birds rise suddenly from the tree-tops, all at once…and swirl round in one cloud…there was no visible sign or communication given. It was telepathic communication* [K pp 298-299]

This rambling exegesis, written on Friday July 7, the day after he returned from town to Thirroul, goes on for 17 hand-written pages without advancing the political sub-plot one jot. It is likely he stopped half-way down p508, suspending session #27 [pp 486-508 c5500 words], and continued the chapter more substantively next day.

However, this long, discursive opening to K chapter 16 poses a problem, for it really shouldn't be there. Plot-wise, the chapter should begin with an account of Somers's trip up to Sydney to attend the *"big public meeting"* (as does the second [section #28] part, written the next morning, Saturday July 8). That is what Lawrence's "research" in Sydney would seem to have dictated. Presumably, that major-key ingredient or narrative element was already drafted in his mind, waiting to be put down on paper. One is tempted to assume that the *"herd-instinct"* opening to "A Row in Town" was written earlier, and is linked in some way to – perhaps a continuation of – the discursive section at the end of the earlier chapter, "Bits", about bullocks being trapped in a muddy waterhole. Yet it is in its correct place, for immediately above it Lawrence wrote the name of the chapter, "A Row in Town", which implies that he did indeed intend to go on later in the chapter to recount the story of the riot in *"Canberra House"*. So why does he begin, apparently irrelevantly with…

> *The thing that Kangaroo had to reckon with, and would not reckon with, was the mass-spirit* [K p294]

…rather than more substantively…

> *Richard came up to the big mass meeting of Labour in the great Canberra Hall, in Sydney* [K p304]

One is tempted to sweep this awkward question under the carpet. Ordinarily, the answer would be that he is "filling in" or "padding out" the text until he had something more substantive to write about. But that cannot be the case here – as it undoubtedly is elsewhere – for he had "more active" ingredients at hand, or in his mind…the results of his newspaper research into the 1921 Domain riots undertaken earlier in the week. The answer must be that this 17-page "herd instinct" section had in fact already been drafted in his mind *before* he travelled up to visit the American Consulate in Sydney on Wednesday July 4, but had yet to be committed to paper (and was indeed a delayed continuation of the discursive ending of the earlier "Bits" chapter). Apparently, this could not be written down until after he returned to Thirroul (and his notebooks) late on Thursday, July 6 – a time of day when he did not ordinarily like to write text. So although he had mentally composed[405] the later and more substantive Row-in-Town material, in preparation for it to be transcribed on Friday July 7, it had to "take its place in the queue", and was only committed to paper next morning, Saturday July 8.

Yet this juxtaposition raises an important question about the relative significance or importance – to Lawrence – of the

---

[405] (or drafted)

novel's substantive secret-army content on the one hand, and its more discursive minor-key elements (such as this herd-instinct section of text) on the other. As explained several times above, it is clear that Lawrence did not comprehend, nor "take in", the significance of the secret-army material that had been disclosed to him, primarily by Jack Scott (possibly supplemented by his *Wyewurrie* neighbour Adrian Friend, who was also a KEA member). So it is most likely that he drew little or no distinction between what we today take to be the major elements (the secret-army content) and minor (discursive) ingredients in his narrative. For Lawrence, they were to all intents the one and the same thing, with the former being no deeper or more important than the latter (for him they had the thickness of "literary wallpaper"). Indeed, that might go some way to explaining his flagrant lack of concern about the possible consequences of what he was doing, reflected for example in the astonishing question[406] later addressed – from Taos – to his U.S. publisher, Seltzer: *"Do you think the Australian Govt. or the Diggers might resent anything?"*...a question so naïve as to beggar belief (and only explicable in terms of "literary wallpaper"[407]).

Be that as it may, the main – second – section of chapter 16 (committed to paper on Saturday morning July 8) duly describes Somers/Lawrence's Saturday trip up to *"Canberra House"*[408]...

---

[406] Cited in *Letters* #2623, written to Seltzer on 7/10/22. Just over a week later Lawrence wrote to his agent Mountsier in New York expressing a similar concern: "Ought one to put in a tiny forward note, apologising to Australia?" [*Letters* #2630]. But what had he said that he thought he should apologise to Australia for? Bruce Steele addresses this – for him, somewhat inconvenient – question by suggesting that "it would seem that he was worried, not so much having given away secret information" [which is my interpretation], "but that his fictional Diggers Clubs might be taken as a caricature of the RSL, the real diggers & their actual political concerns" [*Steele* p xxv]. Still worried about this, Steele adds a same-page footnote, saying: "DHL was also concerned that the Australian Government might take offence" [*Steele ibid*]. Yet take offence at what?

[407] *ie*, he was not interested in what may lie under the surface-coating he was so ingenuously slapping on

[408] Initially, Lawrence calls Struthers' HQ "Canberra House" then changes its name to "Canberra Hall" – in reality the Trades Hall in the Haymarket – a similar transformational mix-up between "Murdoch Street" & "Murdoch Road", on a corner of which, as mentioned above, were "the Canberra Flats" (whence the name "Canberra Hall" came in *Kangaroo*).

Richard got up in the dark, to catch the six o'clock train to Sydney. [K ibid]

…from his Trades Hall meeting with Struthers/Garden, to the end of the "Row in Town" riot [section #28 MS pp 508-518 c5000 words]).[409] Tellingly – and significantly – the content of Struthers' *"Canberra Hall"* harangue is laced with Industrial Workers of the World (IWW) rhetoric, which Lawrence probably picked up from Siebenhaar or (more likely) Garden – both IWW stalwarts. In the "Row in Town" text Struthers advocates positions – such as the welcoming of *"coloured labour"*[K p311] into Australia – that were, at the time, anathema to the mainstream Labor Party.[410] Such views, in direct opposition to Labor's sacrosanct White Australia policy, could not have been publicly voiced by an ordinary party member or an orthodox union leader. Only Garden[411], the IWW/Communist ideologue and secretary of the NSW Labor Council, could have said such things in public, particularly from a platform in the crowded Domain on May Day 1921, and on several subsequent Sundays, when there were further clashes.

---

[409] the morning one being, as described above, a reprise of the original meeting on June 24 with Struthers/Garden in *K* chapter 11, "Willie Struthers and Kangaroo"

[410] In this era – & until the 1970s – the Labor Party (& most of the wider Australian population) were firmly wedded to what was called "The White Australia Policy", which was intended to prevent access to Australia (& Australian jobs) by "coloured" labour from overseas, & in particular China. The masthead of *The Bulletin* (until the early 1960s) carried this unashamedly racist motto: "AUSTRALIA FOR THE WHITE MAN – CHINA FOR THE CHOW". (They dropped "CHINA FOR THE CHOW" in the 1950s after the then External Affairs Minister Richard Casey made a personal appeal to the magazine's assistant editor Malcolm Ellis [personal *Bulletin* knowledge].)

[411] The significant point here being that the CUP edition of *Kangaroo* rejects the obvious connection between "Jock" Garden and "Willie" Struthers. Instead, Bruce Steele suggested that the union leader in the novel may have been based on the (non-union) IWW-supporter William Siebenhaar in Western Australia; or else another local NSW union leader, Arthur Willis; or even on Lawrence's former Eastwood political mentor, Willie Hopkins [see *Steele* p39 (my emphases)]. (He apparently thought a "William" or "Wills" or "Willie" would help counter my more-obvious Scottish "Jock" identification.) Yet, as mentioned above, it was only Garden, the radical (indeed, Communist) NSW union leader who could have lauded IWW ideology, such as welcoming coloured migration to Australia, in front of a union gathering like the "Row in Town" one held in the Domain in 1921 (& got away with it – his acknowledged IWW-radicalism helping neutralise any outrage over his slurs on the sacred White Australia policy)…something that a non-IWW unionist, such as Willis, would never have dared to do.

CHAPTER 17

Thinking of Leaving

AFTER FINISHING chapter 16 "A Row in Town" – the first section on Friday July 7 and the second on Saturday July 8 – Lawrence has two more chapters to write before the novel will be finished and ready to be posted off to Mountsier in New York. He writes to Mountsier on Friday – probably in the afternoon, after his morning session – telling him[412] he had two chapters left to write (which confirms the dating of "A Row in Town"). So on Sunday morning July 9 he almost certainly begins the next section and the start of *K* chapter 17, "Kangaroo is Killed".

The last two chapters consist of 39 *holograph* pages – about 9000 words. It is not easy to distinguish the individual sessions that made up this concluding part of the novel. If he were writing at his "normal" speed – around 4000 words a day/session – this output could have been easily completed in two days, or three at most. That being the case, he could – indeed should – have completed the novel on Monday July 10, or by Tuesday July 11 at the latest. However, there is a problem with such dating, for over a week later on Wednesday July 18 he wrote to his U.S. publisher Seltzer[413] in New York telling him he finished *Kangaroo* the previous Saturday – *ie,* on July 15. So what did he do between Sunday July 9 and Saturday July 15?

This question is made even more difficult to answer by the fact that he probably wrote[414] all of chapter 17 on Sunday

---

[412] *Letters* #2551 [to Mountsier]
[413] *Letters* #2555 [to Seltzer]
[414] no doubt in two writing sessions

July 9 [section #29 MS pp 519-538b[415] about 5200 words]. That, on the face of things, would leave him six days to finish around 3500 words, or 19 MS pages – something he could have easily written in one morning. Moreover, there is no obvious "break" in the writing of the final chapter, nor any "thematic" change, that would indicate a pause or interruption, and so point to two writing sessions – one on Monday and a final one on Tuesday July 11.

The novel's penultimate chapter "Kangaroo is Killed" consists of three segments – two separate visits to Sydney for Somers to see Cooley in hospital (the second time with Jack Callcott present) and a substantial sub-section in-between describing a walk in the evening along the beach below *Cooee/Wyewurk*. The two visits are clearly contrivance and rather weak invention[416] (the killing-off of Cooley is particularly cavalier). But the middle section is totally convincing, and is clearly "splashed down" from reality.

> *So it was when he got back from Sydney and, in the night of moonlight, went down the low cliff to the sand. Immediately the great rhythm and ringing of the breakers obliterated every other feeling in his breast.* [K p329]

Yet that passage is almost certainly, in part, a reprise of his return from Sydney the previous Wednesday (*cf.* the "*liquid radium*" reference above). But now he adds a morning walk, taken later in the week, probably on Friday morning.

> *And in the morning the yellow sea faintly crinkled by the inrushing wind from the land, and long, straight lines on the lacquered meadow, long, straight lines that reared at last*

---

[415] Lawrence also mis-numbered two pages in chapter 17, having two p538s in the *holograph* (see above & below variously about his other *holograph* & typescript mis-paginations)

[416] As indicated below, this part of the text is factitious, & does not reflect any involvement by real-life people (certainly not Jack Scott [Callcott mark #2]). It is one of the limited number of ingredients in *Kangaroo* that are not based on what Lawrence was actually doing in Australia (*ie*, it is "fiction", not [if I may be permitted to coin a word], "faction")

> *in green glass, then broke in snow, and slushed softly up the sand* [K p329]

Again, this is Lawrence at his very best. Now "released" from having to find secret-army narrative-content, he can give his unrivalled writing and reportage skills greater freedom, or sway – for example:

> *Incredibly swift and far the flat rush flew at him, with foam like the hissing, open mouths of snakes. In the nearness a wave broke white and high. Then, ugh! across the intervening gulf the great lurch and swish, as the snakes rushed forward, in a hollow frost hissing at his boots. Then failed to bite, fell back hissing softly, leaving the belly of the sands granulated silver.* [K p340].[417]

There are two almost-identical versions of this wonderful passage, in consecutive paragraphs, and which Lawrence must have seen when revising the manuscript (at least twice), yet left them both in.[418]

Whether writing the last chapter took him two days or one, Lawrence almost certainly begins the final chapter, "Adieu Australia" on Monday July 10, no doubt, as is his custom, soon after breakfast [section #30 MS pp 540-559 c4700 words[419]]. Yet "Adieu Australia" is not the original name of chapter 18. An earlier chapter-heading is "Kangaroo Dies and is Buried". On p540 on the *holograph* manuscript Lawrence crossed these words out and superimposed the published

---

[417] It should be noted that this delightful passage – perhaps the best in the novel – comes immediately after one in which Lawrence wrote: "*It was a time of full moon. The moon rose about eight.*" which could invest these paragraphs with a "real" moonrise date & time that we might correlate with reality. To his credit, Bruce Steele recognised this possible "diary" correlation between fact & fiction, & in an Explanatory Note [*Steele* p408] commented: "If DHL is basing this event on his own experience, it would have been the second week of July 1922." (as indeed it was).

[418] one wonders if his "little devil" had a hand in this disinclination to remove an obvious syntactical solecism (see *Fantasia* for the role his "little devil" plays in his compositional efforts)

[419] again, in probably two sessions, morning & afternoon (even Lawrence could not write c5000 words in one sitting, unless his muse was being paid overtime)

chapter name. There is something odd here too. The death of Cooley – he is still alive in the previous chapter – is mentioned only in the first sentence of the chapter, though Harriett avers to his death in another sentence further on (which would tend to underline the perfunctory treatment of his demise). So what did Lawrence intend with his initial chapter-heading? The assumption must be that he was going to talk more about Cooley and his death. (Where, for example, is his "*great funeral*"[K p342] to be held?) But he does not do this.

There are several versions of the somewhat notorious "last chapter" of *Kangaroo*. The first version, written in Thirroul on Monday July 10, consists this time of two elements: Somers contemplating the township from a viewpoint somewhere above the town, and a second section comprising a conversation with "Jaz" ("*The only person that called at Coo-ee was Jaz*"[K p347]). This first "Thirroul" version of chapter 18 ends with Somers's exchange with "Jaz", and a final sentence.

> *Now Jaz, goodbye. Goodbye to you, goodbye to everybody. I'm finished on this side.* [holograph p559]

(*ie*, that is the ending of the novel in the text he wrote in Thirroul). It is fairly clear where these two ingredients came from. The first element…

> *Sitting at the edge of the bush he looked at the settlement and the sea beyond* [K p342]

…is obviously a reprise of the start of chapter 10, "Diggers" [*ie*, "*He went on till he could look over the tor's edge at the land below. There was the scalloped sea-shore, for miles, and the strip of flat coast-land…*"[K p177]]. The two passages – eight chapters apart – are to all intents identical. The second element – the conversation with "Jaz" – is just as clearly, initially at least, a reprise of the conversation with Jack Callcott/Jack Scott in chapter 15, "Jack Slaps Back". At one point in the exchange Lawrence actually writes "Jack" instead of "Jaz" on his MS [*holograph* p548] and has to cross it out. Lawrence even has Harriett coming out, as she does in "Jack Slaps Back", with a tea-tray and *"pouring cold water"* over the two men. However, this second element soon decays from a reprise of "Jack Slaps Back" into Lawrence preaching about his twin obsessions of *"love"* and *"male power"*, viz:

> *I've looked for love, howled for love…What I finally want is my own male power.* [K p349]

The last 11 *holograph* paragraphs of this sermon do not even contain quotation marks, as if Lawrence has dropped any pretense that it was a conversation with "Jaz", but instead a first-person dialogue with himself (and his muse, or "little devil").

However, the final, published version of this last chapter consists of much more than these two "Thirroul-ending" [*holograph*] elements (which, nevertheless, he largely retained in the final text). They consist of a description of a storm in Mullumbimby/Thirroul; yet another argument or dispute with Harriett/Frieda; a sulky-ride out into the bush when the wattle is in bloom; a trip up to the American Consulate to collect their visas; their preparations for departure; travelling up to Sydney a last time to board their steamer; and, finally, sailing down the Harbour and out into the Pacific, where…

> *It was only four days to New Zealand, over a cold, dark, inhospitable sea.*[420]

---

[420] which is how the text ends on the Berg typescripts & in the Secker & post-Secker "UK" editions (including the international Penguin edition) up until the 1994 edition (where it became part of the 375 TS1R words the CUP edition mistakenly left out – see below)

...which are the last words of the ultimate, published UK version of the novel (and which is in fact Lawrence's chosen ending of *Kangaroo*). However, these words were not written in Australia, but later, after Lawrence and Frieda arrived in Taos, New Mexico, to stay with Mabel Dodge [Luhan].

We will address that separate writing session in a moment. First, however, we have to take Lawrence to his stated, in the above-mentioned letter to Seltzer,[421] finishing point, four or five days later on Saturday, July 15, and his last *Kangaroo* writing-or-revising session in Australia.[422] His final Thirroul words read:

> "Now Jaz, goodbye. Goodbye to you, goodbye to everybody. I'm finished on this side". [*holograph* p 559]

(This *"I'm finished on this side"* ending might well be a reference to the Christian martyr St Laurence of Rome, who was tortured to death on a gridiron, and supposedly said during his ordeal: "Turn me over, Brothers, I'm finished on this side".[423] Lawrence here may have identified himself with the martyr – which would give his final Thirroul words added poignancy.)

---

[421] cf. *Letters* #2555 [to Seltzer] (see above re the Saturday finishing date in that letter)
[422] though he probably finished the text, including his revisions, on Thursday, in time to catch the mail train to Sydney for Saturday dispatch to New York on *Mankura*
[423] cf. http://oca.org/saints/lives/2015/08/10/102258-martyr-and-archdeacon-laurence-of-rome

CHAPTER 18

Departure, Taos and Second Thoughts

WE HAVE little or no evidence on which to base a reconstruction of what Lawrence did between Monday, when we assume he started chapter 18, and Saturday, when he apparently (according to his letter to Seltzer[424]) "threw down his pen".[425] He could have taken his time and written more slowly over the intervening days. He was no longer making any attempt to finish the MS to catch the *Sonoma*, which was due to leave for the U.S. two days later on Wednesday. Instead he now intended to dispatch the MS on the *Mankura*, leaving a week hence on Saturday July 15. So there was no pressing need to hurry. He could have indeed taken several days to finish his text.

But it is unlikely that he would spin out the very thin and rehashed content of chapter 18 for more than one session. So we should assume that Monday July 10 was his last substantive writing session – as far as *Kangaroo* is concerned – in Australia. Yet it would be unusual for Lawrence not to touch his manuscript for up to a week, before packaging it up for sending to America. The strong likelihood is that he spent part of Tuesday to Thursday of that week revising the text. Yet we have no idea what he did on what day, so we will just have to call this editing period: section #31 MS pp 1-559 [revision]. (If, as seems likely, he took several days to revise his manuscript, that would take the number of days he spent

---

[424] *Letters* #2555 [to Seltzer]
[425] echoing the advice he had earlier given to "Mollie" Skinner after she had "written from day to day" & "splashed down reality" [*Fifth Sparrow* p116]

writing and revising *Kangaroo* to 33 – one third of the 99 days he spent in Australia.)

Given how long this might have taken, it implies a substantial revision. Bruce Steele in his 1994 CUP edition of *Kangaroo* pointed out that Lawrence's revision in Thirroul of the *holograph* MS (presumably starting on Tuesday July 11) appeared to have been extensive.[426] Over half of Lawrence's 559 manuscript pages have corrections or revisions. Some, clearly, are "running" changes. But many, if not most, seem to be later revisions, presumably made during this revision/editing period, prior to the dispatch of the MS to Mountsier in New York, presumably from Thirroul post office late on Thursday July 13.

Significantly, there is no sign, in these or any subsequent changes, of Lawrence going back over his text to disguise or "play down" his revelations about Scott and Rosenthal's clandestine organisation. He is still oblivious of the fact that those he called "the Diggers" would be, to put it mildly, somewhat upset about his exposure of their highly illegal, in fact treasonous, activities. Neither did it apparently trouble him what Jack Scott would think when he learned, from reading *Kangaroo*, that he had been portrayed in the novel (in an alternative guise as Victoria's brother "Fred" [Wilmot] [427]) as impotent, and *"can't get his pecker up*[428] *now"*.[K p105]

Two further periods are germane to the composition of *Kangaroo*. The first is what happened between the dispatch of the *holograph* MS to Mountsier in New York on the *Mankura*

---

[426] Steele pp xxxvi-vii
[427] Scott's impotence – with which Lawrence also invested the Scott figure of Jack Strangeways in *John Thomas & Lady Jane* – was apparently known in the circles he moved (see *Research-Diary* 14/6/11 below re his shell-shock in WW1). "Fred Wilmot" is in fact a reference to Victoria's brother, Alfred John [see *K* p30] "*the first Trewhella*" & Callcott's "*best mate*", who had died, fictionally, two years before. In "real life" Scott's best mate had been Major Dudley Oatley – the first husband of Scott's second wife Andree Adelaide Oatley – who indeed died from pneumonia two years previously after swimming off *Hinemoa* [he was certainly not impotent, fathering three children].) Lawrence in *Kangaroo* gets very mixed up about who's who in the real-life Scott, Oatley & Friend ménages.
[428] Then it was called "impotence". Today it's "erectile dysfunction" ("ED"), & a common consequence of post-traumatic stress disorder (PTSD), once known as "shellshock".

on July 15, and Lawrence's later departure from Sydney on Friday August 11. (Several events in that period came to be part of the controversial "last chapter" of *Kangaroo*.[429]) The second is the further revisions Lawrence made in America on the Taos typescripts [TS1aR & TS1bR][430] in October 1922.

The revisions Lawrence made in Taos were extensive, so much so that they necessitated two second typescripts [TS2a & TS2b] so that his two publishers, Secker in the UK and Seltzer in America, could have "clean" final texts to set and print from. We do not know when the two first-typescripts of *Kangaroo* [TS1a & TS1b] arrived from Mountsier in Taos, nor how long it took for Lawrence to make his revisions of them. All that his letters tell us is that he was still waiting for them on October 7, but that he finished the revisions by October 16 – nine days later.[431] As Bruce Steele pointed out, Lawrence's Taos revision involved "hundreds of changes to words, phrases and occasionally sentences".[432] In some cases it involved whole paragraphs – indeed, entire pages. Steele added: "...he rewrote sections of five chapters extensively. Together they amount to some 50 numbered pages of reworked or completely new material"[433]. Steele goes so far as to say that Lawrence regarded the MS he originally wrote in Thirroul (the *holograph*) as "a rough draft", to be revised and polished later.[434] That would go some way towards explaining the extensive nature of his Taos revisions. (Lawrence had earlier told Mountsier that he wanted to go through the MS again.[435]) That might also explain the slap-

---

[429] The peregrinations of the "last chapter" of *Kangaroo* would need an essay in itself to explain, & this is not the place for that. Lawrence's subsequent 16/10/22 letter [#2628] to Mountsier ("Have added last chapter.") merely marked the beginning of the saga (see below & my "Not the End of the Story" [*DHLR* vol 26].)

[430] there were, originally, five *Kangaroo* typescripts [TSS], of which three are still extant & in the Berg collection at the New York Public Library [see below re this]

[431] *Letters* #2622 (6/10/22) & #2628 (16/10/22)

[432] *Steele* p xlii

[433] *ibid*

[434] *ibid*

[435] *Letters* #2554 [to Mountsier] (dated 17/7/22 from Thirroul, three days before he posted the revised typescript [TS1aR] to him in New York)

dash[436], unfinished nature of the last part of his original Thirroul version of *K* chapter 18 (also remarked on by Steele[437]).

It is also worthy of note – and of significance – that he made his corrections on *both* TS1 typescripts [TS1a & TS1b] Mountsier had sent him.[438] In fact he made one set of revisions/editing on one typescript, then transposed his corrections to the second typescript, switching alternately between the two typescripts. This was a result of needing two revised texts, one for Seltzer in New York, and the other for Secker in London – an exigency that was to play a role in the subsequent unfortunate (indeed, catastrophic) confusion over the endings of *Kangaroo*.

Undoubtedly by far the major change was in the last chapter ("Have added last chapter," he told Mountsier.[439]) Into both Taos revised typescripts [TS1aR & TS1bR] he injected[440] an account of the storm that struck the coast of New South Wales on Saturday July 22 (the day the MS went off to America on the *Mankura*), and which lasted several days.[441]

> *Down it came...the wind broke in volleys from the sea, and the rain poured as if the cyclone were a great bucket of water pouring itself endlessly down.* [K p349]

The *"cyclone"* – it was in fact an east-coast low[442] which swept down from the north – immured Lawrence and Frieda in *Wyewurk* for three days.

> *The house was like a small cave under the water. Rain*

---

[436] analogous to the casual finishing off of Cooley in the previous chapter
[437] *Steele* p xxxviii
[438] see *Endings, op cit*
[439] *Letters* #2628 [to Mountsier]
[440] to be seen in TS1aR [Berg 1] pp 464-468 (at this point he was editing/revising both typescripts with the intention of sending them both to Mountsier in New York as setting-texts)
[441] see *SMH* 24/7/22 [p7 for the news report & p9 for the weather report]
[442] such strong storms are a regular feature of winter weather along the NSW coast, & usually last for several days, often causing severe damage to beaches & flooding in coastal areas

> *poured in waves over the dark room...the water swept in, and gurgled under the doors and in at the windows. Tiles were ripped off the verandah roof with a crash, and water splashed more heavily. For the first day there was nothing to do but to sit by the fire.* [K ibid]

Their entrapment leads, through the thoughts of Harriett, to Lawrence later expressing the feeling that had, apparently, been stirring in his mind about the negative side of Australia – and, perhaps, the evil he had encountered in Rosenthal and Scott.

> *Then gradually, through the silver glisten of the new freedom came a dull, sinister vibration...the freedom, like everything else, had two sides to it. Sometimes a heavy, reptile-hostility came off the sombre land, something gruesome and infinitely repulsive...It was as if the silvery freedom suddenly turned*[443], *and showed the scaly back of a reptile, and the horrible paws*[444]. [K p350]

This *"scaly back...horrible-paws"* presentiment is the climactic image in the novel, and I believe is Lawrence's ultimate summing up of his Australian experience. (However, the *"horrible paws"* image might also be a reference to the *"bear-like"* attentions Lawrence was probably subjected to in Rosenthal's apartment on the night of June 17, the ramifications of which are outlined in *Appendix 1* below.)

The storm lasted until Thursday July 27...

> *On the fourth day the wind had sunk, the rain was only*

---

[443] it is, I believe, highly significant that Lawrence wrote these words – his ultimate summing up of his Australian experience – not in Australia, but many weeks later in the safety of Taos, when he had time & occasion to look back on what had happened to him in Sydney & Thirroul

[444] As already mentioned above, from 1950 to 1994 the main circulating edition of *Kangaroo* was the 1950 Penguin text (re-edited from the Secker 1923 edition). Whoever was responsible for editing the Penguin text took it upon themselves to change Lawrence's word "paws" to "jaws" (presumably because a reptile doesn't have paws). Lawrence, however, was not referring to an animal reptile, but to a very human one.

> *thin, the dark sky was breaking.* [K p352]

...during which time the interior of *Wyewurk* was not a happy place.

> *To Richard it was like being caged in with a sick tiger, to be shut up with Harriet in this watery cave of gloom.* [K p351]

The following weekend, the Lawrences had invited the Forresters and Marchbanks[445] down to *Wyewurk*, as Denis Forrester later told Edward Nehls (via Fred Esch): "My memory is that we went down early in the Australian spring."[446] They arrived by train from Sydney in time for lunch, and apparently stayed overnight.[447] On Sunday Lawrence took them up Bulli Pass, in a car and driver he engaged for the occasion, for an excursion into the bush. There they enjoyed a picnic lunch at Loddon Falls. In the Forrester photo-album there are snaps of them, and the driver, in front of the Falls (see *photo-insert* in this volume).[448] Lawrence, according to Forrester, was writing something during their visit – probably continuing his translation of the Verga texts, possibly *Cavelleria Rusticana*. ("D.H. was writing

---

[445] see my "Interlude, and a Trip to the Zoo" chapter above re Lawrence's fellow passengers on the *Malwa* & his contact with them up in Sydney

[446] *Nehls* pp 157-158, from which this account of the visit is reconstructed. (Actually it was the weekend of July 29-30: still winter, for spring does not start officially in Australia until September 1. However, in eastern parts of the continent, August 1, formerly "Wattle Day", is regarded by many as the start of the Australian spring.)

[447] *Nehls ibid* (*Wyewurk* could accommodate up to 13 people, at a pinch)

[448] The "Forrester snaps" are, too, a story in themselves (& are reproduced in this present work). They apparently came from of a roll of film taken by Denis Forrester, initially in Sydney on July 4-5 (both at their rented house at 209 Australia Street Camperdown & in the Botanic Garden), & further snapshots taken on the same reel when the Forresters & Marchbanks later went down to Thirroul on the weekend of July 29-30. These latter photographs included images of the group in the front garden of *Wyewurk*, & also on the picnic trip to Loddon Falls. (The photograph mentioned above was one of the Loddon Falls group.) Laura Forrester must have had them copied & then sent a selection of them to Frieda. Frieda apparently sent some of them to Heinemann for their edition of *The Letters of D.H Lawrence* [1933, Aldous Huxley ed.] while others were included in her *Not I But the Wind* memoir [*op cit* (also see *Research-Diary* 22/2/76 & 25/1/86 below)]. Denis Forrester later wrote a letter to *SMH* journalist Fred Esch describing the event: "My wife & I & two other friends spent a weekend at 'Wyewurk'...we toured the environs of Thirroul with them in a hired car ... They both seemed very happy" (cited in my Forrester article in the *DHLR* vol 20, no 1 [Spring 1988] p40).

something while we were there, because there would be times when he would leave us because he had work to do."[449]) One of the Forrester snaps shows Lawrence, seated on the front lawn of *Wyewurk*, leaning against the wall of the verandah, apparently with a notebook on his knees. (That snapshot is perhaps the most memorable image of Lawrence in Australia [see *photo-insert*].) The English couples no doubt returned to Sydney by the afternoon train on Sunday.

The visit provided Lawrence with another ingredient for the final chapter he later rewrites in Taos [on TS1a & TS1b]. In that revised *K* chapter 18 he describes a sulky ride that Somers/Lawrence and Harriett/Frieda take into the bush. (*"Nothing is lovelier than to drive into the Australian bush in spring."*[K p353]) After returning to *Wyewurk* they deck the interior of the bungalow with wattle.

> *The flowers there in the room were like angel-presences, something out of heaven. The bush! The wonderful Australia.* [K p356]

Two days later, on Tuesday August 1 (*"wattle-day"*), they again travel up to Sydney to go to the U.S. Consulate and collect their visas, which are now ready to be picked up.

> *...it was August, and spring was come, it was wattle-day in Sydney, the city full of yellow bloom of mimosa. Richard and Harriet went up to the United States Consul, to the shipping office: everything very easy.* [K p353]

How they spend the next week or so in Thirroul is not known, as all the text tells us is that...

> *...in the bungalow gardens, birds flew quickly about in the*

---

[449] *Nehls* pp 157-158

> *sun, the morning was quick with spring, the afternoon already hot and drowsy with summer.* [K ibid]

Then it was time to pack up and leave.

> *...the day came to go: to give up the keys, and leave the lonely, bare Coo-ee to the next comers* [K p356]

In Sydney they probably crossed over the Harbour again to visit the Hums in Chatswood. We do not know where they spent their last night in Australia (probably with the Hums), but next morning they are seen off at the wharf, according to the text, by two women, one of whom was probably Lillian Hum, while the other may have been Laura Forrester.

> *On the last morning Victoria*[450] *and Jaz's wife came to see the Somers off. The ship sailed at ten.* [K ibid]

Lawrence's description of the traditional wharf departure, with streamers being thrown by the departing passengers to their friends onshore, became the inspiration for the cover illustration of the U.S. Seltzer edition of *Kangaroo*. Lawrence described the scene:

> *One by one the streamers broke and fluttered loose and fell bright and dead on the water. The slow crowd, slow as a funeral, was at the end, the far end of the quay, holding the last streamer...The last streamers blowing away, like broken attachments, broken* [K p358]

...which is where the Cambridge University Press (CUP) 1994 Critical Edition of *Kangaroo* leaves it. It was also where the 1923 Seltzer edition ended – with a non-authorial full-stop

---

[450] "Victoria", hitherto based on an amalgam of "Maudie" Cohen & ""Fanny"" Friend, has apparently now morphed into Laura Forrester

inserted after the second "broken"[451].

But that is not where Lawrence originally concluded the novel. The extra text he wrote in Taos on TS1a&bR in October 1922 adds the sentence's final word *"attachments."*[452], then went on to describe the passage down the Harbour, past Manly, out through the Heads...

> *...ahead was the open gate of the harbour, the low Heads with the South Lighthouse, and the Pacific beyond, breaking white. On the left was Manly, where Harriet had lost her yellow scarf. And then the tram going to Narrabeen*[453], *where they had first seen Jaz.*[454]

and onward across the Tasman *"...to New Zealand, across a cold, dark, inhospitable sea."*, those being the final words of 1923-1974 UK imprints of *Kangaroo* (Secker, Heinemann, Penguin, etc), and also the 1960 U.S. Viking edition, which replaced the out-of-print Seltzer edition as the American imprint, prior to the 1950 Penguin edition – but not in the CUP version (except in the textual apparatus).

Originally, however, the two typescripts of *Kangaroo* [TS1aR & TS1bR] went on still further to describe a day in Wellington, New Zealand, where inhospitable Customs officials held up Frieda, presumably because of her German ancestry. Lawrence was not pleased, describing New Zealand (in the revised TS1 typescripts) as *"this cold, snobbish, lower middle class colony of pretentious nobodies."*[455] The new Taos ending concluded with Somers and Harriett departing from Tahiti – where an American film crew came aboard and

---

[451] see *Endings* re the "missing" full-stop (inserted by Seltzer's printers)
[452] note the [authorial] full-stop
[453] this is Lawrence's first mention of the name Narrabeen, where the afternoon-tea party was held that first Sunday, May 28, & where he met Jack Scott (who, in this later passage, is once more obliged to put on his "Jaz" hat)
[454] this passage is from TS1aR, & is in all Secker-text editions up to (but not including) the 1994 CUP edition (from which it was, as mentioned above, mistakenly omitted)
[455] the quotations in this [omitted] paragraph come from TS1aR (& presumably TS1bR) pp 476-
[478] [*ibid*]

somewhat offended Lawrence with their "common" behaviour – and Somers/Lawrence talking on deck with *"an American boy"* who had spent *"a year or so"* in Australia. He was *"a blond, honest lad of twenty-two"* called *"Norwood"*, who also *"hadn't a very great opinion of Australians"*[456], comparing them unfavourably to America and Americans. We do not know if this reflects an actual encounter on SS *Tahiti*, but it sounds genuine enough.

While Lawrence and Frieda were in transit to America, his agent Mountsier in New York was having Lawrence's Thirroul manuscript (the *holograph*) typed and converted into two typescripts [TS1a & TS1b], which he forwarded to Lawrence soon after he arrived in Taos. (Mountsier, as mentioned above, had intended that Lawrence would revise both typescripts, and that these would then provide the setting-texts for Seltzer and Secker.) Lawrence apparently proceeded to do this, adding to both typescripts his new ending with its post-July 15 material, up to his encounter with *"Norwood"* on SS *Tahiti* (this is part of his infamous "new last chapter"). But so extensive were his revisions and additions to the two texts [now TS1aR & TS1bR] that he decided to send one of them [TS1aR] back to Mountsier in New York to be retyped to produce the two ultimate setting-texts [TS2a & TS2b]. (Importantly, he retained the other text [TS1bR] in Taos.) In due course Mountsier had Lawrence's revisions retyped, producing the required setting-texts for Seltzer and Secker. However, this was not Lawrence's final say on the text of *Kangaroo* (which was published just under a year later in October 1923 in the UK and U.S.[457]).

After sending one of the revised typescripts [TS1aR] to New York,[458] Lawrence changed his mind again about the

---

[456] [*ibid*]
[457] see *Endings* (Secker beat Seltzer to publication, his edition coming out on 13/9/23, & Seltzer's on 17/9/23 [see *Steele* pp xlviii-iv])
[458] again, see *Endings*

novel's ending. It appears that he sent a telegram[459] from Taos to Mountsier in New York instructing him to cut the text at the shorter "UK ending" (*ie, ...It was only four days to New Zealand across a cold, dark, inhospitable sea.*"). But in doing so he made a grievous error, which led to the two texts, British and American, being published with different endings.[460] For instead of telling Mountsier to cut the text at his now chosen ("*...dark, inhospitable sea.*") UK ending, he tells him to cut the text at the end of the last paragraph "on page 474". However, due to a pagination error – Lawrence's inadvertent omission of p466 in numbering his TS1bR – the two sets of texts now had variant page numbers (in New York TS1aR is numbered correctly, and includes p466). The consequence of this is that what was p474 in Lawrence's Taos TS1bR text is now a page earlier in Mountsier's two retyped setting-texts. Moreover, it is these new TS2 texts that Mountsier is now using, having preserved in them the original, correct – TS1aR – page-numbering (any extra text Lawrence added in Taos being accommodated in additional "A" pages, which preserved the original [pre-A] pagination). Back in Taos however, the text Lawrence was using [TS1bR] still has his intended ["*...four days to New Zealand across a cold, dark, inhospitable sea.*"] ending. The result is that after following what Mountsier believed were Lawrence's (telegram) instructions, the two setting-texts in his New York office [TS2a & TS2b] now end a page earlier, with the ["*broken attachments, broken*"] ending. Lawrence would, nevertheless, have two further opportunities to correct this – not insignificant (yet annoyingly persistent) –

---

[459] my argument for the telegram [message] is to be found in *Endings*
[460] The analysis that follows of the "endings problem" is taken from my *Endings* (*op cit*). It should be noted, however, that Bruce Steele has a very different – though mistaken – analysis in his CUP edition [see *Steele* pp xliii-xlvii]. Interestingly, prior to reading Steele's argument for "his" CUP ending, I too believed that the "*broken attachments, broken*" ending was the correct one. So it may be of additional interest to record how I came to be convinced, contrary to my original belief, that Steele had chosen the wrong ending [for this see *Research-Diary* 31/5/79, 27/9/94, 6/10/94, 8/10/94, 19/10/94, 16/11/94, 22/10/95, & 1/7/96 below]. Although we had both come to the same conclusion about the "correct" ending, it was via a very different route, & one of us had to be wrong. It was fortunate for me – but unlucky for him – that he published first, otherwise he might have stumbled on the truth before I did.

error.

The first came at Christmas 1922, when Mountsier and Seltzer arrived – separately – to stay with Lawrence at his new abode in Taos, the Del Monte "ranch".[461] Mountsier brought with him the U.S. setting-text [TS2a] that he should have sent to Seltzer some weeks previously (relations between Lawrence's agent and his American publisher having broken down), and which Mountsier now intended to hand over to Seltzer at the Christmas rendezvous at Del Monte. Over Christmas the new ending was apparently discussed and Lawrence – to what must have been his considerable dismay – discovered Mountsier's cutting error (though in fact it was Lawrence's mistake in mis-paginating his retained TS1bR Taos text). There wasn't time to correct this error before Seltzer returned on Boxing Day to New York (taking with him his TS2a setting-text), so a day or so later Lawrence copies out, from his retained Taos copy of TS1bR, the missing 375 words (from "...*broken attachments, broken...*" to "...*cold, dark, inhospitable sea.*")[462]. He then posts this to New York with a "covering" letter telling him that herewith is his missing "last page".

Now Lawrence has to send another copy of the same missing 375 words to Mountsier in New York to be added to the TS2b (UK Secker) setting-text. But by then Mountsier no longer had the TS2b text in his possession. It was currently meandering around Europe in the baggage of Gilbert Seldes, the peripatetic editor of the New York literary magazine *The Dial*, to whom Mountsier had entrusted (possibly as far back as December) the UK TS2b text in the hope he might like to use – and pay for – an extract from it (thus showing Lawrence that he had been active on his behalf). When apprised of this situation, Lawrence wrote to his UK agent Curtis Brown (in a

---

[461] a rather primitive log-cabin in the woods outside Taos
[462] which Mountsier had (as per his misunderstanding of Lawrence's telegram instructions) mistakenly deleted from Seltzer's [TS2a] setting text

letter dated 10/2/23[463]) informing him that Seldes should have posted the TS2b text to him for on-sending to Martin Secker (and to tell him if he has not got it yet). In the same letter he encloses an identical missing 375 words from his retained TS1bR text (which are also missing from the TS2b text Seldes has in his possession), and telling him "not to lose it".[464]

At this juncture, around mid-February 1923, both the UK and U.S. setting-texts are identical, both having Lawrence's intended *"cold, dark, inhospitable sea."* ending. And indeed, this is the text-wording that Lawrence finally corrects in proof-form five months later in New Jersey after he received two sets of galley-proofs[465] – U.S. and UK – from Seltzer for his final thoughts and corrections. (Apparently Seltzer had earlier arranged to send Secker's set of corrected galley-proofs to him in London.) This is Lawrence's last chance to correct the anomaly of the variant endings. However, the ending on both sets of "galleys" that he had in front of him in New Jersey was his intended *"cold, dark, inhospitable sea."* one. So he notices nothing amiss, and thus the two sets of author-corrected galley-proofs [TS2a&bR][466] go off to their respective printers to be converted into first editions.

Unfortunately[467], however, it seems that the "readers" at Seltzer's printing plant mistook the cover-sheet that Lawrence attached to the "last page" he sent to Seltzer in January (with his written cover-page heading "end of Kangaroo" on it[468]),

---

[463] *Letters* #2709 [to Curtis Brown]

[464] We do not know of what the "last page" enclosure Lawrence sent to Curtis Brown consisted. It may have been – & probably was – different (by way of itemised content – not wording) to the enclosure he had sent to Seltzer in New York. It may not have had attached to it a "cover-sheet" inscribed with the words "End of Kangaroo" (which was perhaps why Secker did not make the same mistake Seltzer's printers did). Consequently, his UK edition had the correct ["*cold, dark, inhospitable sea.*"] ending to Lawrence's Australian novel.

[465] *ie*, printer's-proofs, *not* author's page-proofs

[466] neither of which has survived

[467] & unbeknown to anyone until recently (*viz* my 1996 *DHLR Endings* article)

[468] The circled words, in Lawrence's hand, "*End of Kangaroo*" are underneath the "A" (extra text) page text on p476 of TS1bR (which Lawrence had kept in Taos) & which Lawrence extracted to show Seltzer where the "missing" text needed to be added. (This then became the "cover page" that Lawrence posted to Seltzer on 4/1/23.) Lawrence's enclosure in his 4/1/23 letter [#2691] to Seltzer comprised that cover-page [p476] together with his handwritten 375 words copied out on a new page from his retained TR1bR, & which then become his "last page"

not as the wording on a cover-sheet, but as a terminating direction under a dozen or so lines of type-written text above. So the New York printers mistakenly cut the following (hand-written) 375 words from the printed text, reinstating the original cutting error. Secker's London printers do not make the same error, thus generating the two variant U.S. and UK endings that were ultimately published. Indeed, it is highly likely that the second UK set of corrected galley-proofs either never reached London, or did not arrive in time for Secker to make Lawrence's editing corrections. So Secker did not incorporate *any* of Lawrence's final proof-corrections in his edition of *Kangaroo*.[469] (It is not beyond possibility that Seltzer deliberately delayed forwarding Secker's set of proofs to London in order to beat his UK rival to publication.) Hence the U.S. Seltzer edition ended *"broken attachments, broken."* (it was the "readers" in Seltzer's printing house who added the "missing" full-stop) while the UK Secker edition included the final word and punctuation of the sentence, *"heartstrings."*, and went on 374 more words to Lawrence's intended final sentence, *"It was only four days to New Zealand across a cold, dark, inhospitable sea."*

Lawrence, seemingly, never saw or read the U.S. Seltzer edition, for he never (as far as we know) made any comment about the different endings...which have, alas, been mistakenly repeated and perpetuated in the current CUP Critical Edition – intended to be the "definitive" edition – due (perhaps somewhat ironically) to yet another, but hopefully not final, editing error. Nevertheless, the 1994 CUP edition at least now includes Lawrence's final proof corrections that Secker failed to incorporate into his UK edition (the main

---

& intended ending (again, see *Endings*). He could not send the actual typewritten TS1bR "missing" text because he had to keep that in Taos so he could send the same 375 words to Secker in London, via his UK agent Curtin Brown [*Letters* #2709] on 10/2/23, telling him: "I enclose the last page of Kangaroo...Don't lose it." (He no doubt sent Secker the actual [his TS1bR] p477 rather than copying out a new one, as he had with Seltzer.)

[469] & hence in all subsequent "UK" [*ie* Secker] editions (& post-Seltzer U.S. editions) up to the 1994 CUP edition (including the global Penguin [1950] international edition)

circulating text[470] up to the CUP edition).

Yet the final – and not altogether inappropriate – irony is that the entire CUP Critical Edition project, whose completion (apart from the final volume of poetry) was celebrated in 2015, had been based on the anomaly of the UK and U.S. variant endings of *Kangaroo*, as the original general editor of the CUP editions, Dr Warren Roberts, pointed out in the early 1970s, when arguing the case for the CUP project:

> *Kangaroo* and *Women in Love* are textually complicated books, and the texts differ in the various editions. *Kangaroo*, I think, is perhaps more complicated than *Women in Love*...I don't think there is now a text of *Kangaroo* in print anywhere with the text he really wanted.[471]

And, irony of ironies – more than 90 years on – there still isn't. *Kangaroo*, poor battered thing, remains crippled and incomplete. (No extant edition, from the novel's original publication in 1923 to the present day, has both his final proof corrections and his correct ending – which means that no one has ever seen, in published form, the text of *Kangaroo* that Lawrence "really wanted".)

---

[470] after 1950, the Penguin international edition

[471] When I was being considered as a possible editor of the CUP *Kangaroo*, Warren Roberts sent me a page of an article containing the above quotation. Alas, I do not have the original source of the article, as I explain in my *Research-Diary* 16/9/15 entry below.

CHAPTER 19

Postscript

WHAT WERE Rosenthal and Scott's reactions when they read *Kangaroo* (which they certainly must have – Scott was later "ribbed" at bridge parties on Sydney's North Shore over his portrayal in *Kangaroo*[472])? Scott in particular would have been very angry indeed – and felt bitterly betrayed – on learning that in Thirroul Lawrence had been writing, literally behind his back, an account of his time in Australia into which he had (ingenuously) put the highly-sensitive secret-army information Scott had so indiscreetly divulged to him, and about which his new "mate" had sworn a solemn oath of secrecy – twice – never to reveal (*"This is strictly between ourselves"*[K p91]…*"Nothing will ever come out through me"*[K p292]). Scott's portrayal as Jack Callcott[473] (and, worse, as the impotent Fred Wilmot, who *"couldn't get his pecker up"*[K p105])[474] in the now-internationally-published book would have angered him, very much indeed. Moreover, unlike Lawrence, he would have appreciated the import and significance of what his erstwhile mate had so naively revealed to the world in his novel of Australia. Thoughts of revenge or retribution must have been curdling in his mind.

So did he or anyone else associated with the KEA do anything to contact Lawrence after he left Australia? Via Hum, and probably through the Friends, they could have found a forwarding address for him, or contacted him through his overseas publishers. Yet there is no extant

---

[472] See *Research-Diary* 14/5/87 below. This reference in my *Research-Diary* came via John Ruffels, & he used "teased" rather than "ribbed". However, I later spoke to Andrew Moore about this, & he confirmed it was "ribbed").

[473] [mark #2, Scott]

[474] & Scott would have known to whom that referred

evidence of any contact. However, there well may have been some. In a subsequent letter to Mabel Dodge Luhan, written over three years later, Lawrence counselled her not to identify "real" people in her writing. "Remember," he warned her, "other people can be utterly remorseless, if they think you have given them away."[475]

Also there are other indications that Lawrence harboured concern that the KEA might attempt to make good the threats Scott and Rosenthal made prior to him leaving Australia (*"I could have you killed,"* Rosenthal had told him). Richard Aldington, for example, thought that Lawrence was worried about something after some military officers made some inquiries about him while they were holidaying together in the south of France in the late 1920s.[476] He told Aldington that they had to leave the resort they were staying at "immediately". Earlier, when travelling with the Lawrences in Mexico in 1923, Witter Bynner recorded that one morning Lawrence rushed into Frieda's room shouting "They've come!", and insisted they depart the town at once. The others in the party thought that Lawrence had been disturbed by local bandits. And perhaps he might have been. But that is not necessarily what Lawrence was referring to.[477]

Whom might Lawrence's "they" have been? Was there any other "they" that he was worried about, other than Scott and his secret soldiers? It is unlikely his "they have come"

---

[475] *Letters* #3675. Some time later, when writing to Mabel [12/4/26], Lawrence said: "Why oh why didn't you change the names! My dear Mabel, call in all the copies, keep them under lock & key, & then carefully, scrupulously change the names: at least do that: before you let one page go out of your hands again. Remember, *other people* [Lawrence's emphasis] can be utterly remorseless, if they think you've given them away." (Earlier, after he was criticised for his portrayal of real people in *The Rainbow,* Lawrence told another writer to change the hair-colour & sex of his characters.) So a not-unreasonable inference to be drawn is that Lawrence later may have been accused (possibly in a letter from Jack Scott) of "giving them away".

[476] see *Spy Letters* re the exchange between Richard Aldington & Adrian Lawlor about Lawrence's behaviour in France in 1928 (& specifically Aldington's letter to Lawlor dated 30/10/48 cited in *Spy Letters*)

[477] See *Research-Diary* 25/1/78 below. I am indebted to the late Rev John Alexander ("DH Lawrence's *Kangaroo*: Fantasy, Fact or Fiction?" [*Meanjin*, June 1965]) for pointing this out (which comes originally from Witter Bynner's *Journey with Genius* [Bynner p96])

could have referred to anything local.[478] It should be kept in mind in this context that secret armies were not unique to Australia. The same social and political circumstances that motivated Rosenthal, Scott and their accomplices to start up a secret army in Australia pertained across much of the Western world in the aftermath of the war. There were numerous "Red scares" in other countries, inflamed by the revolution in Russia and rising militancy among the radical working-class. Australia's secret armies were themselves an offshoot of the anti-labour American Protective League[479], and similar ultra-right bodies were generated in Europe and elsewhere, including the UK and South Africa (and in New Zealand too[480]). The American APL continued on after the war, and in 1919 some of its extensive infrastructure and manpower were absorbed into the nascent FBI. It is by no means beyond possibility that, through links with these shadowy organisations, Scott could have had Lawrence tracked down, despite his former mate's peripatetic inability to have a settled address after he left Sydney. Lawrence would not have had be overly paranoid to entertain fears about the long arm of the KEA and "The Garage".

There are many unanswered questions about *Kangaroo*. It is hard enough to credit that Lawrence, a casual foreign tourist, could have encountered a secret army in Sydney in 1922 (on his second day there!). That one of its leaders should have, almost immediately after first meeting him, divulged to him some of its innermost secrets[481] – and even (if the text is

---

[478] There can be little doubt from a reading of Bynner's account of his time with Lawrence & Frieda in Mexico [in *Journey with Genius, op cit*] that Lawrence was afraid of something. The chapter that describes the "They've come!" incident – it was actually Frieda's report of what Lawrence had said after he burst into her room – is called "The Spectral Visitor". Earlier, Bynner describes the precautions Lawrence took after they arrived in Chapala – bolting the gate & locking the doors. "He was frightened," Bynner recalled [*Bynner* p96].

[479] see Joan Jensen's *The Price of Vigilance* [*op cit* p234]

[480] My own grandfather Robert Darroch was a member of one of their cover organisations in New Zealand ("The Navy League") in the 1930s. He gave my father a letter-of-introduction to one of the Old Guard's leading figures in Sydney, Sir Kelso King [see my *Against the Grain – A Life in the Information Business* [The Svengali Press (Sydney, 2014) pp 85-86].

[481] as outlined in *K* chapter 5, "Coo-ee", & chapter 10, "Diggers"

right) asked him to join it – is stretching credibility to the furthermost limit. Yet that is what must have happened.[482] So the biggest unanswered question is: why did Scott tell Lawrence – a complete stranger – about the ultra-confidential details of the secret army that lurked behind the King and Empire Alliance? Scott himself has left nothing of his own to explain it. We can, however, put forward some possible answers to this highly-relevant question.

The reason why the King and Empire Alliance – along with its shadow secret army "The Garage" (Lawrence's "Maggies") – had been launched in July 1920 (activating a plan drawn up in 1918 for the formation of the Australian Protective League[483]) was the election a few months earlier of the radical Storey/Dooley Labor Government, and the consequent fear that "the workers" might rise up and start a revolution like the one that had broken out in Russia a few years previously.[484] That Labor Government had been roundly defeated at the election in March 1922, a matter of weeks before Lawrence arrived in Sydney. Moreover, it had not turned out to be as radical or revolutionary as Sydney's middle-class had feared. The Rosenthal-Scott secret army never "went into action", apart from some minor scuffles in Moore Park in 1920 and a bit of counting-out in the Domain in May 1921. In fact, the Alliance's rationale for existence, together with that of its shadow secret army, had been decaying for some time (weeks, or more probably months). Now, following the electoral defeat of the NSW Labor Government in March, that fear had all but evaporated. The King and Empire Alliance struggled on for some months before it disappeared from the scene (as described above).

---

[482] else *Kangaroo* could not have been written
[483] details of the Australian APL are revealed in the Brookes Papers at the National Library in Canberra [see *Research-Diary* 19/10/76, 15/3/78 & 19/3/78 below & *Moore* pp 22-29]
[484] here the good citizens of Sydney & NSW would have had in mind the threat from the anarchistic "One Big Union" – the Industrial Workers of the World (IWW), or "Wobblies"

Postscript

The KEA's secret army – "The Garage" – "banked its fires"[485], later to re-emerge as the Old Guard in 1925 and again in 1930-32...but then without its "cover" organisation (and one of whose leading lights was again that inveterate fisher in secret-army waters, Major William John Rendell Scott). Maybe Scott – *"the indiscreet Callcott"* – felt that, following the electoral defeat of Labor, it was no longer necessary to be so obsessively secretive. The temptation to boast about the substantial organisation that he had helped start and build up – and which may soon disappear without a trace – could well have proved irresistible in the presence of a visiting English author whom he wished to impress. For Scott, too, had literary interests. He collected books, and had in his collection autographed copies of Galsworthy.[486] His stepsons later recalled that he also had a number of works by Lawrence, "which he kept under lock and key" (though they thought that was because of their risqué content). Subsequently, following his death in Adelaide after the war, Scott's book collection was valued separately for probate.[487]

It may be that, in the less-highly-charged political circumstances in Sydney in May-June 1922, Scott was tempted to impress a visiting author like Lawrence with his own literary interests and local standing:

> *"Fortunately you haven't anything very risky to trust* [me] *with," laughed Somers.*
> *"I don't know so much about that," said Jack.* [K p55]

In fact, Scott may have used an offer of a writing job to ingratiate himself with Lawrence. He had no reason, at that time, to suspect that Lawrence might use anything he told him to put into a book that would one day be published around

---

[485] a military expression meaning to raise or build a bank behind which activities that otherwise might attract attention could continue to be carried on
[486] see *Research-Diary* 9/6/76 below re Scott's literary interests
[487] see *Research-Diary* 5/12/77 below re Scott's Will

the English-speaking world.

Yet that explanation for Scott's "indiscretion" – a bit of self-indulgent aggrandisement, or "sucking up" – is not sufficient. The clue – indeed, probably the answer – to why Scott "blabbed" lies, I believe, in that almost-mystical Australian male relationship, mateship. In the following extract, taken from *K* chapter 4 "Jack and Jaz", Lawrence gets very close to the essence of mateship, whose primary tenet is "instant trust" – a tradition (as observers of the Australian character have remarked[488]) so necessary in a "frontier" society, where more formal and longer-standing relationships (via family, school or upbringing) are yet to be forged. Jack does his best to explain the principle of mateship to Lawrence.

> *"There's some of us chaps," said Jack, "who've been through the war and had a lick at Paris and London, you know, who can tell a man by the smell of him, so to speak. If we can't see the COLOUR of his aura, we can jolly well size up the QUALITY of it. And that's what we go by. Call it instinct or what you like. If I like a man, slap out, at the first sight, I'd trust him into hell, I would."* [K ibid]

In that exchange Callcott goes on to ask Somers if he can indeed trust him. "'*What with?*'" an ingenuous Somers asks.

> *"What with?" Jack hesitated. "Why everything!" he blurted. "Everything! Body and soul and money and every blessed thing. I can trust you with EVERYTHING! Isn't that right?"* [K ibid]

Lawrence must have given Scott some encouragement in response to his advances inviting Lawrence to "become his mate". (Scott had lost his previous mate, Major Dudley

---

[488] *SMH* Editor John Douglas Pringle commented on this aspect of mateship in his 1958 book *Australian Accent* [Chatto & Windus, 1956 London] – see in particular his chapter 2, "Kangaroo"

Oatley – portrayed in the novel as "Fred Wilmot" – to pneumonia a year or more before.[489]) In the text Somers gives Callcott's mateship "proposal" serious consideration.[490] He certainly shows signs of doing so in the first half of the novel. Two chapters later Somers is still thinking about Callcott's offer to become his mate. Somers has not made up his mind how to respond:

> *He had all his life had this craving for an absolute friend, a David to his Jonathan, Pylades to his Orestes: a blood-brother.* [K p107]

Lawrence's search for a "blood-brother", a relationship with another man, had been a major theme in his greatest novel, *Women in Love*. He thought he had found it in Middleton Murry (who was Gerald Crich to his Birkin in *Women in Love*[491]). But that relationship had turned sour in Cornwall. Now his mind was drifting away from blood-brotherhood towards *"the Dark God who Enters from Below"*. Nevertheless, Scott's approach, his offer of mateship, could have produced what he might have taken as an encouraging response on Lawrence's part. As the text says, Somers was tempted to give Jack his hand there and then, and pledge himself to a friendship, or a comradeship, that nothing should ever alter. Yet something stops him, as if an invisible hand were upon him, holding him back.

> *"I'm not sure that I'm a mating man, either," he said slowly.*

---

[489] see *Research-Diary* 1/3/88 below re the demise of Major Oatley, after swimming at Collaroy (Oatley, unlike the fictional Wilmot, was not impotent, fathering various children – Scott's stepsons – this merely being yet another of Lawrence's identity "switches"/name-borrowings)

[490] not only in *K* chapter 5, "Coo-ee", when Jack first offers his hand in friendship [K p88], but more substantively in the next chapter, "Kangaroo", when he suggests he & Somers "*was mates*" [K p105] & Somers/Lawrence asks himself: *"Did he want to mix and mate with this man?"* [K p106]

[491] remember the wrestling scene

> *"You?" Jack eyed him. "You are and you aren't. If you'd once come over – why man, do you think I wouldn't lay my life down for you?"* [K p106]

To an Australian male – an Aussie "bloke" – that is what mateship implied. Your mate should be almost willing to sacrifice his life for you. In the war that recently ended, the Australian troops – alone of all other forces – had a tradition that on no account should any wounded be left in no-man's-land. If necessary, it was your mate's almost-tribal duty to go out and get you (which might explain why the Australians lost a higher proportion of their troops than any other nation[492]).

If Scott said anything like this to Lawrence – and it is very likely that he did (for where else could Lawrence have got it?) – then that could explain his "indiscretion" in revealing, to an absolute stranger, the highly-secret details of "The Garage" and its cover organisation, the KEA. Scott's revelation about the secret army was not mere indiscretion. It was part-and-parcel of his proposal of mateship. It was his token of what he was prepared to bring to what was, he may well have thought – no doubt with more than a little encouragement from Lawrence – was their developing friendship, perhaps leading towards the more permanent bond of mateship.

Moreover, we must never underestimate Lawrence's highly-developed ability to extract information (*"'You didn't try drawing us out. I should say you did.'"*[K p291]) and spread his limited source material thinly.[493] Many people, down through the years, have remarked on Lawrence's ability to "make something" of limited information. That, after all, was part of his stock-in-trade as a novelist. (Look what he made of a few

---

[492] incurring over 65% casualties
[493] *cf.* my reference to "literary wallpaper" above

newspaper cuttings at *The Sun* office in Sydney.[494]) Also Lawrence's almost preternatural ability to form relationships with people should never be forgotten. His "conquests" in this regard included Lady Ottoline Morrell; Bertrand Russell (with whom he discussed his "philosophy" on an almost equal basis); Ford Madox Ford; Aldous Huxley; Richard Aldington; Norman Douglas; Maynard Keynes; and the whole Bloomsburyerama – not to mention a passing cavalcade of lesser folk. He could charm the proverbial birds out of the trees, especially if he put himself out to do so. Scott would have fallen easy prey to his apparent friendliness and empathy, particularly if Lawrence started talking about such things as Whitman's League of Comrades.

Yet it was not an invisible hand, nor diffidence, that was holding Lawrence back from agreeing to become "mates" with Jack Scott. Rather it was exigency – and more particularly his onward travel plans. For in making his offer of mateship, Scott was assuming Lawrence would be staying in Australia for some considerable time. Mateship was a long-term relationship, to be forged with someone with whom you would be in almost constant contact on an ongoing, permanent basis. Your lifelong pal, in fact. Yet Lawrence was only intending to stay in Australia until his onward fares across the Pacific could be forwarded from America – a matter of a few weeks hence. He had not the slightest intention of becoming Jack Scott's mate. He was only "stringing him along" until his money arrived from New York (while filling in time dashing off a quick "romance"). Lawrence had been talking with a forked tongue.[495]

---

[494] *ie*, almost the whole of his "A Row in Town" chapter. Even Bruce Steele conceded that "so convincing is this [Row in Town] episode that some readers have concluded that Lawrence must have been recording actual events" [*Steele* p xxxii] – which of course he was, as Rawson so perceptively pointed out (in his *Dissent* article cited above).

[495] not, however, as forked as it was when he led Rosenthal to believe (for literary purposes) that he might be amenable to a homoerotic approach, a deception that had near-catastrophic consequences (see "The Worst Day of His Life", above).

THE HORRIBLE PAWS

* * *

AT ONE time, in Australia, *Kangaroo* was regarded as the most profound book ever written about the country.[496] Other opinions were less favourable. Today, it has slipped out of the canon of Australian literature, and is no longer even seen to be (as it once was) a work of Australian fiction.[497] Elsewhere it is not considered one of Lawrence's better works. Perhaps one problem is that there is no consensus on what *Kangaroo* is about. Ever since it was published in 1923, there have been differing interpretations of Lawrence's Australian novel. Its text has provided support for an eclectic range of opinions and theories about Lawrence's life and works, enriching in the process whole library shelves of critical and biographical works, and numberless academic essays and dissertations.

Very few literary critics or biographers (or historians for that matter), locally or overseas, have made any serious effort to come to grips with the politics of its surprising – and highly unLawrentian – "plot". Almost everyone has been content to go along with Richard Aldington's view that Lawrence brought the secret-army plot with him from Europe (and, specifically, from Mussolini's Italy). In his 1950 Introduction to the then-new Heinemann edition of *Kangaroo*, Aldington wrote:

> Where did he get the vivid scenes of political contest between the Diggers and the socialists? Not from his favourite periodical *The Sydney Bulletin*, for at that time no such political violence occurred in Australia.

---

[496] according to John Douglas Pringle (in *Australian Accent* [*op cit*]) it was equal to only Hancock's *Australia* as the most perceptive book written about Australia
[497] In the 1940s, a Professor of English in Adelaide, who had been asked to give a talk on Australian literature, told his audience (words to the effect, tongue-in-cheek) that as he had not been provided with any Australian literature that he could talk about, he would instead give a lecture on DH Lawrence's *Kangaroo*.

Postscript

Aldington could write those subsequently so-influential words – "for at that time no such political violence occurred in Australia" – because he had taken some trouble to find out what was happening in Australia at the time Lawrence was there. His concern about this was first raised (as mentioned above[498]) by Lawrence's behaviour on that holiday with him in the south of France in 1928. Either then or afterwards, Lawrence may have given Aldington some reason to think that, while in Australia, something had happened to him that gave him cause for anxiety. It was the memory of that anxiety, first observed in 1928, that came back to Aldington more than 20 years later when he was composing the Introduction to *Kangaroo*, and preparing his post-war biography of Lawrence (*Portrait of a Genius, But...*), both published in 1950.

He had initially raised the matter with Frieda two years earlier, writing to her in America in 1948 seeking information about what had happened in Australia in 1922. He apparently asked her if there were any truth or fact in the plot of the novel Lawrence wrote there. On November 20 she replied, answering his various questions: "I think Cooley was a mixture of Dr Eder and Kot – No, Lorenzo never went to political meetings – Jack and Victoria something like them were on the boat – No the spy story did not happen."[499] The "something like them on the boat" is probably Frieda's recall of Gerald Hum and his wife Lillian (Frieda had first met Hum on *Osterley* between Naples and Colombo; then met him again with his wife and daughter at Narrabeen; and possibly on other occasions in Sydney as well[500].) Some years earlier Frieda reportedly told Middleton Murry that she believed Lawrence had based Kangaroo/Cooley on Koteliansky (Kot). Murry later raised this with Lawrence himself, and in a letter dated October 3, 1924, Lawrence told him: "Kangaroo was

---

[498] also see the Aldington-Lawlor exchange in *Spy Letters* [*op cit*]
[499] Frieda-Aldington 20/11/48 [*Spy Letters* (*op cit*) p5]
[500] at their home in Chatswood on July 4-5, for example, & probably later on the night of August 10, the day before the Lawrences departed for America

never Kot. Frieda was on the wrong track there."[501] (the implication being that there *was* a right track).[502]

Yet it was that "spy story" that most concerned Aldington, and was probably why he had consulted Frieda in the first place. In fact, he must have asked her, specifically, if Lawrence had been mixed up with some sort of political activity in Australia (note her "no" response). Apparently he had also asked her if Lawrence had perchance met someone in Sydney on whom he could have modelled Benjamin Cooley. Not satisfied with her denials – in which he placed little or no credence[503] – he looked further afield. He consulted an Australian expatriate journalist whom he happened to know in France, Alistair Kershaw.[504] Kershaw supplied him with the address of a literary critic in Melbourne, Adrian Lawlor, suggesting that he might write to him for information about the local scene. Which he did, later thanking Lawlor for his "notes on DHL" and seeking further information about what he called "the spy episode".[505] In his follow-up letter to Lawlor, Aldington wrote:

> If that "spy" scene between Somers and Jack is invented, I should be surprised. There is real rage in it, which I don't think Lorenzo could have worked up over an imaginary episode.[506]

Lawlor, after consulting a local Melbourne historian, wrote back telling Aldington that he had no knowledge of any secret political activity in Australia similar to that described in

---

[501] *Letters* #3256 [to Murry]

[502] Aldington was by no means the only reader of *Kangaroo* who wondered where Lawrence got the political material he put into the text. One Lawrence scholar, Michael Squires, raised this in his 2008 book, *D.H. Lawrence & Frieda: a Portrait of Love & Loyalty* [Andre Deutsch, London], commenting: "It is still a question where he got all his political information." [pp 70-71].

[503] see Aldington's remarks about Frieda's reliability in *Spy Letters* [*op cit*]

[504] See *Rananim* vol 3, no 2 [pp 5-8] re Kershaw. The Aldington material in the following two paragraphs also comes from that 1995 *Rananim* article.

[505] the "spy episode" is his reference to the "Jack Slaps Back" chapter (*cf.* "[He] *had come like a spy to take soundings*" [K p287, my emphasis]

[506] *Spy Letters* [Aldington-Lawlor 30/12/48]

Postscript

Kangaroo. This first-hand local response apparently put Aldington's concerns at rest, and led him to go on and lay down what became the standard post-war interpretation of *Kangaroo's* secret-army plot...that it was Lawrence imagining things – indulging in what Lawrence himself called in the novel *"a thought-adventure"*[507] – and so playing out in print a fantasy of flirting with politics. Thereafter *Kangaroo* became one of Lawrence's three "leadership novels" – the middle one, between *Aaron's Rod* and *The Plumed Serpent*.

But Aldington was wrong, and egregiously so. He had been gravely misled by his Australian informant Adrian Lawlor (whom he cited specifically in his *Kangaroo* Introduction as his "Australian expert"). What he did not know was that the Melbourne historian whom Lawlor had consulted, Brian Fitzpatrick, happened to have been a member[508] of the 1923 White Guard in Victoria, the "brother" secret army to "The Garage" in NSW, and which was (as Lawrence mentions in *Kangaroo*) under the leadership of "Emu", aka Sir John Monash.[509] Either Fitzpatrick had forgotten he was a member of the White Guard – which is highly unlikely – or felt he was still under an obligation of secrecy, and should not allow any information about it and its sibling organisations in the other States to be revealed (for such clandestine secret armies were still active across Australia after WW2). In Victoria the White Guard, which later changed its name to the League of National Security, was

---

[507] In "The Nightmare" chapter Lawrence describes himself as "*a thought adventurer*" [K p238] & in chapter 14 "Bits" he says: "*We insist that a novel is, or should be, also a thought-adventure, if it is to be anything at all complete.*" [K p279]. It is not clear what Lawrence meant by "*a thought adventure*". Steele makes no effort to explain it. Yet if Lawrence believed that what he was writing was a "*thought adventure*", what he may have meant by that term must be important. Did he, for example, think that "splashing down reality" was a "*thought adventure*"? Indeed, was that what he meant by "a romance"? If so, perhaps the "adventure" <u>was</u> the "romance" – an acknowledgement that he intended to deviate from orthodox fiction into the realm of reality (a thought-adventure, in fact).

[508] I have Andrew Moore's personal word on this. Membership of secret armies, as mentioned above, was intended to be secret, & there is no archival way of confirming this.

[509] See K p185: "*The chief in Victoria was a smart chap. They called him the Emu.*" Lawrence goes on to say he was "*a mining expert*". This is clearly a reference to Sir John Monash, who was the leading Australian general in WW1 & a mining engineer by profession.

particularly active in the run-up to the bitterly-contested 1949 Federal election (post-1945 the League was ALSO called "the Association"[510], and Fitzpatrick was no doubt a member of it). In fact, Aldington could not have chosen to ask about the activities, or otherwise, of secret armies in Australia at a less propitious time. Post-war, that activity was still very much afoot. All over Australia clandestine paramilitary anti-Labor organisations were secretly marshalling. No one who had any involvement with such secret activities was going to reveal what was going on, especially to some unknown foreign intellectual (*ie* Richard Aldington) in far-off France.

* * *

KANGAROO is an experiment in novel-writing ("I am going to *try* to write a romance."[511]) It is Lawrence experimenting with a new form or technique of authorship in an effort to get round problems he had been having starting and finishing a new novel, of getting past the Balaam's Ass of his "Burns novel" and his "Venice novel". It was on the boat between Melbourne and Sydney that he decided to "try to write a romance" using an innovative fact-into-fiction technique, foreshadowed initially by the autobiographical approach he had used with the then unpublished *Mr Noon*[512] and a diary technique he had exploited in *Sea and Sardinia*. As mentioned several times above, *Kangaroo* is Lawrence putting into practice the advice he gave to "Mollie" Skinner in Perth: "splash down reality, write from day to day, and when you have done 80,000 words, throw down your pen".[513] (It also followed some profound introspection about his troubled

---

[510] see *Moore* pp 241-246 re "the Association"
[511] my emphasis [*Letters* #2523 (to his U.S. literary agent Robert Mountsier, just prior to his arrival in Sydney)]
[512] as mentioned above, Gilbert Noon is an earlier incarnation of Richard Lovatt Somers in *Kangaroo*
[513] [see *Fifth Sparrow* p116] It may well be this advice was itself a product of Lawrence's previous problems with starting a new novel & of a possible solution to those problems.

creative processes, laid out in *Fantasia of the Unconscious*.)

Kangaroo can be seen, on its ostensible "splash-down" surface, as a novel about a visiting English author encountering fascism in Australia (and, in retrospect, perhaps about fascism more generally[514]). The King and Empire Alliance – and particularly its secret-army inner-core, "The Garage" – was, by any 20th century definition, a fascist organisation. The Alliance's leadership, and specifically Rosenthal's deputy Jack Scott, acknowledged its proto-fascist and illegal nature (*"red-hot treason"* Callcott[515] called it), as did Lawrence in his various[516] authoritarian references in the printed text. For example, the following exchange in *Kangaroo* gets as close to classical fascism as is possible, without the customary salute and click of the heels. In *K* chapter 5 Callcott says to Somers (in the published version):

> "...*we jolly well know you can't keep a country going on the vote-catching system.*" [K p95]

Somers/Lawrence agrees, saying in an earlier passage:

> "...*ideal democratic liberty is an exploded ideal... You've got to have wisdom and authority somewhere, and you can't get it out of any further democracy.*" [K p88]

However, in the *holograph* version – the text he originally wrote in Thirroul – what Lawrence first put down on paper[517] gets much closer to the underlying precepts of fascism. At their talk at Mosman Bay, Callcott asks what would happen if the people wanted to keep democracy. Somers/Lawrence

---

[514] as Bruce Steele, to his credit, acknowledged in his CUP *Introduction* – see *Steele* pp xxix-xxx "[it was] his response to both fascism & socialism"
[515] [mark 2] *ie* Scott
[516] (naïve)
[517] so innocently – for he was merely recording what he thought he had been told, without questioning its significance or ramifications (*cf.* my "literary wallpaper" comment above)

replies (prophetically):

> *"Then, as in war-time, as in cases since the world began, you've got to substitute absolute one-man rule, quick, a sort of military rule and martial law, you've got to have military rule at the back of you. Then you can carry through change."* [*holograph* p115]

Not only did what Lawrence wrote down initially portray Cooley's authoritarian ideals in a benevolent or even adulatory light, but he was, in the first half of *Kangaroo*, apparently advocating something like a Mussolini-type dictatorship...and given his many derogatory references to Jews, perhaps what later became a Nazi-style dictatorship. Lawrence had not the slightest intention of *Kangaroo* being taken as a novel about authoritarianism, but that is one possible interpretation of what it turned out to be.

But whatever his apparent approval of the fascism (represented by the KEA) may have initially been, it changed abruptly in chapter 11, "'Willie Struthers and Kangaroo", and even more sharply in chapter 16, "Jack Slaps Back", when Australia's *"silvery freedom"* suddenly turned, and – to Lawrence's horror and dismay – he found himself, quite literally, face-to-face [518] with the true nature of the society and milieu into which he had so ingenuously blundered, and of which he had been so glibly approving...a revelation that inspired the novel's justly famous "The Nightmare" chapter, surely one of literature's foremost anti-militaristic tracts.

So in that sense, Aldington was right. Lawrence did bring some politics from Italy with him to Australia (in his mental baggage, as it were). And, yes, it was fascism. Therefore *Kangaroo* can indeed be described (as it has sometimes been) as a "fascist novel". But not in the sense that

---

[518] in the person of the "*bear-like*" Rosenthal

many of its detractors have in the past condemned it for allegedly being. For whatever approval of what could be called "fascism" that Lawrence may have evinced in the first 10 chapters of the novel was, in the end, repudiated in his subsequent text. *Kangaroo* turned out to be, not so much a fascist novel, as a novel *about* fascism (in fact *Kangaroo*, on a significant level, is an anti-fascist novel). Ultimately it can be seen as Lawrence rejecting of the ideology of fascism as espoused by Rosenthal and Scott, and embodied in their Diggers and Maggies movement. It is a novel that (not altogether intentionally) reveals the downside, and dangers, of unchecked authoritarianism...a foretaste, in retrospect, of things far worse to come.

* * *

HOWEVER, before we leave the text he wrote in Thirroul (and move on to *Appendix 1* and "The Curious Incident of the Red Wooden Heart") it should be pointed out what Lawrence <u>himself</u> believed his novel of Australia was about, both while he was in Australia, and afterwards. From the start of *Kangaroo* to its final words, what Lawrence believed he had run across in Australia is what he calls, on several occasions, *"an attempt at revolution"*[519]. This is the main political term he uses throughout the text (repeated no less than 40 times).

Kangaroo's political sub-plot is first introduced in *K* chapter 5, "Coo-ee", with Callcott taking Somers down to the beach below *Wyewurk* and there endeavouring to explain the purpose and ideology of the organisation of which he is a part, and into which he wants to enlist Somers. *"What is your aim?"* a rather puzzled Lawrence asks him, *"what do you want, finally?"*[K p95] Callcott/Scott does his best to explain:

---

[519] [*Letters* #2544 (to Seltzer)]

> *"Well," he said. "It's like this. We don't talk a lot about what we intend: we fix nothing. But we start certain talks, and we listen, so we know more or less what most of the ordinary members feel like...The Labour people, the reds, are always talking about a revolution, and the Conservatives are always talking about a disaster. Well, we keep ourselves fit and ready for as soon as the revolution comes–or the disaster. Then we step in, you see, <u>and we are the revolution</u>. We've got most of the trained fighting men behind us, and we can MAKE the will of the people, don't you see: if the members stand steady. We shall have 'Australia' for the word. We stand for Australia, not for any of your parties."*
> [K p95, my emphasis]

Somers/Lawrence initially treats this talk of revolution lightly, as something of a joke. *"Somers laughed...He had thought of himself as many things, but never as a queen bee to a hive of would-be revolutionaries."*[K p95] He soon realises, however, that it is not a joke. After Scott goes back to Sydney, Harriett/Frieda asks what they had been talking about down on the beach. Lawrence – and this has to be him – tells her that they (Scott and his organisation) want a new form of authoritarian government. Not sure what her husband is getting mixed up in, she calls it, derisively, *"their high-and-mighty revolution stuff"*[K p103]. Many times in the text Lawrence ascribes revolutionary rhetoric and terminology to what the Diggers and the Maggies are doing. Early on he says, quite up=front, that Scott and Rosenthal's objective is *"apparently a sort of revolution and a seizing of political power"*.[K ibid] Midway through the novel he informs his American publisher Seltzer what his new novel is about, saying, "the Lord alone knows what anybody will think of it: no love at all [and] <u>an attempt at revolution</u>".[520] Yet in reality that was the very *opposite* of

---

[520] my emphasis [*ibid*]

what Scott and Rosenthal were doing, which was to *prevent* any attempt at revolution (like the one that broke out in Russia in 1917, and specifically amongst the working-class – the Labor party and their possible IWW supporters – in Australia).

Of course, all this depends on what Lawrence meant by the expression *"revolution"*. Early on he tells his wife that it is not about politics, but *"a new life-form, a new social form"*[K p98] – some kind of social revolution perhaps (which was certainly not what Scott and Rosenthal had in mind – though they may well have cloaked their secret-army planning and plotting in more acceptable terms). Nevertheless, Lawrence was well aware of its fascist implications, at one point telling Frieda that *"they"* wanted to bring about *"another sort of government for the Commonwealth – with a sort of dictator*[521]*: not the democratic vote-cadging sort."*[K ibid]

In reality, Lawrence hadn't the foggiest idea (to use a colloquialism) what was behind the King and Empire Alliance and its sinister "The Garage", nor what his new-found Aussie mate Jack Scott and his pseudo-Jewish superior *"the First"* were trying to do. He did not care to examine what might be beneath the literary wallpaper he was so innocently slapping down. To look beneath the surface for anything deeper was not part of his literary experiment. He left Australia as naïve and ignorant as he had arrived 99 days earlier…a proverbial babe in the political gumtrees.[522]

* * *

YET FINALLY…what an extraordinary set of unlikely circumstances led to the composition and writing of *Kangaroo*.

---

[521] having just come from Italy, it is likely the dictator Lawrence had in mind here was Benito Mussolini

[522] Although he himself was not overtly concerned what was under his literary wallpaper, what he happened to be "slapping down" has a great deal of interest – literary & otherwise – to subsequent generations of readers of his Australian "romance". At the very least, it can be said to be one of his more interesting (as well as readable) novels.

Had not Lawrence decided in Sicily to go "west via the east" to America, he would never have gone to Australia. Had he not met Gerald Hum on board *Osterley*, there would have been no one waiting at the P&O wharf in Sydney to meet him. Had not Hum invited Lawrence and Frieda up to Narrabeen the next day to look for rented premises and to attend an afternoon tea-party, Lawrence would never have had the opportunity to meet anyone involved in secret-army activity in Australia. Had not Jack Scott – who just happened to be one of the leaders of the KEA – been present, then Lawrence would not have had an opportunity to be inculcated (at least partially) into the secrets of his clandestine organisation. Had not the KEA lost the editor of its journal one week before Lawrence arrived, there would have been no reason for Scott to think of involving Lawrence in their activities. Had not Scott been interested in literature, he would have had no reason to try to impress a visiting English author with his own literary interests, and local importance. Had Scott not lost his best mate Dudley Oatley some months before, he may not have contemplated asking Lawrence to become, perhaps, his new mate. Had not Lawrence, hamstrung by his inability to compose a new novel, had decided to try a new writing technique in Australia ("splashing down reality"), he would have had no reason to fraternise with Scott, nor to try to *"draw him out"* to get diary-material for his new autobiographical "romance". Had not the KEA been on the verge of dissolution (following the election in March of a safe conservative government), Scott would surely never have been so indiscreet as to tell Lawrence about the organisation he had helped found in July 1920. And, not realising the significance of what Scott (*"the indiscreet Callcott"*) was telling him, had not Lawrence set it down at first hand in his diary/romance, then we would know little or nothing about the KEA's shadow secret army, and Australian history – not to mention

Australian literature and culture[523] – would be so much the poorer. Finally, had not Lawrence written it all down in a manuscript (the *holograph* text of which has survived) in which from his handwriting and other clues we can deduce what he wrote each day – thus reconstructing his "daily diary" – we would never have been able to find out what really happened during the 99 days Lawrence was in Australia, Sydney, and Thirroul in the winter of 1922.

Even though he did not at the time fully realise what he was doing, Lawrence in *Kangaroo* has done us all a very great service…for now we know how a major 20th-century author put together an innovative work of literature, and – as a bonus – how Australia's secret armies were organised in the era of fascism.

---

[523] re culture, see *"Claws in the Arse"* below

APPENDIX 1

*THE CURIOUS INCIDENT OF THE RED WOODEN HEART**

LAWRENCE called his 1923 Australian novel *Kangaroo* "a queer show".[524] To Lawrence, the word "queer" meant something unusual, out of the ordinary.[525] He did not use the word in the modern literary context of queer theory. Therefore, it is more than an irony that, hidden deep in the text of *Kangaroo* – what Lawrence himself called his "queer show" – is evidence of a hitherto unrecognised homoerotic encounter. For Lawrence did not "splash down" everything that happened to him in Australia.

Various scholars and writers have pointed to incidents in Lawrence's life – and fiction – that, they say, give rise to suspicions that he had, if not actual homosexual liaisons, then homoerotic proclivities. In his 1994 *New York Times* review of Brenda Maddox's *DH LAWRENCE The Story of a Marriage*, Professor Walter Kendrick said that Lawrence's fiction "abounds with overheated evocations of male beauty and male bonding". He cited the rubdown sequence in *The White Peacock* and the wrestling scene in *Women in Love* as evidence of Lawrence's ambivalent sexuality, together with Rupert's confession to Ursula: "*I wanted eternal union with a man, too: another kind of love*".[526] Maddox alleged that Lawrence had sex with a young Cornish farmer.[527] Lawrence himself said that

---

* an earlier version of this was published in December 2017 in the DHLA [now online] journal *Rananim*
[524] *Letters* #2542 [to Brewster]
[525] he used the term 55 times in the novel
[526] *Women in Love* [CUP] p481
[527] Brenda Maddox *The Married Man* [Reed London 1994] p243 (the young farmer was William Henry Hocking)

THE CURIOUS INCIDENT OF THE RED WOODEN HEART*

his only "perfect love" was with a young coalminer in Eastwood.[528] Lawrence's involvement with Maurice Magnus, who was overtly homosexual, has been seen by some as suspicious, as has his close relationship with John Middleton Murry in wartime Cornwall.[529]

I believe that an episode in *Kangaroo* can throw light on the question of Lawrence's ambivalent sexuality. I call this episode "The Curious Incident of the Red Wooden Heart". The curious incident occurs at the beginning of chapter 8, "Volcanic Evidence". In it the Lawrence character Somers sends a red wooden heart to his recent Australian acquaintance, Benjamin Cooley (in real-life the Australian architect/soldier Major-General Sir Charles Rosenthal, the leader of the secret army Lawrence encountered in Sydney in 1922[530]). Here I quote the text of *Kangaroo*:

> Harriet[531] *had on her dressing-table tray a painted wooden heart, painted red with dots round it, a Black Forest trifle which she had bought in Baden-Baden for a penny.* [K p150]

Inscribed on the red wooden heart is a German adage: *Dem Mutigen gehort die Welt,* which Lawrence translates, first as *"The world belongs to the courageous",* then as *"The world belongs to the manly brave".*[K p150] With the posted-heart, Somers (*ie* Lawrence) sends a note addressed to Cooley (*ie* Rosenthal), which, according to the text, read:

> *I send you my red heart with its motto. I hope you will accept it, after all <u>my annoying behaviour</u>.[532] It is not the love, but the Mut that I believe in, and join you in. Love*

---

[528] his "love" had, as far as is known, no sexual (*ie* physical contact) aspect to it
[529] Maddox *op cit* p203 ("[Lawrence] could not hide from himself his attraction to Murry's neat, trim body...& dark eyes")
[530] see my *Introduction* above re Rosenthal's leadership role in the King & Empire Alliance
[531] *Harriet* is obviously Frieda, just as *Somers* is clearly Lawrence
[532] my emphasis – for what this "annoying behaviour" might have involved, see below

may be an ingredient in Mut, so you have it all your own way. Anyhow, I send you my red motto-heart, and if you don't want it you can send it back--I will be your follower, in reverence for your virtue--Virtus. [K ibid]

There are in fact a number of curious things about this incident. But before we address them, we should ask what a cheap red wooden heart – what Lawrence calls *"a Black Forest trifle"* – was doing on Frieda's dressing-table, among her womanly accessories, particularly one with such a patently male-chauvinist inscription.

The likelihood is that Lawrence bought it for Frieda in Germany in May 1912, when she was staying with her German family at Metz in Alsace-Lorraine. By then Lawrence had travelled further south to Waldbröl in the Rhineland, where his aunt Ada and her German husband lived. There, for more than a week, he cooled his heels, waiting for Frieda to make up her mind about their future. They exchanged almost daily letters, Lawrence urging her to be resolute; to forsake her husband and children; and run away with him. In one letter he enclosed a poem, entitled "Mutilation":

> *To-night I have left her alone.*
> *They would have it I have left*
> *her for ever.*
>
> *Oh my God, how it*
> *aches*
> *Where she is off from*
> *me!*
>
> *Perhaps she will go back to*
> *England. Perhaps she will go*
> *back*

THE CURIOUS INCIDENT OF THE RED WOODEN HEART*

Perhaps we are parted for ever.

To press his suit, Lawrence endeavoured to make Frieda jealous by taunting her that he was flirting with his cousin Hannah in Waldbröl. She responded by telling him that she on her part was enjoying the company of an old flame, Captain Uno von Henning. Lawrence responded to this counter-taunt by attempting to belittle Henning's masculinity, describing him as *"babified"*, and likening him to a character in a Guy de Maupassant story who is breast-fed on a train.[533]

May in the Rhineland is a time of village fairs and other bucolic festivities. (Lawrence attended a local fair the day he arrived in Waldbröl.[534]) It is likely that he acquired the red wooden heart at one of these fairs and sent it to Frieda as a token of his love, and an earnest of his manliness. So we can now, I believe, deduce where the red wooden heart came from, and the sentimental reasons that Frieda kept it on her dressing-table. But why did Somers (*ie* Lawrence) send it to Cooley (*ie* Rosenthal)? He did so almost certainly because on it was the name of the place it originally came from – the village of Rosenthal, about 300km north of Waldbröl in the Black Forest (whence it no doubt had made its way south by sale and resale to a village fair in the Rhineland, where Lawrence bought it while staying there with his aunt).

It is here, however, where the incident gets curiouser and curiouser. Ten years later in Australia, on the morning of Saturday June 17, Lawrence and Frieda travelled up from *Wyewurk*, their cottage in Thirroul, to spend the weekend in Sydney. That evening the Lawrence character Somers has dinner, alone, with Cooley (*ie* Rosenthal) in his apartment in

---

[533] he did this in a letter to Frieda dated May 17, 1912 [*Letters* #447] (the de Maupassant story was "The Idyll")
[534] in part ii of *Mr Noon*, which is (like *Kangaroo*) a largely-autobiographical account of this period of his life, Lawrence describes going for "long walks" in the countryside around Waldbröl; visiting a local fair; & buying heart-shaped pastries there [*Mr Noon*, CUP p187]

town. On the following Monday, Lawrence and Frieda returned to Thirroul, probably by the afternoon train. Almost immediate they get back to *Wyewurk,* Lawrence does something most peculiar. He strips off his clothes and plunges, naked, into the icy winter surf below *Wyewurk*[535], after which he and Frieda have sex...

> [he] *went into the little wash-place and under the shower, to wash off the sticky, strong Pacific. Harriet came along with the towel, and he put his hand to her face and nodded to her. She knew what he meant, and went wondering, and when he had rubbed the wet off himself he came to her.* [K p146]

This is the famous "sex scene" in *Kangaroo*.[536] We can assume that, following it, the couple remained on amicable terms. This harmony would have surely continued into the next day, Tuesday June 20. Yet around 3pm that afternoon this happy state of affairs was shattered by the mother of all rows. We are fortunate to have independent evidence of this mega-row. An executive of one of Australia's largest companies, who was living in Thirroul, heard a local story of a telegram-delivery boy who had to "stop at the gate of *Wyewurk*" for fear of venturing in, so ferocious was the rumpus inside.[537] And in *Kangaroo* itself, Lawrence describes just such a row. He wrote:

---

[535] As if he wanted to cleanse himself of something, or wash something off (for he could hardly have gone for a swim – at that time of day, in those inclement conditions – just because he fancied a pre-dinner dip in the briny). In fact, Lawrence in his text confirms this "cleansing" interpretation [K p146]: "*Somers turned indoors, and suddenly began taking off his clothes. In a minute he was running naked in the rain which fell <u>with lovely freshness</u> on his skin.*" [my emphasis]

[536] an incident depicted by such Australian artists as Sidney Nolan, Brett Whiteley, Paul Delprat & Garry Shead [see *Appendix 2* "Claws in the Arse" below]

[537] Here I quote from my *Research-Diary* [op cit 14/11/76]: "Shan Benson (ABC producer) to dinner last night. Said Bill Fancourt, PR (public relations) staffer at BHP (Broken Hill Proprietary Ltd – Australia's biggest company), lived in Thirroul & heard a rumour that messenger boys had to stop at the gates of *Wyewurk* because of the virulence of the rows inside.

THE CURIOUS INCIDENT OF THE RED WOODEN HEART*

> *...they had another ferocious battle, Somers and Harriet; they stood opposite to one another in such fury one against the other that they nearly annihilated one another. He couldn't stay near her, so started walking off into the country.* [K p177]

He hiked up the steep slope of Bulli Pass (a strenuous effort for anyone, let alone for someone with Lawrence's fragile constitution) and sat on the edge of the Sublime Point lookout, gazing down on the village of Thirroul below, where soon the lamps were being lit, and he could probably pick out the lights of *Wyewurk*. After an absence of an hour or so, he got up and made his way back down the now darkened pass to where he could have anticipated finding at *Wyewurk* a still-irate Frieda, whom he could have expected to have immediately resumed berating him.

But before he gets there, I think we can deduce what caused that almighty row. It was no doubt ignited by Frieda's discovery that her treasured red wooden heart – which to her was probably the equivalent of an engagement ring (for why else would she keep it on her dressing-table tray?) – was missing. Moreover, she would have extracted from a shame-faced Lawrence what he had done with it: sent it up to the secret-army leader Rosenthal (allegedly because his name was on it) in Sydney.[538] Little wonder she flew into a rage. Yet soon after he walked through the door of *Wyewurk*, the tirade abruptly ceased, and Lawrence was apparently forgiven – and not just forgiven, but they made love again...

> *He went home again, and had forgotten the quarrel...Harriet was waiting for him rather wistful, and <u>loving him rather quiveringly.</u> And yet even <u>in the quiver of her passion</u>...* [K p179, my emphases]

---

[538] a "sacrifice" which indicates how important it was for Lawrence – in that he would risk Frieda's wrath – to set up an appointment to see Rosenthal again

Now, this is not just curious, it is well-nigh incomprehensible. Only a few hours ago they were going at each other hammer and tongs, to the extent that he had to flee, leave her and the house, and trek all the way up steep Bulli Pass. So virulent was the row that a messenger-boy delivering a telegram[539] was afraid to knock on the door. So ferocious was "the quarrel" that its violence was to be remembered in Thirroul for decades to come. What could have caused this astonishing turn-around?

For that we must go back to where Lawrence had been dangling his legs over the escarpment, racking his mind for what he could say to defuse Frieda's incandescent anger, and allow him to return to *Wyewurk* and the amicable state of their relationship, *pre-bellum*. It must have been an exceedingly good explanation, for in the event it not only defused the situation, but led to further love-making. (Sex twice in three days would have been most uncharacteristic – indeed, extraordinary – in their marriage. Sex was infrequent at this time in their lives. They usually slept in separate rooms. No – this is very strange behaviour indeed.) So what was the explanation he came back with, which Frieda not only accepted with something approaching alacrity, but which led to further sexual intercourse?

He decided to tell her the truth. He now revealed to her the <u>real</u> reason he had sent the red wooden heart to Rosenthal. He now confessed to her what had really happened during his encounter with Rosenthal the previous Saturday. He told her that the *"bear-like"* secret-army leader had "made a pass" at him, and that some sort of homosexual incident had taken place.[540] He explained to Frieda that,

---

[539] *Wyewurk* did not have a telephone, so Rosenthal's presumed response to Lawrence's "wooden heart" note earlier in the week – no doubt requesting another meeting – would have to have been sent by telegram (& delivered by the "messenger boy" who was stopped in the side-passage by the virulence of the altercation inside the house)

[540] The relevant passages in *K* chapter 7 "The Battle of Tongues" are replete with homoerotic innuendo & homosexual implications (`for further details, see chapter 9 above, especially the

THE CURIOUS INCIDENT OF THE RED WOODEN HEART*

somehow, he had managed to give Rosenthal the impression that he – Lawrence – was a *"she-man"*[K p291] (in later contrast to Jack Scott's *"he-man"*), and might be receptive to a homosexual approach. As David Ellis and other Lawrence scholars have pointed out variously, Lawrence's several descriptions of this encounter[541] – where there is a lot of touching and feeling – carry clear homosexual implications[542].

Yet Lawrence was not, as I believe I am now able to demonstrate, homosexual[543]. Rather he had been foolishly, recklessly, stringing Rosenthal along, agreeing to have dinner alone with him in his apartment – in essence flirting with him – in the hope of extracting more information to help advance his stalled secret-army plot (which had been *"stuck"* for nigh on a week). So, despite his *"annoying behaviour"*[544] on Saturday, it was imperative for him to renew contact with the leader of the Diggers and the Maggies. That was the reason, he now reassured Frieda, why he had posted the red wooden heart to Rosenthal – with the aim of setting up another meeting the following Saturday.

Of course, his intention had been that Rosenthal would read the adage inscribed on the *"Black Forest trifle"* and taken it as a testament of his heterosexuality, reinforced by the enclosed note about his *"Mut"*, his manliness. When back in 1912 he had sent the same red wooden heart to Frieda, that was the message he had been sending to her – a declaration of his masculinity, to counter the supposed attentions of the

---

text cited there recounting their first meeting in Rosenthal's apartment: *"We are birds of the same feather, aren't we?)*.

[541] Lawrence made three and perhaps four – or even five – attempts to say what had happened that Saturday night in Rosenthal's apartment. The first is the *holograph* or Thirroul account in chapter 7, "The Battle of Tongues", written three days later. The second is his revision of this text made more than three months later in Taos. The third is the addition to the account he later interpolated into chapter 11, "Willie Struthers and Kangaroo" (when, lacking anything more substantive, he needed to "pad out" that chapter). The fourth was possibly his false start to chapter 9, "Harriet and Lovat at Sea in Marriage" [see above re the excised text]. The fifth was probably in the missing chapter Lawrence cut out of the holograph on June 19 or 20 (the stubs of which mention Cooley several times).

[542] *eg*: "Cooley's appeal to Somers has a strong sexual…component" [*Ellis* p45]

[543] in the historical or traditional sense, rather than today's less binary preferred-usage

[544] the annoyance may well have been Lawrence's unsympathetic response to Rosenthal's homosexual overtures

effeminate Henning. Now, 10 years later, she would have accepted, almost without question, that this was now the message he had just sent to Rosenthal. This explanation apparently reassured her sufficiently to overlook the loss of her dressing-table *"trifle"*...and to seal her forgiveness with a kiss. Unfortunately for Lawrence, however, it would not be the *Mut* inscription on the red wooden heart that Rosenthal's eyes would have alighted on, but rather the object itself: the heart, the traditional symbol of love. Incredibly, Lawrence in his apparent naivety had overlooked this (to him, and now Frieda) secondary or subsidiary – yet to Rosenthal far more significant – connotation.

So when, around 6pm on the following Saturday, Lawrence turned up at Rosenthal's apartment for their scheduled *à deux* assignation, the secret-army leader would have been looking forward to a very pleasant, not so say romantic, evening. Imagine, then, his utter horror when he became aware, probably while sipping a pre-dinner *aperitif*[545], that his prospective "toy-boy" was not interested in an encore sexual encounter.   Rather he had come, Rosenthal now realised, to extract more secret-army information from him, and that what he had thought was Lawrence's affection for him was no more than a ruse to fool, deceive, and gull him. Lawrence, he now suddenly apprehended, had been "stringing him along" for his own dishonest and deceptive purposes. It was this sudden realisation – of both Lawrence's secret-army duplicity and his spurning of his offer of love – that transformed Cooley/Rosenthal into a monster, a *"Thing"*. (It is during the subsequent scarifying outburst that Rosenthal threatens to have Lawrence killed if he reveals anything about "The Garage".[546]) This encounter in Sydney on Saturday night

---

[545] which was presumably when Lawrence revealed [see *K* p205] that earlier in the day – that very morning – he had been to see "Jock" Garden, the Communist leader of the union movement in NSW, & the "*bête rouge*" of Rosenthal's secret army
[546] There can be little doubt about the ferocity of Rosenthal's reaction. Lawrence describes what happened: "*He had become again hideous, with a long yellowish face and black eyes close together, and a cold, mindless, dangerous hulk to his shoulders. For a moment Somers was*

THE CURIOUS INCIDENT OF THE RED WOODEN HEART*

June 22 – the worst day in Lawrence's life – led on to "The Nightmare" chapter in *Kangaroo*,[547] and provides dramatic confirmation of Lawrence's repudiation, when push came to shove, of physical homosexual behaviour.

They were not birds of the same feather, after all.[548]

---

afraid of him, as of some great ugly idol that might strike. He felt the intense hatred of the man coming at him in cold waves. He stood up in a kind of horror, in front of the great close-eyed horrible thing that was now Kangaroo. Yes, a thing, not a whole man. A great Thing, a horror." [K pp 210-11]

[547] Lawrence's confrontation with Rosenthal that evening touched off a magna-chamber of repressed memory in his unconscious mind, & it was its volcanic eruption that then fuelled "The Nightmare" chapter. (Lawrence had been having mini-nightmares for several weeks previously – one on the previous Saturday night, after he returned from seeing Rosenthal.)

[548] So where on the queer scale does that leave Lawrence? There doesn't seem much doubt that Lawrence had a homoerotic streak in his complex makeup (which Rosenthal obviously had discerned). I believe, however, that this was essentially part of his more general erotic nature – what he called *"the dark god that enters from below"* – & coexisted with his more dominant heterosexual side, as the red wooden heart episode I believe demonstrates.

APPENDIX 2

"Claws in the Arse"

by Sandra Jobson Darroch

(secretary of the DH Lawrence Society of Australia)

The **Wyewurk** *diptych – left Garry Shead,
right Brett Whiteley*

LAWRENCE'S VISIT to Australia in 1922, and the novel he wrote there, *Kangaroo*, have inspired many leading Australian artists and creative minds. The novel has acted as a catalyst for their talents, producing important works. *Kangaroo* is the common thread that winds through their work, and links them.

Australia's leading composer, the late Peter Sculthorpe,

sensed an affinity with Lawrence in their mutual pantheism and love of landscape. He first wrote a song cycle, "Sun", based on three of Lawrence's poems, and later developed this into a major work, "Irkanda IV". The lines in Lawrence's poem

> *A sun will rise in me.*
> *I shall slowly resurrect,*
> *Already the whiteness of false dawn is on my inner ocean.*

deeply affected Sculthorpe. "It was in this section that I finally managed to recompose my setting of the DH Lawrence poem 'Sun in Me'. The melisma of the solo violin is a reflection of the poem. Thus, in the final bars, there is a high white C. Lawrence in his poem relates sun and atom to God and atom. The high white C, which must be the whitest note of all, represents the word 'God'."

Lawrence continued to inspire Sculthorpe, and in 1963 he composed a work in five movements, "The Fifth Continent". The third movement was revised in 1976 to become a shorter work, "Small Town", based on Thirroul, which he felt epitomised all Australian country towns. The statue of the returned Digger, which used to stand outside the School of Arts at Thirroul, and which Lawrence mentions in *Kangaroo*, led Sculthorpe to introduce an oboe solo, mingled with the bugle sound of the "Last Post", giving a chilling, nostalgic undercurrent to the lyrical piece.

Garry Shead's depiction of the "Maggies", the secret army in Lawrence's Australian novel (from Garry's Kangaroo *series)*

Artist Garry Shead, too, responded to the military undercurrents in *Kangaroo* with his celebrated *Kangaroo* series of paintings and etchings. Shead also uses the image of the Diggers' memorial, while always looming in his pictures of Lawrence and Frieda at "Wyewurk" is the mysterious, sometimes menacing, sometimes slightly comical, figure of a kangaroo. In 2011 Sculthorpe and Shead collaborated on a DVD production using the *Kangaroo* series and the music of "Small Town".

Shead also collaborated with another great Australian artist who was strongly attached to, perhaps haunted by, Lawrence and Thirroul – the late Brett Whiteley. In 1975 the two painters decided to go down to Thirroul and paint a diptych. "Brett suggested one day that we try to soak up the Lawrence ambience there," Garry recalled. "Brett particularly empathised with Lawrence and his stormy relationship in *Wyewurk* with Frieda. There was more than a hint of this in the picture." The two artists wanted to paint from the veranda of *Wyewurk*, so Whiteley, with his two silky terriers in train, approached the door of the bungalow, aware that the occupant at that time, a dentist, did not welcome visitors. "As we were talking to the owner, who was very gruff, one of Brett's dogs ran inside the house. Suddenly we had an excuse to go inside to find the dog," Shead remembered. As they tried to coax the dog out of the house, the pair caught a glimpse of the jarrah table where Lawrence wrote *Kangaroo*, before they retreated. Next they approached the owner of the house next door, who allowed them to set up their easels on her veranda, and they began work. "Brett had cheated a little. He'd already half done his work before coming down, and then he painted on my side of the canvas," Shead said.

Both halves of the diptych depict a stormy scene, with angry waves lashing the shore. Shead's half shows *Wyewurk* teetering on its cliff above a raging sea. The colours are deep purples and blues, contrasting with the olive green of the foliage. Whiteley's trademark white-wisps wash into Shead's scene. Brett's-half echoes the same deep blues, purple and green, but his painting basically depicts a ramp disappearing into the angry ocean – "a ramp leading to oblivion", as Brett described it to Shead. Lawrence's face floats in the foreground. Having completed the diptych, the two artists decided to invite Australia's leading author, Patrick White, to its unveiling at a Sydney gallery. Brett, who knew White well (and later painted what White regarded as the best portrait of him), was aware of White's obsession with Lawrence, who was, in White's opinion, one of the three great writers of the 20th century.[549] In 1939 White made a personal pilgrimage to

---

[549] When I used to go riding in Centennial Park in the early mornings, I would often see White, standing beside the horse track with his two little dogs. I did not know at that time that he always took a volume of Lawrence in his pocket when he went for his walks.

Taos, to pay homage to Lawrence. Dorothy Brett took him to meet Frieda, whom he found "witty and amusing".

Brett Whiteley's portrait of Patrick White

However, White's reaction to the diptych at its gallery "premiere" was not what Shead and Whiteley had expected. "Brett[550] was a person given to the dramatic, so he made something of an event of the unveiling – or rather the unlocking – of the diptych," Shead recalled. "The work consisted of a book-like construction, in imitation of the traditional religious diptyches of medieval times. As White and the rest of the opening-night audience gathered before the closed diptych, Brett unlocked it and swung open its leaves, to reveal the full work in all its magnificence. I think Brett was a trifle disappointed with White's reaction to this ceremony.

---

[550] Whiteley, not Dorothy

"Claws in the Arse"

It may have been White's aversion to public displays of emotion, but he did not go overboard about the work, though in fact it was dedicated to him." Brett Whiteley made regular visits to Thirroul. His last visit was in 1992, when he died there from a drug-overdose, alone, in a local motel room. A life, and a talent, that Australia could ill-afford to lose. He was only 53.

However, this was not to be the only diptych involving Lawrence and *Kangaroo* that was to trouble Patrick White. In October 1982 Sidney Nolan, then perhaps Australia's most famous living artist, painted a series of eight works which he called his "*Kangaroo* series". These have only been exhibited once, briefly, in a gallery in Perth, Western Australia, in 1983. The series included a diptych. The events which led to the creation of this diptych are harrowing, and involve a suicide, a broken friendship, a trust betrayed, a wounded reaction, and a brutal response. Before that, Nolan and White had been, to all intents, the best of friends. Nancy Underhill, who was writing her biography of Nolan[551] at the time I contacted her, told me: "Patrick White first saw Nolan's works in 1949 at the Macquarie Gallery in Sydney, and was much taken by them. White wrote to Nolan asking him to do the cover for *Voss*[552]." Yet White and Nolan did not actually meet until 1956 in, of all places, Fort Lauderdale, Florida. The Nolans – Sidney, Cynthia and her young daughter, Jinx – were on vacation in America, while White and his lover Manoly Lascaris[553] were visiting Manoly's sister Anna in her "claustrophobic" house set "in a mangrove swamp, on a road leading from nowhere to nowhere, in other words, the rest of Florida".[554] Subsequently, for a number of days, White and the Nolans toured around Florida's mangrove swamps, gas

---

[551] *Sidney Nolan: A Life.* New South Books [June 2015]
[552] White's most famous novel
[553] whom White had first met in Alexandria, after being demobbed from the RAF
[554] as Patrick White, inimitably, described it

stations and hamburger joints, forging a "meeting of minds" that was to last until 1981. White was particularly taken with Cynthia, whom he categorised as "steel" to Nolan's "elastic". Whenever Nolan and White were together in the one country, they made a point of seeing one another, and Nolan went on to illustrate the covers of a number of Patrick White's novels. Such close friends did they become that when White was awarded the Nobel Prize for Literature in 1973, he asked Nolan (who was living in England) to accept the Prize on his behalf, preferring not to make the long trip to Stockholm himself.

During this time, White kept up a regular correspondence with Cynthia, describing her as "one of the women I have admired most" – a particular compliment, coming from Patrick White. (Nolan himself was not a good letter-writer, so communication between the Nolans and White was via Cynthia.) Then, in London in 1976, Cynthia committed suicide. White was deeply upset. Just how deep did not become apparent until five years later, when White's autobiography, *Flaws in the Glass*, was published. The book contained a personal attack on Nolan, accusing him of "treachery" for re-marrying too soon after Cynthia's suicide. He didn't blame Nolan for Cynthia's suicide. It was the re-marriage that appalled him. "What I cannot forgive is his flinging himself on another woman's breast when the ashes were scarcely cold," he wrote.[555] "If it had not been for Cynthia I doubt Nolan would have reached the heights he did in his best period," White wrote. "He would have drowned much sooner in the sea of flattery which sucks so many artists of importance under."[556]

Nolan felt bewildered and betrayed by White's turning

---

[555] actually it was 16 months later, & Nolan had known Mary Boyd – a member of an Australian artistic family – for much of his life

[556] Nolan was not, by any means, the only Australian criticised in *Flaws in the Glass*. In it White also made a scathing attack on the Australian *prima donna* Joan Sutherland. The book soon came to be known in Australian literary circles as "*Claws in the Arse*".

against him, and was hurt by the virulence of the attack, particularly coming from such an unexpected quarter. He had had no inkling that there was anything amiss with their hitherto close friendship.[557] For the moment, Nolan said nothing about White's attack on him. However, at the time Nolan read *Flaws in the Glass* in 1982 he was in the throes of painting a new series of canvasses based on Lawrence's *Kangaroo*. (For some time, Nolan had been "illustrating" themes derived from Australian culture and history, searching for iconic figures, such as Ned Kelly, to represent or symbolise Australian themes.) Having read *Kangaroo*, he chose various scenes from the novel to represent – to borrow Lawrence's famous phrase – Australia's "spirit of place".

The first six of the eight pictures are lyrical, almost-pastoral images. In one, "Rainbow", Somers and Harriett are seen walking along the beach at Thirroul. In "Picnic Falls" the couple are dwarfed by the bush landscape around them. "Moon" shows a bright yellow disc suspended over Perth. "Heaven" shows the couple among the wattle blossoms in the bush. "Streamers" depicts the Lawrences' boat leaving the wharf in Sydney, streamers still attached to it side. "Chic" (see below) depicts the couple about to make love after Lawrence went for a swim below *Wyewurk*. It now seems likely that these six works were painted before Nolan read *Flaws in the Glass* – or at least before it had time to sink into his consciousness.

---

[557] the London-based Australian critic Charles Osborne had sent a preview copy of the book to Nolan, seeking his reaction

Nolan's painting (from his 1982-83 Kangaroo series) "Chic", depicting Lawrence & Frieda in the surf below Wyewurk *(actually only Lawrence went in)*

The final two works, however, display a sharp change of mood (perhaps analogous to the "sudden turning" of Lawrence's "silvery freedom" in *Kangaroo*). The cruellest was the diptych, which Nolan called "Nightmare". He had been deeply moved by "The Nightmare" chapter in *Kangaroo* (where the Somers/Lawrence character is called up for army service and humiliated by intrusive physical examinations). However, the diptych which emerged from Nolan's pen and brush in October 1982 went far beyond anything which Lawrence's chapter could have evoked.

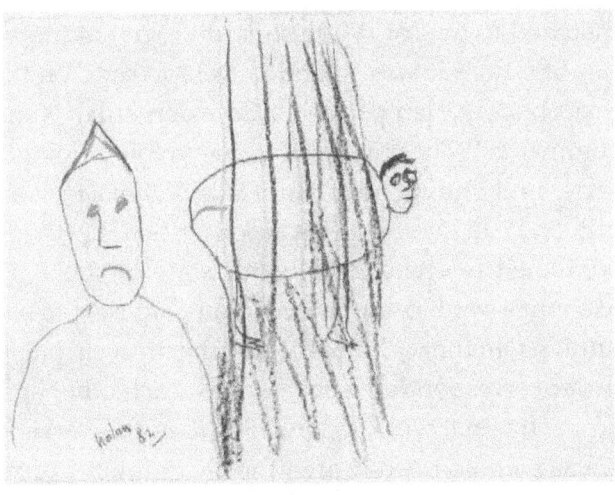

Sidney Nolan's sketch for his diptych "Nightmare" depicting Patrick White and his companion, Manoly Lascaris

The preliminary sketch for the diptych is possibly even more explicit than the diptych itself. It depicts a figure with White's features, wearing what looks like an RAF forage cap. Beside this figure is a large flea-like creature with a slash of crimson on its rear, mirroring the dash of crimson of White's mouth, and with a face unmistakably resembling Manoly Lascaris, White's lover. The Manoly figure, which is scored through angrily, appears to be a reference to Hieronymus Bosch's painting, "The Garden of Earthly Delights". The resulting diptych (painted a day after the sketch, on October 27, 1982) shows on one panel a figure once more resembling White, but this time wearing, not just the RAF forage cap, but a full RAF officer's uniform – the uniform White, who had been in RAF intelligence, might have been wearing at the end of the War when he met Manoly in Alexandria. The features are wizened, the eyes stare madly, and the mouth is twisted in a paroxysm of repulsiveness. The other half of the diptych again depicts the flea-like creature, once more with Manoly's features, but this time in full colour, with a background that resembles excrement. Again, the crimson on the flea's rear is matched to that of White's mouth. So that there could be no doubt whom it was intended to represent, on the side of the flea's body Nolan painted a Greek crucifix. Nancy Underhill comments: "The timing of Sidney Nolan doing his *Kangaroo* series and finding out about *Flaws in the Glass* is a coincidence, but one Sid would seize upon. So The 'Nightmare' is a combined reference to Nolan's state of shock, Patrick's and Manoly's sex-life, and how Nolan paid people back." It is not known whether White ever saw the diptych, but he and Nolan never corresponded, spoke or saw each other again.

The final work in Nolan's "*Kangaroo* series" – the eighth – was painted the day after the "Nightmare" diptych. Earlier, Nolan had also become interested in Eric Campbell's 1930-32 New Guard – another "Australian icon" – and had already created several works depicting the Sydney Harbour Bridge opening ceremony, where the New Guard's Captain de Groot prematurely cut the ribbon "in the name of the decent and respectable people of New South Wales". In the final picture of the series, Nolan introduced the image of a kangaroo, presumably to represent the main character in the novel, Benjamin Cooley, the "Kangaroo" of the title. But Nolan's kangaroo was no ordinary Australian marsupial. He was no "Skippy".[558] Nolan portrayed this kangaroo in a slightly reptilian aspect – a sort of small dinosaur, with "paws" caked up to its armpits in what appears to be dried blood. This reptilian creature is wearing what looks like an Air Force officer's hat, its human shield-like face twisted unnaturally towards the viewer. Given the circumstances of the composition of this final "Kangaroo series" painting, it is difficult to avoid its identification with Patrick White, who has now become, in Nolan's eyes, the fascist leader from Lawrence's Australian novel.[559]

---

[558] an Australian TV series cartoon kangaroo figure

[559] RD adds: the identification may be more pertinent than even Nolan realised, for Patrick White's family were active in the 1930-32 Old Guard, & 10 years earlier had been almost certainly involved with the country section of Rosenthal's King & Empire Alliance, & thus "The Garage" secret army

Nolan's "Kangaroo" – note what seems to be caked blood on the creature's paws and forearms

The luminaries in Australia's cultural pantheon who have been influence by Lawrence and *Kangaroo* cannot be fully plumbed here. Indeed, I cannot make up a definitive list. However, Tom Bass – Australia's greatest sculptor – must be mentioned. Bass, who died in 2010, called Lawrence "my inspiration, my mentor, my guide". It was Lawrence's poetry that first attracted him. "Lawrence spoke to me directly. I can't think of any other man who has been on my life's journey with me as intimately and constantly as Lawrence," he said in an interview published in *Rananim* in 2004. In 1974 one of Lawrence's poems "The Story of the Man Who Has Come Through" inspired Bass to cast a Lawrentian bronze, which he named "Introspection". "I was especially affected by that poem," he said. "It was particularly important to me at a time when it seemed that almost every aspect of my life and my values were crumbling. I felt that my whole sense of myself and my career had been invalidated. I felt like a medieval man stranded in the middle of the 20th century. Then, when I read Lawrence's lines that there is 'the fine, fine wind that finds its way through the chaos of the world' and that he would be 'like a fine, an exquisite chisel, a wedge-blade inserted driven by invisible blows, the rock will split, and we shall come at the wonder' I felt he was speaking to me as a sculptor."

The late Geoffrey Dutton – poet, author, publisher, and eminent all-round man-of-letters – was a fan of Lawrence from an early age, and even made a pilgrimage to the Villa Mirenda near Florence where Lawrence had written *Lady Chatterley's Lover.* In his autobiography *Out in the Open*, Dutton claimed to be the only person who had read the collected works of DH Lawrence while flying an aircraft. As a very young pilot in WWII, flying a Wackett Trainer, Dutton discovered that a book could be balanced on the cowl above the instruments, and propped again the windscreen.

For John Douglas Pringle, a Scot who came to Australia in the 1950s and later became editor of the *Sydney Morning Herald*, *Kangaroo* was a "masterpiece". In his much-acclaimed 1958 book, *Australian Accent*, Pringle devotes his second chapter to *Kangaroo*. Pringle was certain about Lawrence's importance to Australian life and literature. He praised Lawrence's "faultless" observations in *Kangaroo* of the landscape and the bush: what Lawrence called "the spirit of the place".

One of the few Australian artists to actually gain access to *Wyewurk* is Paul Delprat, who was also inspired by Lawrence and *Kangaroo*. He went down to Thirroul and *Wyewurk* several times, the first in 1976 (when he created a series of 20 pen-and-wash illustrations for one of Robert Darroch's articles about Lawrence and *Kangaroo* published in *The Australian* colour magazine). On a later visit Paul stationed himself in Craig Street, opposite *Wyewurk*, and was completing a sketch he had done of the street-side of the famous bungalow. "An occupant from the house noticed me painting and took time to examine my work. I told him that I was an artist from Sydney, and that I was interested in DHL. He offered to let me view the interior of the house and the garden. I was invited to walk through to the front of the bungalow, down the steps, and across the lawn facing the sea, to the cliff edge. It was just as Lawrence had described it."

Paul Delprat's depiction of Lawrence chasing his hat into the surf at Wollongong

Delprat's 1976 series depicted a number of scenes from *Kangaroo*, showing the Lawrence/Somers figure bathing in the sea; walking in the bush; watching a football match; and writing at the jarrah table which Paul saw with his own eyes – as had Whiteley and Shead two decades earlier – the day he was invited into *Wyewurk*. Paul summed up: "Having read much of his work, I believe I am able to say that I am 'Lawrentian' in the sense that I have been affected, as have so many others, by his poetic vision, and by *Kangaroo*."

What other literary text could have inspired so many significant Australian works-of-art, or had such an influence on Australian culture?

WHAT LAWRENCE WROTE EACH DAY

#	date	day	pages	total	words
1	31/5	Wednesday	1-9a	9	c2000
2	4/6	Sunday	9b-26	16	c3050
3	5/6	Monday	26-33	11	c2640
4	6/6	Tuesday	34-51	17	c3010
5	7/6	Wednesday	51-66	15	c3300
6	8/6	Thursday	67-86	19	c4180
7	9/6	Friday	86-104	18	c3960
8	10/6	Saturday	104-126	22	c5040
9	11/6	Sunday	127-148	21	c4800
10	12/6	Monday	148-159	21	c4950
11	13/6	Tuesday	160-186	26	c5780
12	14/6	Wednesday	187-213	26	c6240
13	15/6	Thursday	214-228	20	c4140
14	16/6	Friday	229-236	7	c1680
15	19/6	Monday	236-249	22	c5040
16	20/6	Tuesday	249-270	21	c4800
17	21/6	Wednesday	270-290	20	c4140
18	22/6	Thursday	290-309+10	19+10	c7250
19	23/6	Friday	310-336	26	c5780
20	26/6	Monday	337-359	22	c5060
21	27/6	Tuesday	359-381	22	c6600
22	28/6	Wednesday	381-403	22	c6380
23	29/6	Thursday	403-430	27	c7560
24	1/7	Saturday	431-447	16	c4000
25	2/7	Sunday	447-468	21	c5250
26	3/7	Monday	469-486	17	c4250
27	7/7	Friday	486-508	22	c5500
28	8/7	Saturday	508-518	10	c2500
29	9/7	Sunday	519-539b	21	c5250
30	10/7	Monday	540-559	19	c4750
31	11/7	Tues-Thurs	revision		c140,000

The table above is compiled & derived from the obvious and presumed changes in Lawrence's handwriting, & associated *holograph* evidence, correlated with other information, including his assumed comings-and-goings in Thirroul & Sydney; his and Frieda's letters; current events; newspaper reports (including *The Bulletin*); weather information (including details of the sun, moon & tides); shipping arrivals & departures (*ie*, "the mails"); & other contemporary accounts (*eg*, in *Nehls*); etc. It is an approximation.

Research-Diary 1972-2018

These (selected) entries in roman type are the original diary entries - here heavily edited-and-truncated - as they were originally written and dated. The entries in italics are a subsequent gloss/comment, inserted after the written diary-entries were digitised in 2002. The uncut diary is at http://www.dhlawrencesocietyaustralia.com.au/

In the Fall of 1972 Dr Warren Roberts, Director of the Humanities Research Center (HRC) in Austin, Texas - where we had been examining Ottoline's letters - suggested we look into Lawrence's time in Australia. After we had finished the manuscript of Ottoline *in mid-1974, we came out to Australia, arriving in Sydney in early September to do some preliminary research. In March 1975 we had to return to London because of copyright problems with* Ottoline. *This diary/log now takes up the story. The main record of this early stage (mid-1974 to late-1975) of the research is contained in letters to-and-from various people. The first relevant letter, dated 6/8/74 & sent from London, was to the HRC and its assistant director.*

6/8/74

Kensington Park Road
London

Dear Dr Farmer*

Many thanks for your letter. I had a long talk with Charles Ross* last Saturday up at Oxford where he was receiving his degree...My book on Ottoline is now virtually completed...I have two projects in mind. The first is a short-term idea which my husband and I will collaborate on. We would like to do a fairly small book or monograph on D.H. Lawrence in Australia: his stay there, its influences on him, and the work he did there...we plan to finish [it] within 12 months...

Sandra Darroch

[**Dr David Farmer was assistant director of the Humanities Research Center at the University of Texas at Austin. *Charles Ross was a Lawrence scholar, & was to go on and edit* Women in Love *for the CUP.*]

In Sydney we began examining "back copies" of newspapers & other records. We returned to London to sort out some copyright problems with Ottoline. *Then our minds returned to Lawrence and Australia*

London 10/6/75

"Claws in the Arse"

Dear Charles* - We were pleased to get your letter...It was good to hear also about your DHL work which is of great interest to us now that we're busy on DHL in Australia...Already we have unearthed a great deal of interesting material...and have begun developing a theory that much more in Kangaroo is based on Lawrence's actual experiences in Australia...we did a great deal of work in the Mitchell Library in Sydney...Now we are back in London dealing with the final details of Ottoline...When you get to Texas would you please give our regards to Drs Roberts and Farmer...

[*Ross] *At first, the research continued to be mainly in newspapers. But we also made a trip down to Thirroul in early December 1975, primarily to see* Wyewurk. *Our artist friend Paul Delprat accompanied us & did some sketches of the occasion. The highlight of the visit, apart from the rude reception we received at the front door of* Wyewurk, *was an interview with the son of the woman – Mrs Lucy Callcott – the letting-agent who rented* Wyewurk *to the Lawrences in 1922. I wrote to him a week later, & this is his reply.*

Dear Mr Darroch - I am in receipt of your letter of 9/12/75...You have requested that I send certain photographs to the Mitchell Library...I do not think it advisable to have these pictures of my parents reprinted and possibly used for publication...The Lawrences were nonentities whilst in Thirroul. A rather odd couple...I feel that there would be no purpose having pictures of my parents copied...and I would strongly resent it...I do not like any of the named characters in the book, nor their activities, especially Jack Callcott, the young returned soldier with revolutionary ideas who lovingly embraced Somers in a tense moment on the rocks at Thirroul at night - L.R. Callcott

These problems aside, the research was progressing. But it was very much on the surface. We needed to get below that surface. Then luck, or coincidence, or the smallness of Sydney, or something else took a hand, and the process of discovery, or uncovery, began. The first crucial event was an Australia Day party-cum-wake at Evan Williams' place on January 26, 1976 [Evan had been Whitlam's Press Secretary]. I found myself sitting next to Tom Fitzgerald, a SMH [Sydney Morning Herald] *journalist & former editor/publisher of an intellectual magazine,* Nation. *I knew from my preliminary research that he had written an article ("The Beard of the Prophet") in* Nation *in 1958 about Lawrence & Thirroul. I told him about my current research &, when he evinced interest, said words to the effect that, after examining some of the 1921-22 Sydney newspapers, I had come to the conclusion that there was a lot of factual material in* Kangaroo. *I was unearthing an unexpected number of correlations between what Lawrence said in the novel & contemporary events in Sydney in 1921-22. I then went on to make this comment: "I am almost beginning to suspect that there might be some truth in the secret army plot." At this, Fitzgerald said: "Strange you should say that. Before he died, I had lunch with Eric Campbell [leader of the New Guard, a public semi-fascist "army" that was active in Sydney following the 1929 election of Labor Premier Jack Lang]. Campbell asked me: 'Do you know why we were called the New Guard?' I replied, no. Then he said: 'Because there was an Old Guard.'" He [TF] suggested I read Campbell's book,* The Rallying Point. *This I did. This diary (at first undated, but the early dates are inferred from my general diary) began with the results of that reading.*

[27/1/76] Mosman (where we were staying temporarily): [*reading* The Rallying Point] Interesting points. Campbell says (pp 27-29) that after Lang came to power in 1929 he rang up an old friend, John Scott, about the danger of "civil disturbance" & the two of them met & decided to recruit a similar para-military force to that they had organised in 1925 on the instructions of [*the then Prime Minister Stanley Melbourne*] Bruce. But apparently another group, called "the Old Guard", was also organising what seems to have been some sort of secret army. Initially Campbell & Scott joined forces with what Campbell called "the Gillespie-Goldfinch organisation", but Campbell apparently grew dissatisfied with this group's obsession with secrecy, & decided to break away & "go public". Scott stayed (p50) behind with the "Old Guard".

237

[Between 29/1/76 and 5/2/76]: *Did a lot of research, with Sandra, at the Mitchell and Fisher libraries & was given the name of an historian, Peter Spearitt, who might be helpful. He gave me a long list of possible leads, such as the George Waite papers, the Vol Molesworth papers, the Haughton James papers, the De Groot papers, etc. I also sought permission to examine at the Attorney-General's Department reports by NSW police on the 1930-32 crisis, delightfully named "the secret bundles". These reports also touched on earlier precedents. This Research-Diary now picks up the story:*

5/2/76 Mitchell Library [*the main repository of Australian books & documents in Sydney*]: Reading the "secret bundles". Some sort of trouble in the Domain on Sunday 15/5/21 [*a year before Lawrence arrived*]. Magistrate there to read the Riot Act if necessary. Union Jack burnt. Examining *Sands Directory* [*listing all Sydney residents & businesses*], looking for "John Scott". No luck

6/2/76 Mitchell: [*reading the George Waite papers*] Waite denounced the May Day 1921 riot. Copy of an interesting magazine, *King & Empire*, dated October 1922. [*just how interesting was yet to unfold*]

22/2/76 Fountains Restaurant [*King Street*]: Met [*Bruce? Brian?*] Nyland. He's been working on DHL for over a year. Mainly interested in Thirroul. Ready to go into print [*he didn't*]. Started on the same line I did, but switched to Thirroul & "Spirit of Place". Encountered similar hostility. Nyland had contacted Fred Esch [*the author of a major article on Lawrence in Australia*]. What Esch knows: [*Denis*] Forrester [*Lawrence was befriended by two English couples on the boat from Perth to Sydney, the Forresters and the Marchbanks. They kept in touch while L was in NSW & Forrester took the only photos of the Lawrences while they were in Australia, & also wrote a memoir which was included in Nehls's Composite Biography of DHL.*] Forrester contacted Esch after his SMH article on Lawrence & sent him 5 photos. Nyland mainly interested in the missing photos [*much later we – John Ruffels & I - found the missing photos, unrecognised, in Forrester's son Norm's photo album in Strathfield*]. (later at the Mitchell:) In 1935 Sands found reference to WJR Scott "attorney" for The Cornhill Insurance Company Ltd 26 Bridge Street.

14/3/76 ditto: Saw 1922 *Who's Who*. Lists Major William John Rendall Scott, DSO, insurance agent.

8/4/76 Mitchell: Read copies of *King & Empire* (journal of the King & Empire Alliance) 1921-23. Vol 1 No 1 January 21 1921. K&E Alliance formed "recently" to combat disloyal elements & enemies of Britain & the Empire. Meetings in Sydney Town Hall in July & August 1920. "…thousands of residents of city & suburbs" joined the K&E. Major-General Sir Charles Rosenthal secretary. Jan 1922 10,000 members, 34 branches. Rosenthal & WJR Scott "organisers & inspirers of the Alliance" (John Scott of Campbell notoriety?)

13/4/76 Mitchell: Looked at electoral roll for Mosman & Neutral Bay & 1924 Sands for someone in Murdoch Street who might fit some of the clues in K. [*In the novel Lawrence mentions a house in "Murdoch Street" but later alters that to "Road".*] Also looked at [*Warren Perry*] bio of Rosenthal. Some interesting stuff. Finished first tranche of K&Es.

22/4/76 ditto: Finished whole of *K&E*. Tried to trace elusive WJR Scott. Some info. Scott & Broad, insurance brokers, 92b Pitt Street (room 7, 5th floor), just down Daking Place from Rosenthal's office at 8a Mendes Chambers, Castlereagh Street. Major William John Rendall Scott, DSO (2 mentions in dispatches) born Bingara NSW 21 June 1888.

"Claws in the Arse"

Around 23/4/76 I began compiling my first article on Lawrence and Australia. It was published on 28/4/76 in my then newspaper, The Australian. *It was called "The Mystery of Kangaroo" and had a "break-out" headed "The Scott Connection" in which I speculated that much of the "mystery" of* Kangaroo – *its Diggers and Maggies secret army material – might be explained had Lawrence run across a man called Scott in Sydney in 1922.*

12/5/76 ditto: A night of discovery! Sandra & I went through the Haughton James research Research-Diary. HJ says the New Guard flowed from the Old Guard or "The Movement" which, says James, sprang up spontaneously in 1930 after [*Lang was elected*]. Groups of men appeared out of the woodwork in the affluent Sydney suburbs offering to help police maintain order & guard essential services. They had insignia & were armed with pickaxe handles. There was also four "Country Movements" – Riverina, Western, New England & Eden Monaro.

13/5/65 ditto: According to a "secret bundle" the Old Guard was formed in Sydney in November 1930. It was affiliated with a similar organisation in Victoria called the White Guard. The Old Guard's "staff" were General Heane CIC; Col Somerville QM; Col Bertram Admin;, Philip Goldfinch Finance; & Colonel Jack Scott General Staff branch. (Scott!)

14/5/76 ditto: Re-read *The Rallying Point* last night (read it too quickly earlier). Campbell's account of how the New Guard started can't be correct. Scott could not have been "amazed" to discover another group was organising, for he must have been part of that other group (the Old Guard). The NG had to be a public breakaway

17/5/76 Victoria Street: At tennis yesty Sally Rothwell [*a school-friend of Sandra's*] said she was related to [*Jack*] Scott!!!!! When she saw the *Kangaroo* article she rang up her uncle who was actually brought up in Scott's house!!!! He, the uncle, was Scott's stepson!!!! She told me that Scott was married three times (the second wife was her grandmother); that Scott & Broad still exists; that there were a lot of DHL books in Scott's house; that Scott split with Campbell; that when World War 2 broke out Scott went round interning Germans. He was also something of a womaniser, she said.

9/6/76 Journalist Club: Today I met John & Peter Oatley, two stepsons of Scott. They first remember Scott coming to their house in Gordon, then later to their home in Collaroy when they moved there in 1922 or 1923. They remember him as a tall (over 6ft), thin man with a hooked nose and a pointed face & chin. He was a ladies' man. They also remember Rosenthal ("Rosey") coming to their home. In 1939-45 Scott was "in intelligence". He was very interested in Japan & covered the war in Manchuria for the Sydney Morning Herald [*SMH*]. He died in the 1950s, possibly in Adelaide. He had collected books, & dealt in these. He was a mad gambler & would try to recoup his losses on the races at the dogs at night. He had a collection of DHL books, which he kept under lock & key (they thought because of their risqué nature).

7/7/76 ditto: Given another New Guard "secret bundle". Police confused over what is New Guard & what is "the other organisation". In March 1932 each NSW police district was ordered to investigate & report. Lismore report that there are about 260 New Guard members & 700 "Country Defence Association" members. Other "the organisation" names: Bathurst, "The Western Movement"; Eugowra, "The Western Districts Movement"; Mudgee, "The Anti-Socialist Party"; Gulgong, "The Country Movement"; Moss Vale, "The Peace Association"; Bourke, "the Citizens' League"; Orange, "The Western Division"; Oberon, "The Country", etc, etc. March 1932 conference in Mudgee where selected men were summoned & empowered to go back to their districts & choose 12 men to accompany them to Sydney, when required.

21/8/76 Victoria Street: Humphrey McQueen [*lefty historian*] to lunch. His info: secret armies from 1917 onwards. Much secret army activity in Brisbane (in 1919?). Red Flag riots. & in Perth, too (wharfies & soldiers combine, police defeated). Suggested DHL could have learned about Digger clashes there. Brisbane 1921 riots organised by Herbert Brookes [*of whom more soon*]. Told me about Bill Richards, "the mad psychiatrist". Heavy, heavy conspiracy stuff.

8/9/76 ditto: It is becoming increasingly obvious that DHL's time in WA is significant. H McQ asked if DHL met KS Prichard [*WA lefty writer*]. He didn't, but her husband Hugo Throssell did [*wrong*]. Could he have been an early model of Jack Callcott? [*no*]. But Throssell is the sort of person who could have provided L with Digger material [*wrong again*]. Also, the figure of Trewhella is becoming the key that cd unlock the secret of *Kangaroo* [*right*]. Who is he?

15/9/76 ditto: Last night, in *Kangaroo* ch 3, read that Callcott is an "expert on Japan". Scott! Today got a letter from Shan Benson, who is adapting *K* for the ABC. Has done some research & confirms that L's description of the weather on May 27/28 was accurate. Would imply he [*Lawrence*] began *K* early that week starting May 29. [*actually Wednesday May 31*]

12/10/76 ditto: Quite obviously, the secret army organisation is like this: begins with a top officer or officers/civilians deciding to form some standing paramilitary organisation. Scott (why Scott?*) and Rosenthal got something together in 1920, maybe 1919. [*No – it flows from an earlier contingency plan*] But in 1930-32 real danger surfaces & within weeks the contigency plan goes into operation & 5000 men mobilised. [**Later: Major Scott was deputy to General Rosenthal organising the repatriation of the Australian troops from France and England in 1918-19.*]

6/11/76 ditto: Today I became convinced that my theory about DHL, Australia & *Kangaroo* is correct. I now believe that: 1. Lawrence did lead a secret life in Aust;. 2. The Diggers plot in *K* is true; 3. There was a secret army in Sydney, identical to the Diggers & Maggies; 4. Lawrence met its leaders, Rosenthal & Scott; 5. They are Cooley & Callcot in K; 6. They sought DHL's aid (possibly to edit or contribute to their *K&E* mag; 7. He sucked them dry, mainly to get plot; 8. They warned him not to divulge anything. (However, he was already writing *Kangaroo*.) How do I know that what I believe about L & *K* is correct, while the orthodox account, so widely-held & universally accepted, is wrong? First, the novel was written in odd circumstances – suddenly, quickly, about a place & subject L knew nothing about. Yet *K* is surprisingly factual. The key is surely the Mollie Skinner quote about doing a novel in diary form [*L advised her to "splash down reality" and write "from day-to-day"*]. The final convincing came from re-reading the "Jack Slaps Back" chapter. Knowing now that there was a secret army & that DHL's descriptions approximate it, then the dialogue in this chapter ("You've found out all you wanted to know?") can mean only one thing – I'm right.

14/11/76 Victoria Street: Shan Benson [*ABC producer*] to dinner last night. Said Bill Fancourt, PR [*public relations staffer*] at BHP at Port Kembla, stayed in Thirroul and heard a rumour that messenger boys had to stop at the gate of Wyewurk because of the virulence of the rows inside between Lawrence & Frieda.

15/11/76 ditto: Did L meet an Australian, either on the *Osterley* (between Naples & Colombo) or in Ceylon or on the boat between Colombo and Perth? His conversion from Perth to Sydney seems a bit sudden. [*yes, he did – Gerald Hum, see below*]

"Claws in the Arse"

18/11/76 ditto: *Bulletin* report (4/5/22): "The anti-Labor side in the NSW [Legislative] Assembly is stiff with ex-soldiers of ability & character – professional men like Rosenthal". [*cf in K Lawrence said Cooley is praised by the* Bulletin] DHL read (& extracts quotes & passages from) *Bulletins* 8/6/22 & 22/6/22 [*and probably 15/6/22*].

4/12/76 ditto: Looks like Colonel Ennis [*Maggies leader in* Kangaroo] is [*Brigadier-General*] Macarthur Onslow.

December 1976 marked the end of the first year of research into Lawrence & Kangaroo*. It had led to the formulation of what later was to be known as the "Darroch Thesis". It had started with a growing suspicion that Lawrence was leaning on reality in* Kangaroo *to a degree hitherto unsuspected. Next came the revelation that a real secret army existed in Sydney while Lawrence was there. This was tantamount to heresy in the context of Lawrence scholarship, but the facts led to no other conclusion. Then came the discovery of Scott and Rosenthal and their King and Empire Alliance. This converted, in my mind at least, probability into virtual certainty. After this the focus of research changed to trying to find the link between Lawrence and Jack Scott.*

7/12/76 ditto: Yesty I made a discovery. I think I know the solution to the secret army puzzle in K. The problem is to link what DHL describes with what we know of real secret army organisations. Here are the facts: [*fiction*] L has Digger Clubs of 50, organised with three office-bearers, master, jack & teller. Maggie squads organised in 20s with three officers, leader lieutenant & secretary. [*reality*] 1923 White Guard emerges organised in 10s. 1925 Scott-Campbell force has 500 "stalwart ex-servicemen". Old Guard emerges in 12s in 1930. New Guard has "action groups" of 500 & overall 1112 or 1012 (including leaders). Pack of Cards squads have 49 (4 x 12 plus joker). All this can be explained with two leaders getting 10 jokers each of whom get 50 by getting four jacks to enlist one teller or secretary who gets 10 men. $10+1+1=12$ $4 \times 12=49$, plus one joker=49. This could explain the 10 & 12 phenomenon [*over this I wrote in 1981 "no, no, no – see entry 6/8/81"*]

18/1/77 Victoria Street: Big "Pack of Cards" article [*in The Australian*] published last Saturday. No reaction yet. Interesting thought: after L arrived in Sydney he did two unusual things. He went straight to Thirroul, about which he knew nothing, & he began writing a major novel, after saying the same week he had no such intention. Something must have happened to cause this.

27/1/77 ditto: Last night went to [*bibliophile*] Walter Stone's Australia Day party. He introduced me to another bookman, Col Alex Sheppard. We had a long chat. He said that during 1930-32 the Army helped the New Guard (sic) with weapons, etc. [*like many others, Sheppard mixed up the Old Guard with the New Guard, at least in retrospect, for the Army would have had nothing to do with the New Guard*] A senior [*militia*] officer had asked him, "Are you in the Guard? I thought you would be." Said Rosenthal wasn't big, but had a booming voice & overbearing manner. His Jewishness wasn't very obvious.

8/3/77 QF007 to London: What would make sense is this: Scott is Jack Callcott & Jaz is the Thirroul person who lives next door. None of Scott's personal life is put in – quite the contrary. He is just used physically & politically. All the personal stuff – relations, etc – are Jaz, or whoever Jaz is. He had to use real Australians, so to disguise them he would use half of one real person & tack half of another on to the "fictional" character, making a composite that would acquit him of guilt for using real people. [*this speculation turned out to be one of my better ones*]

15/5/77 London: It is interesting how L disguises things. The reversal technique is his favourite - ie, if you have something you want to use that is sensitive, just reverse it: eg, Scott single, Callcott married; Cooley single, Rosenthal married; etc. We might get somewhere going through *K* simply reversing things. [*This observation about Lawrence's disguise methods was to become important later - see my Perth 1994 entries*]

18/5/77 ditto: Ralph Maud (Southerly 1956) makes the point that the ideas L puts into Cooley are reminiscent of L's ideas expressed in a letter to [B]*ertram* [R]*ussell*] in 1915: "There must be an aristocracy of people who have wisdom, and there must be a ruler..." etc. [*at this point I was doing a lot of reading of books and articles*] According to John Alexander [*Meanjin, June 1965*] L wanted to write a novel about each of the five continents. According to Alexander, L averaged over 4000 words a day for the 42 days he took to write K. He makes some good points: "On the basis of previous writings, it should be assumed that Lawrence will work closely with actuality most of the time." And: "The onus of proof of 'unreality' is on the critic, not on Lawrence." He says that Struthers' religious utterances sound oddly in the novel. But [*Jock*] Garden was a lay preacher!

30/5/77 ditto: In a letter to JMM [*John Middleton Murry*] 3/10/24 L said (obviously about something JMM hd sd in his letter about something that F had told him) re Kot [*Lawrence's friend Koteliansky*]: "Kangaroo was never Kot. Frieda was on the wrong track." So F did not know who K was based on, which means she could not have met Rosenthal.

3/6/77 ditto: I don't know if it means anything, but in a letter to MDL 12/4/26 L said (re her memoirs): "...why oh why didn't you change the names! My dear Mabel, call in all the copies, keep them under lock & key, and then carefully, scrupulously change the names: at least do that: before you let one page go out of your hands again. Remember, other people [*Lawrence's emphasis*] can be utterly remorseless, if they think you've given them away."

10/6/77 ditto: Well, today was to have bn an historic day in L research – a day of make or break for Darroch's theory. I took the vital microfilm of the K holograph to the BM and looked at it – all. [Some weeks previously I had been approached by Michael Black of the Cambridge University Press, who had learned of my interest in Kangaroo, with the idea that I should put in a proposal to edit Kangaroo for the forthcoming CUP edition of Lawrence's works. To do this I was given access to the necessary primary sources, such as the autograph manuscript (holograph) of the text Lawrence wrote in Thirroul.] I assumed I wd find copious corrections & changes, as L went back to disguise things so as to render his progressive discovery of Scott's secret army less sensitive. [this was, and is, a very important point] I found no such thing, which was worrying, to say the least. What I did find were minimal changes & not one single alteration (that I cd find) that wd amount to disguising. Conclusion: either I am very wrong, or he disguised it perfectly as he went along. [which was intrinsically unlikely – a worrying moment in my research quest] **30/5/18 Bondi:** *As it turned out, he did not disguise it as he went along, because he did not question or inquire into what he was recording in "his gramophone of a novel". The possible sensitivity of what he was writing about never occurred to him. He just "slapped it down" unthinkingly.*

8/8/77 Victoria Street: Resuming after a while. [*We had returned to Sydney that August, lured back with a job offer on The Bulletin, in whose employ I spent the next 25 years or so, & continued my research, initially in its Sydney office.*] Got Scott's Army record & reference to him in the Official War History. Will start a file on him. More interestingly, Ernest Whiting has come good. [*Ernest Whiting, a gentleman from Melbourne, had written to me after one of my early articles had been published saying that he had heard that the man who told Lawrence about secret armies, etc, had met him on one of the ships bringing him to Sydney. I had written back to him seeking more information, and asking where he got the information. This is now his reply.*] He originally said that he heard that L had

"Claws in the Arse"

learned of the secret army from a man on a ship. But Whiting cd have read that [*speculation*] in one of my articles. But he has now written back to say that the secret army contact who told him this had now died. So, unless he is lying (& there is no reason why he would), then he did hear from someone knowledgeable that K's genesis was on Malwa. He said he is now consulting his other contacts (who include Colonel Spry, ex-ASIO chief) & promises further detail. Perhaps I may yet find my smoking gun!

7/9/77 Mitchell: Read H.M Ellis papers. Nothing on DHL. [*Again, a blunder, for it turned out that there was something of considerable interest in these papers – a letter, which unfortunately I did not diarise, to Jack Scott mentioning "the Garage" – see 23/2/97 below. In the Ellis papers I later found a letter from Ellis to Jack Scott referring to a trip Scott was proposing to make, Ellis asking if "the garage" was going to pay for it.*]

14/9/77 ditto: An important day. This afternoon got a letter from Ernest Whiting. He sd L was met on the wharf in Sydney by a man who took him to the North Shore for three days. [*in fact he said that Scott matched the description of the man who took L to stay on the North Shore for three days*]. How does Whiting know this? Yet his letter (see full text) has the ring of authenticity about it. EW also talks about the post-WW2 "Association". This, too, sounds authentic. [*note, in particular, the reference to "three days", a period that Whiting could not possibly have known was the precise time* L spent in Sydney before going down to Thirroul (*but see note 16/4/98 below)*]

5/12/77 ditto: Last week in Melbourne (covering a story down there) I saw Scott's will. He left his estate, valued for probate at £939, to his widow, Gip. However, & interestingly, his book collection was valued by the firm of H.A. Evans at £81. So he did collect books. [*Naturally, I asked his surviving family if the collection had any Lawrence books, but his stepson, Tony Street, the Foreign Minister, assured me that it did not.*]

18/1/78 ditto: Have I stumbled on the truth? Today, looking through back files of *The Bulletin* for Jan-June 1922, I came across an item to the effect that "little Mrs Arthur Scrivener" organised at Rawson House in aid of seamen a concert for "the Harbour Lights Fund". This surely must be the Harbour Lights concert Jack Callcott mentions in *K*. & on *Malwa* was a Captain Scrivener! [*This "lead" proved one of the biggest, most persistent red herrings in the long saga, & was to lure me and John Ruffels, who had yet to hove into sight, into a great deal of wasted effort.*]

25/1/78 ditto: In Alexander's MS [*the Rev. John Alexander had written an article on Lawrence and Kangaroo for Meanjin – see earlier note 18/5/77 - which was part of a longer work, which he had just sent me to read*] he cites an incident in Chapala, Mexico, about May 1923 when L told Willard Johnson & Witter Bynner that they all had to quit Chapala immediately. F explained why. In the night L hd woken & thought someone was trying to break into his room. "He rushed in saying 'They've come'," sd Frieda. L hd obviously been terrified. This could, of course, bn a dream, or local bandits, but it might also have bn L thinking that Scott's men hd tracked him down & were about to realise the threat Rosenthal may indeed have made (if what Cooley said actually happened) that night in Sydney ("I could have you killed."). This is the only indication I have come across of the (anticipated) fear L must have hd of some retribution from Australia.

20/2/78 ditto: I have made many (perhaps premature) claims before in these my notes, but I shall now venture a prediction: that I now know, roughly, the circumstances of L's writing K. Here are the facts I draw this conclusion from: 1. on the ship [*Malwa*] L met [was a fellow passenger with] three Army captains, one of which was cpt A Scrivener. 2. in K Somers says "a chap on the Naldera" told Cooley about him (Somers) – ie, independent of Callcott, Cooley knew of Somers from someone met on a ship. 3. the cpt was cpt Arthur Herbert Scrivener, at one time of Cremorne [*Sydney northside Habourside suburb*] 4. the Bulle that [*mentions*] L&F's arrival in Sydney also mentions that Captain "Bertie" Scrivener arrived "with his English bride" & was spending his leave with "his people at Hunters Hill" 5. the only Scrivener listed in Sands near HH is A.S. Scrivener (the only A Scrivener in [*Sands*]) of Lucretia Ave Longueville (a stone's throw from HH). 6. in the Bulle of March 23, 1922 (p 42) there is an item which says that "little Mrs Arthur Scrivener" provided "a capital concert" for the sailors at the Rawson Institute. Item goes on to say, or imply, that one of the organisations that organised the evening was the "Harbour Lights Guild" and, further, that the evening was "a special night of sing-song". 7. now, in K Jack Callcott mentions singing a duet at "the Habour Lights Concert" [*a sea-song in fact – "Larbord Watch Ahoy"*] 8. "Little Amy Scrivener" gave a recitation at KEA function at Junee in 1922 From these facts I deduce a chain of associations: L & Capt S on boat - contact from boat to Rosenthal - Callcott (Scott) connected with Harbour Lights concert - probably Scrivener's mother ran these – some possibility of association between Scott & Scrivener & maybe Scrivener family (at least at Junee). It's thin, but it's possible – or rather it makes the impossible, possible. If I can place Scott at HLG concert, then the chain is strengthened considerably. Meanwhile could Scrivener be Twewhella? [*almost totally wrong - beware of chains of association!*]

15/3/78 ditto: Yesty I read through the NL [*National Library, which had photocopied the material and sent it up to me in Sydney*] file, in the Herbert Brookes papers, referring to the "Self-Defence League". The first-glance discoveries were dramatic. It seems that following the Red Flag riots in Brisbane in March 1918 [*this was an error – the riots were later, in March 1919*] Brookes held some talks with the Federal Govt (Acting PM Watt) which led to Brookes being summoned to Watt's office in Melb in May 1918 to discuss, with several others, the formation of some auxiliary organisation connected with the Secret Intelligence Bureau [*forerunner of the IB*] & designed to spread throughout Aust & garner information about anti-government activity. Discussions apparently continued throughout 1918 & the last dated reference is a note by Brookes that the scheme, enunciated in his notes, was accepted about Oct 1918. This scheme involved a secret connection with the SIB & a downward organising hierarchy of State leaders who would contact the various loyal bodies in each State & secretly propose [*the formation of*] a secret organisation throughout each State to get information, & for "other purposes", on "disloyal" & anti-Govt activity. Here, apparently, we have the genesis of the KEA and L's Diggers Clubs. [*correct, but see next note 19/3 below*]

19/3/78 ditto: I now believe I know what happened. Brookes was almost deranged by the "disloyalty" that surfaced in Australia following Easter 1916 [*the IRA uprising in Dublin*], the two conscription referenda, the 1917 general strike, & the Bolshevik revolution in Russia. Apparently the precipitating crisis was the St Patrick's Day march in Melbourne on Saturday March 17. [*it was contributory rather than precipitating*] The "disloyalty" so blatantly displayed caused some sort of brain-storm in Brookes, & he resolved to devote "the rest of his life" to combating such "evil". This led to the May 1918 letter from Watt. [*incorrect – as we shall see (see Rananim 9.1) the letter was the result of a visit to America by a Melbourne dentist called Elliott*] During the March 1919 [*the right date*] riots in Brisbane plan was activated, & this led to the NSW meetings in 1920 & the KEA. [*correct*]

31/8/78 ditto: My operative in Thirroul, Joe Davis, has come up with a few interesting things. Wyewurrie (next to Wyewurk) owned by Sydney hardware merchant WS Friends in 1922. Mrs Wynn (a name in *Kangaroo*) probably employed by Callcotts at their estate agency. This info from Mrs Smith, 84. [*Joe Davis, then still a student, contacted me following one of my articles and sought advice on research into Lawrence's time in Thirroul. I advised him to ignore printed sources, except Lawrence's letters, and to do his* *own research. He did, to very good effect. He later did a PhD on Lawrence in Thirroul, and subsequently a book,* D.H. Lawrence at Thirroul.]

13/12/78 Mitchell: Resuming after a long delay, spent mostly trying to convince Cambridge [University Press] & the DHL editorial board [of the Complete Works project] that I should edit K. But to no avail. [I had just been informed by Michael Black of the CUP that my proposal, prepared after many months of effort, had been rejected.] I am a DHL pariah. So I turn my nose from such gilded & perfumed pavements to the dirt track back in Australia. First thing of note: apparently among the books KSP [Katherine Sussanah Prichard, a young and aspiring WA author who had missed meeting Lawrence in Perth due to the immanency of her confinement. They later corresponded, in Australia and when Lawrence was in America.] sent L in Sydney was Eyes of Vigilance (which L retained and commented on). This work, published in 1920, was by Furnley Maurice, pseudonym of Frank Wilmot. (cf Fred Wilmot, Jack Callcott's "best mate", mentioned in K).

[*I took this rejection rather badly, assuming (perhaps not totally correctly) it was mainly due to my interpretation of Lawrence's time in Australia, & in particular the secret army background to the writing of the novel, which I had outlined in my proposal. However, from then on, I abandoned any idea of what Julia Roberts called, in a slightly different context, "Sleeping with the enemy", & struck out on my own.*]

[**c. 16/1/79**] *Around this time I was beginning to have some problems with my job on the* Bulletin. *I had made something of a niche for myself with my expertise in extreme-right politics in contemporary (as well as historical) Australia, following on my work in 1975-77 at* The Australian. *This was my own choice, & no one else was to blame. However, the then main target of this extremist activity was the NSW Liberal Party, whose higher ranks the extremists – nicknamed "the Crazies" or "Uglies" (for those interested, their actual name was the "Sinless Perfectionists") – were trying to infiltrate, using various front & disguise methods. I, being the acknowledged expert in such methods and disguises, had become too closely associated - indeed, involved - with uncovering and thwarting of such activities. In an effort to acquit the Party of involvement with extremists, the then Secretary NSW division of the Party, John Carrick, made a public denial (or at least made public statements downplaying such influences), & this sabotaged (as it was designed to do) a series of articles I had written for the* Bulletin *on the subject, & which were to be published beginning that week. I was somewhat discredited as a result of this, & a promised promotion to deputy editor was aborted. My personal life was somewhat disrupted, too. Soon after this I decided to resign & return overseas. But while I was still in Sydney, I tried to chase up & accelerate all my outstanding research leads.*]

26/1/79 at work and Victoria Street: I had earlier this week rang Peter Oatley. I wanted to check up some details I had omitted to inquire about when I interviewed him & his brother three years ago. In 1922, he is pretty sure, they moved from Gordon to Collaroy [*one of Sydney's northern beach suburbs*]. Their address there was in Florence Avenue. The house had a Maori name: Hinemoa. [*Jack Scott*] was "the Major". He married Mrs Oatley, who was a widow, around 1928, but before that he was a frequent visitor to the Collaroy house. But, most importantly, I read out to him L's description of the house I had presumed had been at Narrabeen [*the next beach and suburb further north, where Lawrence says in* Kangaroo *Somers went to after arriving in Sydney*]. The description goes: "The bungalow was pleasant, a large room facing the sea, with verandahs and other little rooms opening off. There were many family portraits, and a framed medal & ribbon and letter praising the first Trewhell.so the party sat around in basket chairs and on settles under the windows…". Peter Oatley said this was a precise description of their house in Florence Avenue, Collaroy. [*see below re "Billabong" at Narrabeen & the end of my Quest for Coioley*]

5/2/79 Mitchell: Today I discovered, in a set of electoral rolls the existence of which I had not known about before (State, not Federal rolls), Jack Scott's 1922-23 address! It was 112 Wycombe Road, Waterleigh (ie, Mosman West). So, Scott was there, in Mosman, a stone's throw or so from 51 Murdoch Street in 1922-23!

6/2/79 Victoria Street: The day has arrived. I have my proof. After yesty's discovery of Scott's Mosman address, I drove over to Wycombe Road. Sandwiched between two large blocks of units was 112-114: a convalescent home. I told the manager, a Mr Ken Young, my tale of research & Lawrence. We went upstairs to see the view. Then we went back outside into the small backyard. Disappointment: too small, no summer house [*which Lawrence described in ch. 2 of Kangaroo*], nor room for one, nor a potential view from one [*which, again, Lawrence put into ch. 2*]. Hopefully, I asked if there [*had been*] a flame tree in the garden [*also described by Lawrence*]. No, sd Mr Young. But perhaps Norm wd remember – & he called to an old chap who was passing by, or working in the garden. He proved to be Norman Arthur Dunn, 75, who lived at the rear of the 112 place. Did he recall a flame tree in the garden? No – yes! What about a summer house? Yes – and there was something on the roof. A lookout. And now he remembered it clearly – it was built to see over the 2-storey house in front. That's it! As I left I drove up Bennett Street, almost opposite 112-114 Wycombe Road, & what should I find at the end of the street, but 51 Murdoch Street. [*The significance of this discovery was that I could now, crucially, place Scott and Lawrence in the same place in May-June 1922.*]

7/2/79 ditto: Took typed statement to 112 Wycombe Road. Found Norm – good old Norm – & he signed it in the presence of Mr Young, who witnessed. Norm made a few slight alterations (not sure it was a Mr Summers, etc). Later, at ML: searched (& copied) Wollondilly [*electoral*] roll for Thirroul, 1923. No sign of K house names [*Lawrence in K cites many house names*]. Odd. No other clues (such as name of motor driver [*who drove Lawrence around district*], etc). Also: at VG's [*Valuer-General's*] Department [*main repository of land information in NSW*] I finally found the full details of Craig Street [*Wyewurk was in Craig Street, Thirroul*]. Barrister had two houses down from Wyewurk, and Fanny Easton of Leura owned Wyewurrie [*the house next door, north, to Wyewurk*]. Fanny! Isn't that a name crossed out in the MS? Across the road, the two facing houses were owned by a Burwood [*Sydney suburb*] businessman & a Lucy May Friend (of WS Friend – wasn't that the firm that Arthur Scrivener worked for?) [*no, but we were getting warmer*]

c.8/2/79 Sydney: [*Someone suggested that it might be useful if I were to visit a gentleman called Walter Friend in Beach Road, Collaroy, just round the corner from Florence Avenue and Hinemoa. I explained to him that I was trying to track down Lawrence's contacts in Sydney & had come to see him because I believed he had some connection with Hinemoa and Collaroy. He denied any knowledge of what I was interested in, but he did say one thing that at the time I did not place much importance on, but which is the only written legacy of that encounter. For some reason he suggested that I might like to write to his brother, explaining my quest and the reason for it (& I retain a copy of this letter). He gave me his brother's address in country NSW, & I did write such a letter later from London, to which I received no reply. His brother in the country was Robert Moreton Friend, who is almost certainly part of the characters Jack Callcott & Jaz Trewhella in Kangaroo, and was probably the person who took Lawrence and Frieda down to Thirroul and installed them in Wyewurk*]. [*No, I was wrong, for it was not Robert Moreton Friend but his younger brother Adrian, as will become clear in 2011 – see below*]

31/5/79 KPR: [*back in London*] Long time, no discoveries. But now a few things to note. Since arriving back at KPR I have been examining Sydney papers at Collindale [*the BM newspaper library*] and correlating this with the MS of K. I now have a very good picture of L's time in NSW…weather, sunrise/sunset, ship arrivals, newspaper items, politics, etc. I can, perhaps, now work out how he wrote K – what his inputs were, what he wrote each day, etc. No sign of a Row in Town, but will keep looking. Reviews of current literature, description of storm, passenger list of Tahiti [*ship Lawrence left on*], background of KEA start and finish, etc. The other major piece of research is the last chapter problem. Here I did make some progress (see my letter to Warren Roberts and draft of [*my*] article). Proved that last chapter, contrary to what critics say, was written in Thirroul. Developed analysis of progress of text from MS to publication of editions & also a theory of how the variant endings came about. To this last night I added the interesting thought that the cover [*of the U.S. Seltzer edition*] tends to confirm the theory of a deliberate or preferential predilection (I know that's poor grammar) for the "broken attachments" ending. (By whom?)

While preparing my rejected submission for the CUP, I had looked into the vexed problem of the variant endings of Kangaroo (the Seltzer or U.S. edition ending considerably short of the Secker or U.K. edition). Warren Roberts, the U.S. general editor of the proposed CUP Complete Works edition, had sent me a copy of an article on this by a U.S. academic named Jarvis. I had also seen in a U.S. journal his (Roberts') statement that the two editions were quite different. (I also spoke to him personally on the matter when he gave me lunch in Austin in early March 1979.) After I looked into the question quite closely (having photocopies of all the relevant texts, courtesy of the CUP, & having recently examined the holograph in Austin & the TSS in the Berg collection in the New York Public Library [where the inks & nature of top copies and carbons could be checked]), I found that that variants, the endings apart, were not as considerable as he had made out, & told him this. When I reached London, I decided to compose an article on my analysis of the endings, as I thought I had discovered why they were different, or at least had developed a possible theory on this, which involved Lawrence letting accident determine the ending. But I did not publish the article. Later, in the 1990s, as I shall relate, when the CUP edition of Kangaroo, *edited by Bruce Steele, was published, I saw that he had come to the same conclusion – that the U.S. "short" version was the correct one. However, his argument for this was utterly different to mine, & I realised at once that we both could not be correct (mainly because of Steele's insistence that Lawrence had sent a different "last page" to Secker & Seltzer).. This led me to re-examine the matter even more closely, & I then discovered that we were both wrong, & that the longer Secker variant was the correct one. (See my article in the* DHLR *26.13 &* Rananim *9/1, "Not the End of the Story".)*

9/8/79 KPR: L must have had a good idea of what he would find at Thirroul on that Monday, for he went late & arrived late, about 4pm. Had he been looking randomly [*as Frieda maintained in her memoir*] he would not have risked this. Someone must have told him about this specific place [*Thirroul*] & that particular house [*Wyewurk*] - someone who knew it was empty & available.

19/10/80 ditto: Nearly a year since my last entry. Yet, although I have made no dramatic discoveries, the pace of progress has been brisk. In having to write a book about D.H. Lawrence in Australia [*commissioned by Macmillan Australia in June 1980 to coincide with the coming out of copyright – on 31/12/80 - of Lawrence's works*] I have been obliged to bring together all my facts & discoveries & stretch them over the topic. For the most part they cover pretty well, & the process has added greatly to my knowledge & understanding, especially of the chronology of what L did in Australia, & also of the techniques he used to make characters & events do double duty. I can now say, with some confidence, that I know roughly what he did in NSW & how he came to write *K*.

6/8/81 ditto: Re numbers in K. In ch 10, "Diggers", L says squads number "1400". What is the significance of this figure? 28x50? 70x20? In June 1922, according to the K&E, the KEA had 34 branches. But we are talking about the Maggie squads here. Perhaps L is mixing up the Diggers & the Maggies (ie, branches & squads). Also, note the figure 20 that

Callcott cites in the "Cooee" chapter. In K&E p 4 28/8/22 it is mentioned that 20 people my form a KEA branch. Same issue has ad for WS Friend & Co, architects & builders. (Owen Friend director of CBC, Scott's father's bank, and the KEA's bankers.) *So that's where L's figure "20" came from! - enough men to fill four cars with five secret soldiers each.* (inserted here on 2/6/18)

10/9/81 Burran Avenue: Found another helper. He [*John Ruffels*] knows someone – whom he won't say – who knew Scott. [*That person*] describes [*Scott*] as "a bit of a womaniser" and also confirms his pent-up energy. [*John Ruffels proved to be a very remarkable researcher, and has been of considerable help in my quest. A postman by profession, he has the ability to track down leads and tips that few others would have the tome or persistence to do.*]

20/12/82 QF002 London-Sydney: Just before leaving for Sydney, Leo Chapman [*a journalist colleague*], who had read my book & also a bio of [*General Sir John*] Monash, sd I was wrong about Rosenthal being Jewish! And sure enough, on re-reading Perry's monograph on R it turns out he was a Methodist, & an active one (his parents were Danish & Swedish, I think). Something of a blunder. And yet, it may be even better that he was not Jewish. For L does not say [*initially at least*] that he was Jewish: merely that he looks Jewish (long, pendulous face, thick lips) & remarks "…surely he had Jewish blood in him…the man surely had Jewish blood".

Although there had been nothing to note in the diary for that two-year period, the research effort had not been inactive. John Ruffels had been beavering away back in Sydney trying to track down Scriveners &, in particular, members of the Harbour Lights Guild, & tracing a network of social, business & political links among members of the Sydney Anglican elite, including a growing number of members of the Friend clan. Andrew Moore had also been very active & has sent many items about secret army activity in NSW between the wars. These came in their regular letters to me in London.

1/2/85 WPR: Three years [*just over two, actually*] since my last entry! However, there has been a trickle of information, mainly in Ruffels' letters [*see separately*]. But here it is worth recording what I learned on my [*recent*] trip to Cambridge to see Jack Lindsay [*literary son of Norman Lindsay*] (who was last in Australia in 1926!). He had mentioned in his autobiographical The Roaring Twenties that he had just missed [*meeting*] L in 1922 in Dymocks [*bookshop in Sydney*]. I wanted to test his memory further. He reiterated that he went to Dymocks one day in 1922 & saw his friend Frank Johnson, who was some sort of under-manager, who told him (words to the effect): "Guess who was just in here…D.H Lawrence…". Lindsay, now 85 but mentally OK, knew, read & admired L's works, so the incident was significant for him. He sd that he recalled that later, after K was published in Aust, literary circles in Sydney wondered how L hd got his information (they also marveled at how L "covered his tracks" & had "kept to himself"). [*there was speculation that he might have based Cooley on a Sydney left-wing lawyer – see 3/2/86 below*] One might speculate what L was up to in Dymocks. Was he simply up in Sydney on one of his regular trips & had some time on his hands & just wandered into Dymocks (in George Street, not far from Martin Place, where he picked up his mail [*wrong – he picked up his mail from Cooks in Martin Place*] for a gentle browse? Or was he looking for books about Australia [*Dymocks had both a lending library and a second-hand section*]? I think we can dismiss any idea that he was looking for literary company. Incidentally, Lindsay remembers nothing about the 1919 Red Flag riots, though he was in Brisbane at the time.

6/8/85 WPR: R[*uffels*] has come up with a small point or two worth noting. He shows (see his letter July '85) that the only person on Malwa that fits [*Frieda's*] description of "a young Army Captain" who recalled the rain on the roofs is Captain Scrivener, the others being eliminated by age or nationality. He has also turned up the Meston Volcanic Evidence reference in the DT of May 11, 1922. This shows that L was reading [*old*] newspapers at least back to that date, possibly at Wyewurk [*which maintained a stock of old newspapers for fire-making purposes*]. Incidentally, Bob Carr has put a preservation order on Wyewurk following my representations to him last March. Also: re the lack of an Irish-Catholic element in K (raised by R in his letter 7/85), this cd be a case of the dog in the night [*which did not bark*], & makes it more likely that Struthers is Garden (who was protestant and Scottish), as most NSW Labor figures in the 1920s were Irish-Catholic, Garden being the conspicuous exception.

29/1/86 London: (*back in the UK as ACP's London bureau chief*) It seems that the Friend connection shld be chased up. Joe Davis says Mrs Smith sd Wyewurrie [next to Wyewurk] was owned by WS Friend. What wd make sense is that it was a Friend who, possibly that day at Hinemoa - Jaz? – told L that Wyewurk was empty. Only this degree of info wd surely have allowed L to go to Thirroul on Monday. Will chase up. [*a prophetic insight, as it turned out*]

30/1/86 ditto: [*Keith*] Sagar [*prominent British-based Lawrence scholar*], in a letter to me, makes the point that Torestin [*where, in Kangaroo, Somers goes after arriving in Sydney*] was probably L paraphrasing Wyewurk (and Wyewurrie). Possible. More likely he [*Lawrence*] saw it [*the name*] in Australia. [*wrong – Sagar was right*]

10/2/86 ditto: I have come to the belief that the Scrivener original-contact scenario, on which a lot of my assumptions have been based, does not adequately explain how L so quickly stumbled into that Scott-Kaeppel-Friend milieu immediately after his arrival in Sydney. That HLG concert reference is simply not enough. What we really need is an earlier contact with someone like one of the Friends. For, after all, L within 48 hours or so of his arrival went to two places where the Friends had homes – Narrabeen [*actually Collaroy*] & Thirroul. It would be much more likely that it was through a Friend that L met Scott. Also I am haunted by what Ernest Whiting told me, that if one seeks the answer to how L found out [*about the secret army*], look in the passenger list of the ships in which L came to Australia. Again, the Scriveners don't satisfy this. So I looked back over the three lists, having come to a provisional theory that L may have met someone on the *Osterley* [*between Naples & Ceylon*], as he did Mrs Jenkins, & this was the person who told him about Sydney (for he booked through to Sydney in Colombo), & that this was his contact [*in Sydney*]. If I could find a name I recognised, then this would explain a lot. [*as I was to find out soon, it was Gerald Hum, who joined the Osterley in Naples, as did Lawrence*]

14/5/87 PA100 US-UK: A year since my last entry. Going home to Sydney soon, hopefully to the final denouement (in the wake of the [*Kangaroo*] film and the various flattering mentions of my work). [*that was about to change*] It now seems that we have a possible explanation, ie, that L met someone, either on the *Osterley* or in Ceylon, who was his initial contact with the Friends. One extra tidbit: according to AM [*Andrew Moore*] (via JR) he has found a lady (Mrs Jeffery), a radical, whose father was a doctor in Killara whose habit was to play cards with Scott. And they used to tease him about him being portrayed in a book. I wonder which one…

We came back to Sydney in August 1987. I think it was John Ruffels who first focussed attention on Gerald Hum, though I would have seen his name on the Osterley *passenger list, along with Mrs Jenkins. What, however, brought him to the very forefront of our research was the fact that his name was also in one of Lawrence's address books, which implied that Lawrence had not only run across him, almost certainly on the* Osterley, *but that he may have had ongoing contact with him. The significance of this was that Hum was the only Sydney name in Lawrence's address book (a photocopy of which I had just acquired).*

8/1/88 Brougham Street (*then our Sydney office*): L left Naples intending to go to Ceylon to stay with the Brewsters before going on to Taos. On the *Osterley* his mind turned to going to the U.S. via Australia. He struck up a friendship with Mrs Jenkins & received an invitation *[from her]* to go to Perth. He also, apparently, met D[*avid*] G[*erald*] Hum of Sydney, & noted his address [*in his address book*]. Probably he knew he [*would eventually*] go on to Sydney from Perth & needed information & a contact there. In Ceylon he decided, probably very early, to go to Perth. He wrote to Mrs Jenkins, teeing up accommodation. He almost certainly would have also written to Hum in similar terms. In any case, Hum wd apparently have replied helpfully, probably to Perth (check mails). Probably L wrote [*again*] from Perth giving details of his arrival on *Malwa* (this explains L's short stay in Perth). So the likelihood is that it was Hum who was waiting to greet & help him [*when he did reach*] Sydney.

The possible, even probable, identification of Hum as Jaz was reinforced by another coincidence. My closest friend, the artist Paul Delprat, who had gone down with us to Thirroul in 1975, was a member of the renowned Ashton family in Sydney. Paul's mother could actually recall Hum and his cousin Howard Ashton sitting in their Mosman home every Sunday listening to music and discussing art and politics. The description Mrs Delprat, Paul's mother, gave of Hum fitted Lawrence's description of Jaz down to the last detail ("stuggy", etc). But the clincher, to use an Americanism, was the fact that she could remember her father Howard remarking that Hum was "a typical Cornishman". Hum is, of course, portrayed in Kangaroo *as a Cornishman.*

25/1/88 Brougham Street: Yesty JR mentioned that he had spoken to Hum's son, who lives up the North Coast, who told him that his father used to go to a rented holiday cottage at Fisherman's Beach on Sydney's north-side. He described Fisherman's Beach as being just behind Long Reef [*ie, Collaroy, or, more accurately, Collaroy Basin*]. Which is where, of course, Hinemoa is. Hummmm....

This revelation was extremely important, for it placed Hum, at least in holiday mode, in the same, small area – Collaroy Basin comprised only a few blocks between the beach and Pittwater Road – that we were pretty sure Lawrence visited on his first weekend in Sydney, and made it very likely that it was indeed Hum who took him to Hinemoa. [*Later: no, that was Scott – see 5/8/11 below*]

1/3/88 ditto: On Sunday last I had lunch at Sally and John Rothwell's at Gordon to meet Carl Oatley, her brother or step-brother (I'm not sure which, and I didn't feel it right to ask). He's an [*Air Force?*] intelligence officer & ex-Duntroon [*Australia's military college, where Paul Eggert also lectured*] lecturer, about 30. Somewhat skeptical of my thesis, but co-operative. I think he slowly came round to believe that his grandmother, Andree Adelaide [*Kaeppel*], might have known the great secret. He brought a photo album that had shots of AAK, possibly at Hinemoa around 1922. Has more, apparently. She was vivacious, literary, & very loyal to her first husband, Dudley Oatley, whom she chased to London & Egypt with three kids in tow. The family picture of Scott, her second husband, is of a poor soldier, rather scatty & incapable of much plotting. The gun incident [*when he threatened to shoot himself*] confirmed. Some Friend or Street connection vaguely recalled. Quite knowledgeable about Carl Kaeppel, the family wastrel [*AAK's brother*]. Some hint that Scott may have been chasing AAK before she married Dudley Oatley. The surviving daughter [*sister to Carl and John Oatley*] lives at Moree, & Carl promised to contact her. AAK went to Japan with Scott in the 1930s. She may have bn the first female BA at Sydney University (so if Scott had Lawrence in tow, it would have impressed her).

4/5/88 ditto: Why do I believe it was Hum [*who led Lawrence to Scott*]? On the face of things he seems [*according to his surviving family, interviewed by Ruffels*] an unlikely cohort of Scott & his secret army plotting. Yet he has qualifications. First, appearance (stuggy, etc). Second, he fits the Whiting ship stricture – & he was the only Sydney person L put in his address book, before or after Sydney. He cd also, in concert with Whiting's "tip" [*in EW's early letters to me*], be the someone who "met Lawrence on the wharf and took him to stay on the North Shore for three days". (It now makes more sense that it was Hum who drove L&F back to his Chatswood home & perhaps it was Hum who took L to Mosman Bay to meet Scott [*wrong*].) Hum had a big Nash [*car*], so he wd have been a useful section [*squad*] head. And his non-involvement in the AIF [*Australia's WW1 military force*], when he was conspicuously eligible for active service, may have obliged him to be active on the home front. His wife may have been in the [*Anglican-run*] HLG. (Their daughter went to Abbotsleigh.) And they holidayed at Collaroy, where the Friends, & Scott, also holidayed.

8/5/89 ditto: ...Meanwhile, Bruce Steele, a lecturer in English at Monash University (Victoria), and a CUP editor, delivered a lecture at Duntroon & later published in an Australian journal Meridian an article severely criticising my account of how Kangaroo came to be written ("...not a shred of evidence has been found of a secret army...all are speculations".) This counterblast turned the (hitherto largely favourable) tide, both here and overseas, against what Andrew Moore (in a riposte to Steele) came to call "The Darroch Thesis". This counterblast was given extra impetus when Joe Davis converted into a book his PhD thesis, gained under the supervision of Wollongong University Professor Ray Southall, who, despite this, became the first President of the D.H. Lawrence Society of Australia, & who wrote an introduction to Davis's book (*DH Lawrence at Thirroul*). Davis in his research was assisted by my collaborator John Ruffels, who was himself beginning to entertain doubts about the Darroch Thesis, doubts that others, including Bruce Steele, gratefully picked up on. Needless to say, Ruffels was too good a researcher not to later come to realise that these waverings were temporary, & he has since assisted me materially, & is a stalwart of our DHL Society, down to this day. As the counterblast gathered strength it began to be taken up by other academics and reviewers, such as in a *SMH* review of Davis's book by Professor A.P. Riemer who went so far as to ask the Friend family, whom he knew, if there was any truth in assertions that their forebears were involved, or could have been involved, with Lawrence or secret armies, an allegation that they categorically denied (& thus lied through their teeth).

2/1/90 ditto: A new decade, and still going. *Wyewurk* lost, Steele contemptuous, J. Davis abusive, Southall ditto, Professor Riemer ditto, ditto, ditto. The dogs of doubt are baying at my heels. Such is the life of one who holds heretical ideas. Anyway, it is certainly time for a new entry, & justified I think. A lot of small stuff not worth recording (the Vernon papers [*see below*], research at Collaroy [*where we now had our holiday cottage*], etc), but it was Sandra who came up with, or rather crystallised, something significant re Hum. Why did L not correct the two mistakes he made in Hum's address? Of course, he cd have dealt with Hum in Sydney via his office address in Carrington Street [*city*], but there is another possibility. Maybe Hum was not living at his "Chatsford" address when L arrived. Perhaps he was on holiday at Collaroy! (That wd be a far better reason why L&F went up there that first Sunday.) By the way, I have had some disturbing news from Hum's relatives overseas [they had sent me their "family tree"]. He was not a Cornishman! Yet Rosalind [*nee Ashton*] was adamant that her father Howard called him "a typicalCornishman". Why? Was this some sort of twisted joke on Howard's part, & a reference, rather, to Hum's portrayal in Kangaroo? [*it was a family joke, Paul Delprat told me*] Worrying.

20/3/91 ditto: Have tracked down everyone [*I can find via the electoral rolls*] at 112. It seems that 3-4 people moved out between rolls, & 4 moved in, incl Scott. 112 clearly a guest-house, so it wd seem that, for the Ls to stay there, there would have hd to be a spare room, which is possible, given the comings & goings. R supplies the extra info that Tinson snr was a cordial manufacturer at Quirindi (this from a surviving relative). Bertha Pearshouse, a 112 resident, signed the KEA petition [*complaining about some Labor iniquity*]. R thinks WP Friend worked for AA Hemsley [*a leading Sydney law firm*]. Nothing obvious here to follow up, but am still poking around. Read [*David*] Ellis piece on "The Darroch Controversy" in the DHLR at weekend and got v. annoyed. [*English academic and anointed CUP biographer of L's period in Australia David Ellis had done a nice hatchet job on me.*] But silence is best until Steele bursts forth [*with his CUP edition of Kangaroo*].

11/6/91 Colombo Airport (after midnight): Having four hours (so far) to wait for my London plane, I will indulge myself in a little speculation. Last night in Kandy I woke up at 3am and, having nothing else to do, started re-reading parts of K. What tripped an idea was the passage in "Battle of the Tongues" [*chapter*] when Somers returns [*to the Callcotts' place in Sydney*] after his argument with Cooley to find them all waiting for him. He "found a little party". [*Trewhella*] was there, and Victoria had made, "by coincidence", a Welsh rarebit. Why "by coincidence"? The coincidence seems to be focused on WJ [*Trewhella*]. But he is Cornish, not Welsh. (So if comestible coincidence were involved, she should be making Cornish pasties.) The words might mean nothing, but, on the other hand, there cd be a more significant explanation, & this is where speculation comes in. Let's consider what sort of disguise L might have adopted if he were using real people in K. For them to be of any use to him, he wd have to retain some of their characteristics. So what wd he change? Gross matters, probably – marital status, job, address - but nt, apparently, physical appearance. Scott might be the guide to what L changed & what he left in. Scott & Callcott are very similar (thank God) – appearance, character traits, probably behaviour. So what does L do to make [*the borrowing*] less obvious? He changes his name, marital status, Army rank [*incorrect – it was Rosenthal's rank he changed*], job – but that's about it (he cd hardly change his sex). Not much real disguise, but any more & it wd vitiate the utility of the exercise. So, let's now turn to Victoria. Her name is not that, and she may nt be married. But what else? Age, perhaps. What incidental [*ie, not important for characterisation purposes*] detail might be changed? In the novel she comes from Somerset. That cd be changed. Could she be, rather, from Wales? Cd that be the coincidence? Rank speculation, except for two things. First, there is the famous "slip of the pen" when L uses the name "Tanny" or "Fanny" in the MS, then crosses it out and replaces it with "Victoria" [*incorrect – see below*]. Second is the fact that Fanny, or Mywfanny, is a name used in the (originally Welsh?) Friend family. OK, nothing very solid, but the Friends' Fanny bears closer inspection.

12/1/92 Bondi: Another year begins - the 20th since we first got the idea in Austin, Texas, at the HRC to look into L's time in A. If we had but known. The nub of the matter can now be reduced to three questions: 1, was there a secret army in NSW in 1922?; 2, is this the secret army L describes in *K*?; 3, how did L find out about it? The answers to the first two questions are yes, yes. The third question remains to be answered.

28/4/92 ditto: (Reorganising my files & research scraps.) On going through my Willie Struthers file I came across the l[*etter*] from Frank Hardy [*a left-wing author*] to JR[*uffels*] dated 16/1/83 in which FH says he recalls speaking to Jock Garden in about 1948-48 re DHL. FH sd: "In the course of the conversation, the q[*uestion*] of L[*awrence*]'s K[*angaroo*] came up somehow and G[*arden*] told me L[*awrence*] had visited the [*Sydney*] Trades Hall while in Sydney asking q[*uestions*] about the political situation…". FH said the memory of what Garden told him was now very vague, but he seemed to recall that L was interested in the political position of the returned soldiers. This tends to confirm what Garden's biographer Arthur Hoyle told R in a letter (28/3/83) that he was "reasonably certain" that Lawrence's character Willie Struthers was based on Jock

Garden. This is reinforced, of course, by the content of Struthers' speech in the "Row in Town" chapter, where he talks about being friendly with "Brother Brown & Brother Yellow", a line no ALP-affiliated unionist wd dare espouse in the White Australia of 1920-22, but which Jock Garden would say, being both a Communist (founding secretary of the Australian Communist Party) & a prominent "Wobbly" [*IWW*] supporter [*both of which advocated an international brotherhood of all workers*].

5/9/92 ditto: Went to the ML last Fri to read the letter from Aldington to Adrian Lawlor. [Andrew Moore had discovered that a cache of papers belonging to Adrian Lawlor were in the La Trobe (University) Library (Victoria), & that they included this particular letter. This was quite important, because in his so-influential Introduction to the Heinemann edition of Kangaroo – since the 1940s the standard British and American text of the novel – Aldington had stated, categorically, that there was no secret army of the sort Lawrence had described in the novel in Australia at the time, citing as the authority for this statement information he had received from an Australian contact, Adrian Lawlor (who was a literary figure in Australia in the 1930-60 era). How & where Lawlor himself got this (totally misleading) information was a matter of some significance, as it was partly, even principally, responsible for the incorrect interpretation of Kangaroo. The La Trobe library had refused to send me a copy of the vital letter, but had arranged for it to be sent up to the Mitchell in order that I could read it there, which I had now done.] Something of a revelation. I hd always blamed RA's Introduction for being largely responsible for the no-factual-basis interpretation of K. But this letter now undermines that view. It is dated 30/10/48 & in it RA tells Lawlor that, "If that 'spy' scene between Somers & Jack is invented I should be surprised. There is real rage in it, which I don't think Lorenzo could have worked up over an imaginary episode." [Aldington had known Lawrence personally; the "spy" scene probably refers to the "Jack Slaps Back" episode] RA earnestly sought Lawlor's opinion of "DHL's insight & even prophetic vision", going on the refer disparagingly to other discussions of Kangaroo (such as Hugh Kingsmill's) as "invented twaddle". Yet, despite these very valid doubts & insightful questions, RA went on eventually to set in literary concrete an altogether different impression in his Introduction, plugging for, if not for such twaddle, then at least invention. One supposes that RA's initial insight was altered by Lawlor's negative reply. I am writing to Alister Kershaw, who was RA's secretary, re this, for AK is also mentioned in the letter as having sent RA Lawlor's "very interesting" notes on DHL. Will follow this up.

24/9/92 ditto: A[lister] Kershaw has replied from France. It turns out that he is RA's literary executor, so I now have all the permission I need to access Aldington material, world-wide. He enclosed a copy of the vital letter from Lawlor to RA [sent in response to RA's letter cited above]. In essence, AL denied to RA any possible "fascist background" to K. Indeed, he had taken the trouble to consult a local historian on the matter. The expert was Brian Fitzpatrick, the Labor historian. [*&, I later discovered – see below - a member of a secret army in Melbourne post-1945*]

24/9/92 ditto: We are having a meeting at Thirroul on Nov 14 to see if we can set up a DHL Society. Only thing we can do now to help preserve Wyewurk. Wendy Jollife [*Thirroul librarian*] commendably keen. No response from Steele or Eggert, however. Sagar wrote supportively, as did UK DHL Society.

2/11/92 ditto: [*I noted that this date was exactly one year since our discovery in Sri Lanka of Ardnaree. A propitious date, I remarked, and adding "but please, not another year". However, what I should have written was "decade", not "year".*] JC rang first thing this morning in a state of hardly suppressed excitement. She thinks that she has, finally, come across the real model & inspiration for Victoria Callcott. She is a Friend, at least by marriage, & her name is Myfawny (yes – Fanny) Beatrice Owen. In 1918 she was married to Ernest Adrian Friend, one of the 7 sons of the Friend doyen, A.G. Friend, principal of WS

THE HORRIBLE PAWS

Friend & Co. She's the right age (born 1897, so 25 in 1922). Recently married to EAF, he 28 in 1922. Father a retired clergyman (Edward Owen) & mother a Phillips, a well-known South Coast family. Father at Nowra (definitely on the SC) in 1922, JC thinks. Some dairy farm connection. Strong [*Anglican church*] connection (father once rector at Hunters Hill). Connected with the [*Banjo*] Pattersons [*cf above re Ernest Whiting's family*]. Not proof positive, but... [*as it turned out, she was correct – see below*]

16/11/92 ditto: On Saturday we all trooped down to Thirroul to form the DH Lawrence Society of Australia.

9/1/93 ditto: I have bn re-reading [*Witter*] Bynner's *Journey with Genius* to check up on what L's habits might have been pre-*Mexico* [*see next note*]. However, it is interesting also what B says about L's writing regime or system. He observed that L seemed to make up in his mind – ie, compose - vast sections of text, then just copy them down, as if by dictation [*my emphasis*].

This observation is one of the most important ever made about Lawrence, and will be pursued below (independent of Bynner's acute observation) – see July 1994 et seq below). It is, I now believe, one of the key aspects of a proper interpretation of Kangaroo, and how it came to be written. It is interesting to note, however, that it is very similar to the observation made by Aldous Huxley in the Introduction to his Letters – see 14/10/79 above.

c. 9/7/93 ditto: To what extent has any work bn done on L's use of reality &, more importantly, his methods for disguising or transforming real-life events & people into fiction? I am beginning to suspect that disguise or camouflage isn't really the right way to look at it. What L does in *K* (from what we know of reality) is not disguise, at least in the sense of changing things to make them, for example, less sensitive. Rather he seems to be using some sort of automatic transformation technique.

22/9/93 ditto: Something quite amazing happened yesty. I was lunching at the Union Club with [*fellow member*] Robert Douglass. He hd written to me saying his father had heckled Jock Garden in the Domain. Rob has promised to do a piece for *Rananim* on Jock and the Garden family.

26/9/93 ditto: Sally Rothwell rang on Friday with some interesting information about a Miss Marky (for Margaret) Vernon. Her father knew Scott quite well [*hence the Vernon papers in the ML with their file on the Old Guard and its North Shore nominal roll and dispositions*]. Even more interestingly, however, Miss Vernon not only knew Enid Hum, but was "the girl-friend" [*Sally's description, not mine*] of Sir Phillip Goldfinch [*the executive head of the Old Guard and general manager of CSR*] Obviously a lady whose closer acquaintance I will be endeavouring to make.

5/10/93 ditto: This morning I went to see Miss Markie Vernon. Knew all about the Old Guard. Knew Scott, but not very well. But here's the really important thing - I felt she was keeping something back. Her answers were guarded, and seemed to come from a deeper level of knowledge than the one she was exposing. At one stage I was rabbiting on about Hum, Scott, Collaroy, Hinemoa, and how I now thought it had all come about, when she said, as I paused for breath, and quite softly: "Are you sure?" "Well, not really," I replied, and, after a moment, went on. But she *knew* something, something that she was not prepared to reveal. Again, I was on the threshold of the truth. [*but it would take another 18 years for its door to swing open*]

"Claws in the Arse"

12/10/93 ditto: Got permission from the Botanic Garden Trust to hold our inaugural DHLA meeting in the [*Rose Garden pavilion in*] the Palace Garden [*where Lawrence and Frieda strolled in May 1922*]. First' issue of *Rananim* also goes out today. One of AM's prospective new ferrets rang. "I'm still skeptical," she told me. Thanks a lot, dear.

13/10/93 ditto: Often have I wondered how all this wd end – with a bang, perhaps, or just trailing off, with all leads exhausted, & no final answer found. The main hope has always been some sort of dramatic discovery – a lost file on Scott, mentioning Lawrence & Kangaroo, or some aged relation suddenly fessing up. Well, just such an event seems to have occurred. Andrew [Moore] rang yesty with the news that he had received a letter from the archivist at The Kings School, Parramatta. This gentleman [the archivist] had written, apparently, after Andrew's book [*The Secret Army and the Premier*] had been remaindered, and he had acquired a copy. In his letter to Andrew, the archivist said that one of the Friends, who went to TKS, had told him that Lawrence "had been given the key [to Wyewurk] by a Friend" (or words to that effect). Now, this might be the key that unlocks the final door. For reasons that I won't go into here, I have concluded that someone who met L at Collaroy that first Sunday accompanied him down to Thirroul the next day (the Monday) and installed him & F in Wyewurk. Who is this particular Friend, identified by the TKS archivist? Walter? Dawdie? Andrew is sending me the [archivist's] letter. After the comparative disappointment of yesty's entry re Markie Vernon, this breakthrough, if it is one, comes at a propitious moment. We might just have some interesting news to announce at our Palace Garden's meeting.

13/10/93 ditto: Came home about 2pm to find a message on the answer-phone from a very excited AM. He had spoken to the TKS archivist (whose name is Peter Yeend). In May 1974 - note the date! [*ie, 18 months before we returned to start our Lawrence/Kangaroo research*] - Yeend went down to Bowral to interview an [*TKS*] old boy, N.H. Wright [*Yeend was interviewing TKS old boys for the school records*]. In the course of a conversation about the Old Guard Mr Wright said words to the effect that, "This [*the Old Guard*] was the organisation that D.H. Lawrence portrays in *Kangaroo*." Moreover, Wright sd he had bn told this by none other than his brother-in-law, Walter Friend. Well, well, well, so that dirty old dog Walter Friend knew all along! Ferrets scattering in all directions. Exciting days - exciting hours!

20/10/93 ditto: Ferrets still investigating. Yesty got [*a copy of*] the crucial Yeend letter from AM, plus Research-Diary of his conversations with same. I will quote the exact wording from AM's letter to me: [*Yeend told AM*] "Also you will be aware that D.H. Lawrence stayed in a cottage provided by the Friend family who publicly denied they told Lawrence about the rural army...". In one of AM's follow-up calls, Yeend told him that somewhere in his file on the Friend family there was a reference saying that WSF [Walter Friend] gave L the key to Wyewurk.

This note marked the end of one of the most productive years of the Lawrence research, second only perhaps to 1976, when I found out about Scott and the secret army, & slightly ahead of 1979, when I discovered the geographic link between Scott & Lawrence (at 112 Wycombe Road). Yet a lot was still unknown. Most particularly, the precise nature of the link between Lawrence & the Friends was still a mystery. This question was to dominate the next few years of research - that & the matter of the endings of Kangaroo

26/1/94 ditto: The image, propagated by many (incl Joe Davis), of L sitting passively at *Wyewurk* dreaming up the contents & characters of *K* is nonsensical. There is far too much Sydney, etc, reality, fact, etc, in the novel for that to be the case. The more accurate image is of L darting hither & yon, garnering ingredients for his novel. He went to the library, to

255

Dymocks, to the KMT [*Kuo Min Tang*], to Trades Hall, GPO, etc, etc. He was a busy little bee, buzzing all over Sydney & Thirroul in search of material to supplement his daily doings & introspective musings.

In March 1994 I went over to Perth to take up a job as publisher of some mining magazines, & Sandra joined me soon afterwards. We remained there till October, during which time we did a lot of research on Lawrence's period in Western Australia. Its productiveness cannot be over-estimated, & included the first Yeend letters, the correspondence with LD Clark over the endings of Kangaroo, *the solving of the mystery of the Old Dairy, the development of "the Darroch shift", finding out about Rosenthal's WA background, &, most significantly, the uncovering of the true identity of Victoria Callcott.*

4/5/94 Perth: On Monday came a letter from Dennis Jackson of the *DHLR* accepting the piece I sent last year, "The Case for the Darroch Thesis". Enclosed with it was a letter from the "reader" to whom the article hd bn sent for appraisal. This turned out to be LD Clark, the eminent Lawrence scholar (*The Minoan Distance*, *The Dark Body of Night*, and the CUP editor of *The Plumed Serpent*). His assessment was an enthusiastic recommendation to publish my piece ("unreservedly"). He even praised my writing! Then, next mail, came the "Simon Leys" article from the *New York Review of Books*, "Lawrence of Australia". This pretty much pedalled my line, with attribution. A good 24 hours, & I cd nt have asked for more, with Steele's *K* about to hit the bookshops. [*In the event, the* DHLR *did not publish my "Case for the DT" piece. Within weeks, Bruce Steele's CUP edition of* Kangaroo *was published, & the Lawrence world began to turn against me.*]

26/5/94 ditto: Quite a bit of L work. Was going through my files [*I had brought most of my Lawrence research materials over from Sydney, intending to stay some time*] & came across the [*1919 Brisbane*] Red Flag & [*1921 Sydney*] riots file. They were in a bit of a mess, so I started to tidy them up. Reading them, I decided to try to write a piece on the Row in Town & use it for our first DHL seminar, "In the Footsteps of Lawrence", which will be held at [*our house in*] Collaroy on our brief return to Sydney in a few weeks. In doing so I realised that Struthers' speech before the riot is pure IWW rhetoric. I checked in Ian Turner's Is Sydney Burning? [*the standard work in the IWW in Australia*] & this was pretty much confirmed. Then I read my notes & cuttings on the background to the 1921 May Day incident & the disturbances this led to. The start of it all was a meeting held in the Sydney Town Hall on May 1 to mark the death of Percy Brookfield, the Labor MP who was shot on Rivirton [*near Broken Hill in western NSW*] railway station some weeks earlier [*by a deranged Turk*]. That May 1 Town Hall meeting, at which Garden spoke, has according to the cuttings, the precedent of Willie Struthers' speech in the Row In Town. And the riot that occurred in the Domain a week later had all the ingredients of the subsequent fictional fracas in K. Here are all the elements that go to make up "The Row in Town" chapter, including the shooting & death of Cooley (Brookfield was shot in the stomach – his "marsupial pouch" - & succumbed some time later.)

26/5/94 Perth: Peter Yeend asks: Did it have to be Walter Friend, adding: "His father and several brothers have equal claim." Then came these words: "Now my predicament is that as Archivist I cannot allow access to the Friend material any more, yet I do hold a strong piece of evidence which your thesis needs." He went on to imply that I was wrong about Florence Avenue - or at least that I shld nt be limiting my search to it. "I'd be more interested in Beach Road," he sd. "A check on the owners of cottages there might be very productive." [*see 5/8/11 below re Adrian Friend the Friend house in Beach Road*]

12/6/94 ditto: Letters to Peter Yeend & Fiona Friend went off last week. The hooks are in the water. We shld soon get some bites. In the meantime, I have gone back over my

"Claws in the Arse"

Collaroy research, focusing (naturally) on Beach Road. But going over it has, alas, revealed nothing fresh, nothing apparently overlooked. The houses & their inhabitants stand there, like ghosts, waiting to come to life. I peer at & around them, but can see nothing. Yet, I know, lurking in the half-light is someone, something, somewhere.

28/7/94 ditto: The major development has been a burst of research by Sandra & myself on L in WA. L definitely arrived intending to stay for some time (for he told a reporter who boarded the boat before it docked that that was his intention). Yet within hours of his disembarking he had changed his mind & instead decided to catch the first available boat to Sydney. Almost certainly this was because he opened a letter from Hum in Sydney that had bn waiting for him & whose content made him change his plans.

8/8/94 ditto: Two very interesting things have come out of this current spate of research. I have bn going through the cancelled [*crossed out*] parts in the holograph, and something quite odd is emerging. There is, I have observed, a subtle & totally unexpected pattern in them. Surprisingly, the more he re-writes, the closer (as a rule) he reverts to the original reality (when one wd expect the exact opposite). But it is the second find, which comes from reading the three versions of *Lady C*, that is of real significance. In the second *LCL* a character called Jack Strangeways appears. It looks as if he is based on Jack Scott (as I had suspected might happen, which was why I was reading Lawrence's works).

15/8/94 ditto: (Definitely a right-hand-page entry.) Something interesting has happened. It looks as if I may have discovered a major clue. (Though I shld have thought of it earlier.) As my 8/8 previous entry indicated, I have bn pursuing a line of research that started with my decision – pending news of the Friend front – to go through the entire run of DHLRs & extract anything about K, etc (partly for information, partly as a reflection of knowledge on the matter over a period now spanning over 25 years). This line led me to Prof Adams' article on LCL & CBP. This in turn led to the discovery of Jack Strangeways in LCL #2. Yesty I read Derek Britton's 1988 book on The Making of [*LCL*], which actually has a chapter on Jack Strangeways. Britton identified JS as JMM [*John Middleton Murry*]. But, of course, he knew nothing of Jack Scott. (And JMM doesn't really fit, for he was not noteably a fascist, & I don't think he wd have machine-gunned the proletariat [*as Jack Strangeways urges in LCL #2*].) But Britton also mentioned The Virgin & The Gipsy, which preceded LCL & largely pre-figured it. It features a military figure, too. He is Major Charles Eastwood. We know where the name Eastwood comes from. But where did L get Major Charles? Well, in the novelette (unpublished in Lawrence's time) he is described as "surely Danish". Does this ring a bell? Cooley in K is described as "surely Jewish". Moreover, [*Major-General Charles*] Rosenthal was Danish (though he looked Jewish). But leaving that aspect aside for the moment, this led me on to think what L might be doing, generally, when he needs the names of characters (& places, for that matter). I think he has some mental equivalent of a rag-bag, filled with names & other ingredients he needs for his fiction. This bag is stuffed with names he has come across, from his childhood in Eastwood, down to his present day. If I am right (& I think I am), then that bag wd contain names like Scott, Rosenthal, Hum, Friend, etc &, more importantly, their characteristics, both appearance-wise & behaviour-wise. In subsequent works these patchwork "bits & pieces" wd be pulled out, when necessary, to do their fictional duty. (I must catch up on my L reading, for a Robert Moreton Friend, or parts of him, might be lying there, out in the oeuvre somewhere.)

29/8/94 Perth: It turns out that Victoria Callcott is, in large part, none other than Maudie Cohen, wife of Eustace Cohen, the couple that befriended fellow guests L&F at Mollie Skinner's guest-house-cum-convalescent-home, Leithdale. She's recently married (like VC) [*in fact the young couple were on their honeymoon*]; her mother (a Brazier) came from Somerset (like VC); her father was a surveyor who had given up surveying and taken up dairy farming on the South Coast (of WA, not NSW, as everyone had assumed); and she was the eldest of a large family. (And her father came from Victoria [*like VC*]!) There is no question now where L got the family & other details he invests VC with. Nor is there much doubt they are grafted on to someone in NSW who is the real VC, and who we now have to track down. [*no easy task*]

12/9/94 ditto: Peter Yeend has written. He says he will soon approach key members of the Friend family to plead my case, "for the greater good". Let us hope they cleave to his entreaties.

23/9/94 Collaroy: Yeend has approached one of the key Friends, with quite negative results. His exact words are: "I was given a strong hint last night by one of the Friend family that their problem is they want no publicity and that is where the problem lies." He enclosed a page of handwriting. It was numbered [*page*] 3 & was clearly part of a longer document. It detailed how, in 1917, a group of TKS boys marched to Victoria Barracks in Paddington to enlist. It is probably the Friend memoir he told me about, & I will be much mistaken if that Friend is not Robert Moreton Friend*. I wrote back begging for more. However, in the wings, other forces are now at work. M Jones [SMH *literary editor*] rang to say she hd learned from Ruffels that Steele's *K* is out, & that it rubbishes me. [* *I was mistaken, for it was Adrian's, not Robert's memoir*]

27/9/94 ditto: CUP *Kangaroo* arrived yesty. Steele utterly rejects - contemptuously - the Darroch Thesis (which, according to him, "has now been found to be without foundation"). I don't even warrant a cue-title, though Joe Davis does!

6/10/94 ditto: I have now analysed Steele's argument for the Seltzer ending [*to the CUP Kangaroo*] and, though I myself originally cleaved to this ending, I now suspect that he is wrong, mainly because of his interpretation of how Lawrence's "last page" came about. It is inconceivable that this Secker "last page" is not the same last page he sent Seltzer on 4/1/23, yet Steele alleges just that.

8/10/94 ditto: I have bn analysing Steele's argument for the Seltzer ending. I am convinced now that he has blundered. Moreover, as a result of the analysis I think I now know what happened: how the different endings did come about. I may do an article on this.

8/10/94 ditto: Two, somewhat enigmatic, letters from P. Yeend. He has spoken to Brian Friend, son of Robert Moreton Friend. Answer still no. BF told Yeend that "the young men" (ie, his father & elder brother Walter) shld nt be blamed for "what they did" (presumably joining Jack Scott's secret army in 1920-22).

19/10/94 ditto: Finished first draft of my *Kangaroo* endings article ("Not the End of the Story"). Pretty devastating re Steele. Also proposed to Yeend that he set up a meeting with the Friends (Brian & Bill), perhaps at the U[*nion*] C[*lub*]. Coincidentally, I'm playing golf on Friday at *RSGC* [*Royal Sydney Golf Club*] in the annual Union Club vs Australian Club match, and in the four behind me is none other than Brian Friend! (He's a member of the AC.) It's a small world.

16/11/94 ditto: Finished second revise of my "Not the End" article & sent it off to LD Clark for unofficial appraisal & advice. Spent most of the last four weeks polishing what is now a powerful & convincing piece. Steele will not be left with much credibility after this. He actually had the gall to write to Lacey & say that he thought *Rananim* was "concentrating too much on L's Australian period", which was only "a brief interlude". The cheek of him!. Wait till he reads "Not the End" He went on to deign to offer (in reponse to an invitation from Lacey) to provide a few thoughts, when he cd spare the time, on "some of the editorial decisions" he made with his CUP *Kangaroo* edition. Jolly D of him. [*In his deeply flawed explanation of how the variant endings came about, Steele deliberately failed to mention perhaps the most germane point - that the Seltzer ending, & now his chosen CUP ending, ended in mid-sentence.*]

22/10/95 ditto: Almost a five-month gap. My main activity has been re-polishing my endings article for the *DHLR*. Warren Roberts, bless his big Texas heart, has taken it under his wing, & himself sent it to the *DHLR*, with his blessings. As he's the general editor of the CUP project, & an ex-head of the HRC [*Humanities Research Center at the University of Texas, publisher of the DHLR*], I think it's in with a chance. Meanwhile I'm planning to go to Nottingham for a DHL International Conference in July, where I will detonate my endings bombshell. Our new DHLA president, Eggert, has apparently hitched his caboose to the Steele bandwaggon. Even though he *knows* about the Yeend letters saying that I am right & Steele is wrong! [*but CUP editors have to stick together*]

20/3/96 ditto:. Yeend wrote, bleakly: "No change in the Friends' position," then adding, "I still have the matter in my daily work file, for you are right, but we are prevented from proving it." Nice to know.

11/4/96 ditto: According to one of my young helpers, Sacha Davis, whose family is German, the name Rosenthal means "valley of the roses", and there is a village called Rosenthal in Germany! Must visit it.

1/7/96 ditto: I'm off to Nottingham tomorrow for the DHL conference & to give my (brief) paper - aka bombshell - on the endings. Chuck Rossman, who will be at the conference, now has the article. Says he will publish later this year. Will also go to Germany & try to visit Rosenthal. Had a thought last night. The car trip back from Collaroy that Sunday wasn't in Hum's car, but in Robert Moreton Friend's car, garaged, as L says Jack Callcott's was, in town, no doubt in the Taylor's garage. [*no, it was Adrian Friend's car – see below*]

6/7/96 Frankenberg: An exotic dateline, as exotic as any I have penned. I arrived here at 8pm, so the Rathaus bell just told me. It's a hilltop, early medieval town, in Hessen. Am now 13 km from Rosenthal, according to the sign down the hill. Passed Waldbrol, Numbrect & Dallenberg on the way (all places L mentions when he was in Germany in 1912). Too far [*for him*] to walk or ride. But a train line all the way. And Frankenberg *is* a major tourist spot. Just the place to bring a bored & frustrated nephew [*Lawrence had been staying at Waldbrol with his German relatives*]. Tomorrow to Rosenthal. Shall report further. Now, a stroll round town, dinner & bed.

6/7/96 Frankenberg: After writing the previous entry, I went for a pre-prandial stroll. As luck (fickle mistress!) wd have it, I came across a poster on the front of a [motor] garage advertising a "disco nite" at the nearby village of Rosenthal. Nice souvenir, & some indication that Rosenthal performs some sort of festival function, at least vis-à-vis Frankenberg. But back to the hotel. And dinner. I was placed in what seems to be the guests' dining room. I ordered. As I waited, my eyes drifted around the room. Suddenly they were arrested by the sight of a plate hanging on the wall, not more than 8ft away. An ordinary plate, glazed brown, & somewhat garish. But in the centre was something that riveted me: a heart, and, far more significantly, a heart with dots around its perimeter [*just as Lawrence describes in* Kangaroo].

13/7/96 Nottingham: .I drove to Rosenthal the next day. The road was through a forest of great firs. As I arrived, the outskirts were marked by a sign, on which a rose was carved & painted. But it was a small hamlet, not really a tourist venue, though there was a hotel & a village green that sported a marquee, so some sort of festival was in progress, adding weight to impression the poster imparted. Roses in abundance & carved wooden weather vanes. But no wooden hearts.

13/7/96 ditto: Am now in Nottingham, at the uni, for the DHL conference. It is an interesting experience, face-to-face at last with the orthodox Lawrence world. Pained politeness on their part - Worthen, Kinkead-Weekes, Ellis, etc. It will be interesting to see what happens when I give my talk on Monday. [*It was received politely, and ignored, (though [CUP general editor] Professor [Geoffrey] Boulton, who attended with Ellis in tow, came up afterwards and asked: "Have you spoken to Bruce [Steele] about this?", and when I replied that we had not spoken since the Wyewurk inquiry day, added, wistfully, "Pity."*]

19/2/97 Bondi: I now believe that there are two Lawrence "voices". There are almost two Lawrences. There is the "authorial" voice - the "dear reader" voice of his letters, essays & parts of his fiction (but not, I think, most of his poetry). Then there is the voice of what he called* "his daemon" - the creative voice. Time & time again, he refers to this latter "beast", whom he can't seem to control, & which (for it seems a "thing" rather than something animate) he has to conjure up, or else it makes unscheduled, uninvited manifestations of itself, & which is the "real author" of much of his fiction, & perhaps all his poetry. This, if I'm right (& I'm investigating further), cd help explain some profound puzzles about, in particular, *K*, such as why L seemed incapable of changing some things, such as the repetitions. Maybe, & I realise I'm drawing an enormously long bow here, maybe these bits were "written" by the daemon, & the "other" L cdn't (or wdn't) change them. [**actually he called it "his little devil" – but it is of interest that Aldous Huxley came to the same conclusion in his preface to his volume of Lawrence's letters*]

23/2/97 ditto: An amusing thing has happened. AM related it on our annual DHL Harbour Cruise [*on the Lady Hopetoun*]. A woman from *Ermington* [*a Sydney western suburb*] rang AM to tell him about her father, Jack Davies, who was high up in the Old Guard (the Country Movement) in 1930-32 around Scone [*a country town/center north-west of Sydney*]. His name is on the cigarette case. [*Andrew had found a cigarette case, presented I think to Colonel Hinton (see note c. 1/1/78 above), bearing the engraved initials of all the Old Guard "top brass", including, of course, "JWRS"*] She told AM a lot about the OG around Scone & the Hunter [*River*]. As she reached the end of her recollection, Andrew, ever alert to possibilities, asked her if she was aware, by chance, of any link between her father's organisation & DHL & Kangaroo. Yes, she said, brightly. She knew of a book that had been written locally to explain how the OG came into existence, & it included the story of how Lawrence came to be involved with the organisation. She sd she would get the book & show it to Andrew, who made the earliest possible appointment to see the lady & her book. Had our ship come in at long last? She greeted him at her door with an apology. She did indeed have the book, & it did give a history of the OG, at least in the Scone area, but it had nothing about Lawrence. She had mixed it up with another book that had mentioned Lawrence & secret armies, a book by a chap called Andrew Moore. However, that aside, she did have some important information. The local book (by Sandy McTavish or some similar name) recalled that the local OG branch was run out of someone's house, & that they used to meet in its garage. The two chaps in charge of the local group were called "the two rats from the garage*". Interesting. [**We now believe that one of the pseudonyms or euphemisms for the 1920s NSW predecessor of the Old Guard was "the garage - which makes Callcott's profession in Kangaroo ("garage proprietor") more than a little pertinent.*]

30/4/97 ditto: I received from Yeend a short note saying that he had referred the matter to the Headmaster [*of Kings*] - what authority & power does that title conjure up! - & who is now "reviewing" the correspondence. (Also I have bn having a rather dusty exchange of emails with John Worthen [*Lawrence biographer and head of the DH Lawrence Centre at*

Nottingham], whom I have apprised of the existence of the TKS letters. He says he prefers to remain one of the sceptics, however, & not "break ranks".)

7/3/98 Bondi: More than six months since my last entry. Nothing very exciting to report. FF never replied, despite various reminders. No doubt "got at" by the Friends (inheritance concerns, etc). Nothing, too, from Kings, so the Yeend opening is totally closed now. The vault door has slammed shut, & I am back in stygian gloom again. Ellis's volume covering L's time in Australia has bn published, but though I asked Peter Preston [*of the Nottingham DHL Centre*] for a photocopy of the Australian bits, I got no reply. Have ordered a copy via The Spectator. I hope it is dismissive [*it was*] as it helps keep up the pressure on the Friends, Kings, etc (*but not with any hope of success*). Been corresponding with Taos [*where the next DHL Conference was to be held, and to which Sandra and I planned to go*] but silence since I revealed my non-academic background. No reaction to either my endings piece in the DHLR or my nomenclature series in Rananim [*5/1 etc*]. Warren Roberts, my good & true friend, died, & I did a little item about him – having inspired me, etc – which I sent to the DHL list [*a short-lived website run by Chuck Rossman out of HRC*]. Our DHLA society hangs on, but by a thread, with membership & enthusiasm ekeing away. But to end on a positive note. Last night at the ATP [*Australian Technology Park, where our Internet company had its office*] I met the financial controller, Charles Summers. He is egregiously Scottish (so we got on well!) & revealed that his family came from Cruden Bay, near Aberdeen, & confirmed that Summers is a Scottish name. (The Murdochs also come from Cruden Bay, & Charles's father [or grandfather] knew Keith Murdoch, Rup's pop.) However, this [Scottish information] might help with a Darroch-shift transformation: {Lawrence} = {RLS} [Robert Louis Stevenson] = {Richard Lovatt Somers}. Well, it's possible.

10/9/01 ditto: Again, over a year since my last entry. A year in which our DHLA society has fragmented, due to Paul Eggert's defection. [*Paul Eggert had made overtures to some academics at Wollongong University about taking over the running of the DHLA and "refocusing" its activities from Sydney to the South Coast. This did not work out and led to an exchange of letters between myself and Eggert, published in* Rananim *9.1. At the next AGM John Lacey became the DHLA President, and Eggert did not renew his membership.*] John Lacey is our new President, and our main activity now, socialising apart, is building our DHLA website. But that is not the reason for this entry. Rather it is my realisation, when subbing my "Nothing to Sniff At" article, that Scott is probably Lawrence's cover for Robert Moreton Friend. [*no – the cover for his younger brother, Adrian*]

4/4/02 ditto: Seven months since my last entry. I had thought that there wasn't, miracles apart, much scope for further advances that wd warrant new entries. But now something has cropped up, quite unexpectedly, from "left field". I won't go into the whole thing here, for it is outlined in the article "The Man Who Wasn't There" I am writing for *Rananim* [10.1]. The absent man is George Augustine Taylor - not a name that has impinged on these notebooks hitherto. I hd never heard of him until AM sent his letter about him to me a couple of weeks ago. Now he is the centre of attention. His use of the name Cooley (twice!) and his closeness to Rosenthal make for some fascinating possibilities. Exciting days again!

11/4/02 ditto: I have just finished the Cooley/Taylor article, leaving the answer to the mystery quite open. I ended it by posing the question: Is it a coincidence that Taylor conjures up the same unlikely name Cooley that L uses in K to describe their mutual friend, Rosenthal? Clearly not. There must be an explanation. Moreover, the clue to that explanation must lie in K, or elsewhere at hand. What cd that answer be? One possibility is that Taylor put some element of his hero Rosenthal into The Sequel. That's possible, given their mutual interests & close association. (Ruffels is equally fascinated by the mystery, & is using his very considerable skills & resources to probe further.) If L found Rosenthal charismatic & visionary, so wd Taylor. Did he associate Rosenthal with the name Cooley via his contact with The Public & The Arena (ie, via Henry George)? [*see Rananim article*] But how, when & via whom was the information imparted to L, esp as Taylor wasn't in Sydney at the time?

29/5/02 ditto: *This entry marks a turning point, or watershed in the diary. From now on the entries will be electronic, not in hard copy. (The notebooks have come to an end.)*

24/11/10 ditto: There is now little doubt that George Augustine Taylor was either editor of the K&E journal, or a substantial contributor to it. Having just gone through the 36 monthly copies of the K&E I can report that it reeks of GAT influence & interests (aviation, wireless, planning, etc). My best guess is that it was a joint effort by Rosenthal & Taylor - as I think *The Soldier* (contemporary with the *K&E Journal*) was. R might – probably was – the "titular" editor, but I think Taylor did all the journalistic work. I think he also sold the ads, for it is full of building supplies ads (eg, WS Friend and Co). A major element of its editorial content was an almost obsessive interest in promoting aviation – Taylor's main interest at this time. It has an article about a visit (no doubt by Rosenthal) to Taylor's aircraft factory at Mascot, urging its value to, for example, the defence of the Northern Territory (a need Taylor expressed in his 1916 novel, *The Sequel*).

26/11/10 ditto: A somewhat seismic email from Robert Whitelaw yesty. He has discovered that there **is** an end house at Narrabeen, and a rather significant one too. It apparently (& Robert is checking further) was (as Lawrence's text says) standing sideways facing the lagoon. It was owned by a Mr and Mrs Shultz (certainly not a name I have ever come across). But – & here's the vital part – it has a crucial Taylor connection. For Taylor apparently stayed there when he was conducting his aviation experiments in 1909 over the sandhills nearby. (Not only that, but Robert has found a snapshot of Rosenthal & Taylor in the front garden of Billabong having afternoon tea c.1908!) [See *photo-insert*]

Cleveland Street 22.10.11: I recently became convinced (where I was merely speculating before) that the meeting with "Trewhella" at Mosman Bay was in fact a meeting with Jack Scott. This would explain an anomaly about Ernest Whiting's remark about being told that my description of Jack Scott matched the description he had been given of the "man who met Lawrence at the wharf & took him to stay on the North Shore for three days". I now believe that this was the first time Scott met Lawrence (& that the wharf was not at Circular Quay, but at Mosman). It then occurred to me that Lawrence must have come back to Sydney that first Friday to retrieve his trunks (I bet that ferry collision in the Harbour, mentioned in Kangaroo, occurred that Friday [*it did*]). That was when someone took him to see Scott, having previously told Scott of Lawrence's arrival in Sydney & his possible availability as a fill in for Taylor. I now think that, after the interview, Scott had invited Lawrence up to his place at 112 Wycombe Road, where Lawrence mounted the summer-house & stayed the night. The "second meeting" with Callcott at 112 probably occurred later that same day - when Lawrence returned in the evening by ferry & tram, as per the text. (Next morning - Saturday - L & Scott no doubt walked back down Neutral Bay/Cremorne to Mosman wharf to catch the ferry into town & thence the train at Central.) Scott & Lawrence must have gone down to Thirroul on that Saturday. Then it clicked that was when they watched the football game on the field opposite the station.

Bondi 1.03.11: Robert (Whitelaw - now my right-hand) & I are leaving no stones unturned in our quest to find the clinching evidence that will show what really happened to Lawrence in Sydney & Thirroul. Our interviews with the surviving descendants of the Irons and Southwell families have yielded much valuable "background" material, yet so far nothing conclusive. But we still have some stones left to turn, & I think we both believe that we will soon uncover something reasonably convincing, if not the proverbial "smoking gun". (The key, we now believe, is who was at that Sunday tea-party at Narrabeen - & we think we can get close to answering that vital question before the Sydney DHL conference kicks off in June.)

Cleveland Street 5/8/11: An email from Mike Sutherland, & a rather momentous one at that. Potentially it could herald the end or culmination of my 40-year quest. (Actually it was from his aunt, Janet Walker, onpassing it to me.)

Michael, I spoke with Jim Friend this morning. He knew about Lawrence and Kangaroo. He said his grandfather's brother Adrian was a supporter of the King & Country League but did not believe he would be plotting to overthrow the government. Somewhere he has seen a record of a donation to the league. His Uncle Walter was indignant about the inferences and as you said Brian has just died and I believe he was the last of the family historians. Walter had a house at Collaroy. Jim had not heard of Billabong at N Narrabeen He suggested the King's archives. It appears Rob and Sandra know Fiona McGuinness (nee Friend). This is one of Jim's daughters, who has just returned to journalism after many years child raising. I'd suggest leaving it to Rob and Fonia. I have Jim's phone numbers. – Janet

I rang & went to see Jim Friend in his apartment in Millers Point. He was most amicable & promiused to approach Brian Friend to see if he would grant permission for me to see the Friend Memoir (which I still thought was written by Robert Moreton Friend). He emailed me later to say Brian had refused. I had thought I would not get anything more from the Friend family. But in the course of bringing everything together [*for my 2014 draft book*] I began to think I was wrong about "the Friend Connection". I wrote again to Jim Friend.

Jim - I thought you would like to know that I have just completed my new book on Lawrence. I have sent it to the Cambridge University Press, who seem interested in it. It is my final say on the matter The Friend family are, obviously, mentioned. But I think I am wrong about Robert Moreton Friend being the main Friend link with Lawrence. It was - as I think you hinted - Ernest Adrian Friend, and more particularly his wife Fanny Beatrice (nee Owen). She provides, I now believe, the main ingredients for Victoria Callcott in the novel (not, as I had thought, Dawdie Friend). You might pass this on.

Later in the day I received this email from his wife (now widow):

Dear Robert, I regret to inform you that Jim died on March 10. He had secondaries from his lung cancer which progressed to both hips and then throughout. He spent 3 weeks in palliative care from February. As you know he was interested in your work on Laurence and would not have been at all surprised of your conclusions re Ernest Adrian and Fanny. I shall be interested to read the book when published. Kind regards, Judy Friend.

If that is not a smoking gun, I don't know what is. He (Jim Friend) "would not have been at all surprised of your conclusions re Ernest Adrian and Fanny". So it was not after all Robert Moreton Friend whom Lawrence encountered at the Narrabeen afternoon-tea, and subsequently, but his younger brother Adrian (& his 25-year-old flirty wife Fanny). Of course, I went back and changed "Robert" to "Adrian", & added Fanny. (Fanny! So that's the name Lawrence crossed out in the holograph! And all these years I thought it was "Tanny", & hence Frieda)]

BONDI 08.01.16: When revising *Scaly Back* I came to the part when I was describing what Peter Yeend had said about the Friends having a holiday place in Collaroy Basin – in Beach Road in fact. Yeend had said in his letters to me, several times, that the "house I was looking for" was in Collaroy Basin. He indicated that this was where the Friends holidayed. When I mentioned Seaview Parade – the Hum vacation venue - Yeend told me that I would be better off looking in nearby Beach Road. Yeend said that in the 1920s and '30s Friend family spent school holidays in The Basin. However, later research (following my realisation that Hum drove the Lawrence back from Narrabeen that first Sunday afternoon to change cars there to Adrian Friend's Austin) indicated that L&K and Jack Scott had walked along the track from Seaview Parade to Florence Avenue between the houses & the Basin to Hinemoa (so Scott could show off Lawrence to Mrs Oatley, who was living in Hinemoa), where they waited for Adrian Friend and Fanny to bring the Friend's Austin from where they had bene staying the weekend in Beach Road.

BONDI 10/9/17: I am editing my Silvery book text. I see in my end notes a reference to the holograph and it being sent to me in 1977. I have now added how this came about, which I have not noted before. In 1977 I received a letter from Gerald Pollinger, the Lawrence estate agent, informing me that Dr FJ Jarvis had been murdered (which is no doubt why Dr Roberts approached me in 1972 to put in a proposal to edit Kangaroo). Had I known this at the time, I might have tried harder to stay in the editing race (which I spurned in disgust after I was turned down by the CUP).

BONDI 05.06.18 – yesty I finished my last, final revise of my book text (with a check of the footnotes). We will now construct a website for the book, which will initially go up on our new DHL in Australia website. It can then he read, freely, by anyone. (This is the modern equivalent of having a book published.) So my "life's work" is now completed. I can die, or fade away, content that I have left something behind that I can be proud of, and which will probably last, well, forever (for I am reasonably sure no one else will ever have a better interpretation of Kangaroo and Lawrence's time in Australia). I believe I have handled the matter of his homoerotic relationship with Rosenthal adequately. This is, of course, not to say that nothing will ever emerge to improve on what I have said. Some ASIO or other file may one day be found that will make the matter clearer – but it will, I am sure, merely confirm what I have written. I am very lucky that I have been granted the opportunity to do this. I falls to few people to be able to do something significant in their lives. My life has had a purpose, and an important one at that. I am very grateful (and happy) for this. If I have another task, it is to re-edit Kangaroo to provide "the text he really wanted". So that is what I will do next.

BIBLIOGRAPHIC NOTE

IT IS NOT feasible to compile a comprehensive bibliography for this book, which has been, at time of writing, more than 40 years in the making. (In my library up at Blackheath I have literally hundreds of Lawrence books, and it would be impracticable to list a meaningful sample of them all here.) What I will do, however, is indicate how, when and where my research was undertaken, and outline the main sources I have relied on for its content and conclusions.

The idea to write a book about Lawrence in Australia, as I describe in my *Introduction*, came out of a visit to Austin Texas in 1972 where my wife and close collaborator, Sandra Jobson Darroch, was researching the life of Lady Ottoline Morrell in the archives of what was then the Humanities Research Centre at the University of Texas. We had already learned much about Lawrence through his involvement with Ottoline. Her papers at the HRC included many letters from Lawrence.

From early in 1976 I began to keep a diary of my research – a legacy of our work on *Ottoline* – which became more detailed and comprehensive as time went on. The chronicle of that research, which outlines where I obtained my information about Lawrence, *Kangaroo* and his time in Australia (the libraries and archives visited; the books and journals read; the letters and primary documents consulted; the leads identified and the clues followed up; the hundreds of interviews reported and recorded) can be found on both our DH Lawrence Society of Australia website[560] and our new DH Lawrence in Australia site[561] (edited selections from the research-diary are included above, for easy access to the

---

[560] http://www.dhlawrencesocietyaustralia.com.au (click on "Kangaroo Research Notes")
[561] http://www.dhlawrenceinaustralia.com.au (*ditto*)

references cited from the diary mentioned in my text). Not all my diary-entries were relevant or germane, by any means. There were numerous false scents and many dead-ends. Some people were helpful and encouraging; others less so.

Initially, the various biographies of Lawrence (and Frieda[562]) gave me a broad outline of what was already known about Lawrence and *Kangaroo*. Harry T Moore and Keith Sagar's biographies, in particular, were useful. Richard Aldington's work – knowing Lawrence personally – was especially helpful.

Yet it was Lawrence's letters that were central to my research. The 53 he posted in Australia (and a number subsequently) were perhaps my primary resource – bar one. For by far the greatest source of information was *Kangaroo* itself – once I realised that it was a fictionalised "splash-down-reality" account of his time in Australia

I came to rank my various sources in order of importance and reliability. At the top was Lawrence himself, both in his letters and in the text of *Kangaroo* (and what he told other people, as recorded in several memoirs and reminiscences).

In the second rank were contemporary newspaper, journals, timetables, and other published sources. (These helped, for example, to establish what trains or ships he caught; when he received or send mail; what the weather was on particular days; and so on.)

Contemporaries of Lawrence and those who knew and wrote about him came in the third rank (people like Aldington, Dorothy Brett, Mabel Dodge Luhan, Witter Bynner, etc). Below that, and very subsidiary, were the sources that attempted to speculate what might have happened to Lawrence when he was in Australia. Most of these were unhelpful.

---

[562] but not her autobiographical *Not I But the Wind* (see below)

INDEX

A Roo by Any Other Name, 84
a typical Cornishman, 169, 255
Aldington, Richard, iii, iv, 2, 47, 125, 130, 153, 196, 203-207, 210, 258, 271
Alexander, the Rev. John, 2, 9, 196, 247-248
American Consulate, 162, 164, 171, 178
Ancora Press, 139
Ashton, Howard, 168-169, 255
ASIO, 59, 148, 248
Australian Accent, 200, 203, 237
Australian Communist Party, 143, 258
Australian Protective League, 6, 148, 198
Bacchus, 106
Barkell, Lieutenant, 53
Bass, Tom, 236
Baynes, Rosalind, 21
Beach Road, 18, 42, 251, 261-262, 268
Bennett Street, 61, 105-106, 251
Benson, Shan, 219, 245
Berg typescripts, 100, 178
Billabong, ii, 39, 42, 250, 267-268
Birds, Beasts & Flowers, 163
Bits, ii, 56, 150-152, 154, 160, 170-171, 207
Black Forest, 23, 85, 122, 216-218, 222
blazing row, 131
Boldrewood, Rolf, 21
Bosch, Hieronymus, 234
Botanic Garden, 28, 31, 147
Boy Scouts, 30
Boyd, Mary, 231
Brett, Dorothy, 229, 271
Brewster, Earl, 95
broken attachments, broken, 188, 190-191, 193
Brookes, Herbert, 6, 72, 245, 249
Burns, Robert, 23
Bynner, Witter, 196, 248, 271
Callcott, Jack, 4-5, 11, 15-18, 25, 39-41, 49-50, 54, 57-58, 61, 63-72, 74, 79-80, 82, 86, 88-89, 92-93, 105-107, 109-110, 112, 115, 125, 134-135, 143, 145, 154, 156, 161, 175, 178, 181, 195, 199-201, 209, 211, 214, 242, 245-248, 250-251, 253, 257, 264-265, 267

Callcott, Mrs AF, 47, 49
Callcott, Victoria (Vikki), 12, 25, 79, 107, 115, 258, 261-262, 268
Cambridge University Press, i, iii, v, vii, 3-5, 7, 10-11, 13, 15, 53, 56, 58, 62, 64, 69-75, 80-81, 83, 85-86, 93, 97-99, 110-111, 114, 117, 120, 122-123, 125, 127, 130, 134-135, 143-144, 156-157, 167, 172, 176, 182, 188, 195, 197-198, 202, 204, 207-208, 212-213, 216, 220-223, 227, 235, 242, 244-248, 250, 253-254, 256-258, 260, 263, 268
Cameron Sutherland, 39
Camperdown, 165, 169, 185
Canberra Flats, 8, 46, 61, 172
Canberra House/Hall, 138, 140
Cape York tiger-cat, 56, 86, 94-95
Carlton Hotel, 110, 145, 149-150
Carswell, Catherine, 20, 24, 124, 160
Carter & Co, 140
Casey, Lord Richard, 173
Castlereagh Street, 82, 85-87, 92, 95, 99, 110, 129, 140, 145, 169, 243
Cavelleria Rusticana, 186
Central Railway Station, 45, 63
Ceylon, 20-23, 27, 34, 45, 51-52, 54, 57, 75, 81, 95, 138, 245, 254-255
Chapala, 197, 248
Chapman, Leo, 253
Charleroi Bank, 60
Chatswood, 12, 29, 105, 141, 162, 167, 187, 205, 256
chic, 118-119
Circular Quay, 27-28, 31, 35, 55, 59-60, 99, 103, 138, 141, 267
Clark, Dr LD, 261, 263
Claws in the Arse, ii, viii, 118, 152, 214, 219, 225, 231
coal-jetty, 95, 97, 131
Cohen, Eustace, 25, 262
Cohen, Maudie, 262
Collaroy, 16-17, 35, 39, 42, 201, 244, 250-251, 254-256, 259-264, 268
Commonwealth Investigation Bureau, 148
Conservatorium, 28, 45
Cooley, Benjamin, ii, 5, 9-10, 14-15, 17-18, 62, 80, 82, 84-90, 93-95, 100-102, 113-114, 122, 128, 133,

INDEX

141, 143, 150, 155, 161, 167, 175, 177, 183, 205-206, 209, 216, 218-219, 222-223, 235, 245-248, 253, 257, 262, 266
Cooley/Rosenthal, 85, 88, 93, 133, 141, 150, 155, 223
copyright problems, 241
cornstalks, 101
Cornwall, 40, 145, 149-150, 169, 201, 216
Covent Garden, 31, 138
Craig Street, 47-49, 60, 64, 237, 251
Cremorne, 61, 103-104, 151, 249, 267
Cullen, Sir William, 30
CUP Critical Edition, 194
Curtis Brown, 192
Customs officials, 188
daemon, 265
Dark God, 98, 103, 132, 161, 201
Darlington, 12, 22, 24-25, 33, 48, 57
Darroch Thesis, i, vii, 246, 256, 261, 263
Darroch, Sandra (Jobson), i
Delprat, Paul, ii, 152, 169, 219, 237-238, 242, 255-256
Demos, 33-34, 44
DH Lawrence in Australia, i, 10, 270
DH Lawrence Society of Australia, iv, 12, 225, 259, 270
Diggers, i, 5, 54, 56, 64, 69-72, 74, 80, 85, 88, 94, 99, 110-111, 113-114, 117, 131, 133-135, 167-168, 172, 177, 181-182, 197, 204, 210, 212, 222, 227, 244-245, 249, 252
Diggers Club, 71, 88, 111, 172, 249
Dodge, Mabel, 93, 96-97, 116, 127, 129-130, 179, 196, 271
Doolittle, Hilda, 125
Douglas, Norman, 203
Douglass, Robert, 259
Dutton, Geoffrey, 237
Dymocks bookshop, 138
Eastwood, 44, 67, 84-85, 95, 173, 216, 262
Eastwood, Major Charles, 84, 262
Eder, David, 87
Eggert, Dr Paul, 24, 255, 266
Elephant, 27, 45
Ellis, Malcolm, 70, 173
Empire Day, 30
Emu, 86, 207
Ennis, Colonel, 75-76, 246
Esch, Fred, 49, 54, 165, 185-186, 243
ex-servicemen, 3, 71, 168, 246

Fancourt, Bill, 219, 245
Fanfrolico, 139
Fantasia of the Unconscious, iii, 24, 80, 103, 208
Farm Cove, 140
Farmer, Dr David, 241
Farraher, Mrs Clarice, 54
fascism, 73, 88, 102, 150, 208-211, 214
FBI, 59, 197
ferry collision, 55, 58, 267
final proof corrections, 194
Friend, Fiona, 261
Fitzgerald, Tom, 3, 242
Fitzpatrick, Brian, 207, 258
Flaws in the Glass, 231-232, 235
Florence Avenue, 46, 250-251, 261, 269
Forrester snaps, 185-186
Forrester, Denis, 78, 165, 169, 185
Forrester, Laura, 164-165, 169, 186-187
Frankenberg, 264
Friend family, 13, 17-18, 42, 47, 65, 112, 115, 155, 256-257, 260, 263, 268
Friend, Adrian, 18, 25, 39-40, 42-43, 79, 89, 105-106, 110, 172, 258, 261, 264, 268-269
Friend, Brian, 263, 268
Friend, Jim, 268
Friend, Judy, 268

Friend, Lucy May, 47, 251
Friend, Robert Moreton, 251, 262-264, 266, 268
Friend, Walter, 251, 260-261
Game, Dr David, 21
Garage, the, 81, 248, 265
Garden, Jock, 257, 259
George Street, 82, 137-139, 253
Gillespie-Goldfinch organisation, 242
Goldfinch, Sir Philip, 83, 244
Gould, Nat, 152
Government House, 30, 140, 143
GPS schools, 112
Graham, Dr Alexander, 21
Gutenberg, v, 36
Harbour Lights Guild, 11, 48, 249, 253
Hardy, Frank, 137, 257
Hinemoa, 16-17, 42, 181, 250-251, 254-255, 259, 269
his little devil, 265
his own devil, 127
Holbrook, May, 21
holograph, iii, 7, 10, 12, 18, 25, 52, 70, 76, 94, 96-97, 100-102, 104, 118, 120, 125, 128-129, 133, 135, 138, 149, 156, 161, 167, 175-179, 181, 183, 189,

INDEX

209, 214, 222, 240, 247, 252, 262, 268
homosexual, 90-91, 93, 101, 103, 120, 215, 222, 224
Hopkin, Willie, 173
horrible paws, i-ii, 184-185
Hoyle, Arthur, 137, 257
Hum, David Gerald, 11, 17, 20, 22, 29, 34-36, 38-40, 42, 57, 60, 62, 83, 97, 105, 111, 138, 140-141, 147, 158, 162, 167, 169-170, 195, 205, 213, 245, 254-256, 259, 262, 264, 268
Hum, Lillian, 187
Humanities Research Center, vii, 1, 241, 264
Huxley, Aldous, 186, 203, 259, 265
Imperial Service Club, 62
In the Valley of the Roses, 122
Industrial Workers of the World (IWW), 24, 173, 198
Jackson, Dr Dennis, 261
Jaffe, Else, 95
James, John Haughton, 6, 243-244
Jeffery, Mrs, 254
Jenson, Joan, 85
Jerger, Father, 85, 168
Jewish, 49, 86-87, 213, 253, 262
John Thomas and Lady Jane, 84

Johnson, Frank, 139, 253
Jones, Colonel HE, 148
Journey with Genius, iii, 196-197, 259
July 4, 162, 171, 185, 205
Kandy, 21-22, 44, 257
Kangaroo, i-viii, 1-2, 4-10, 12-19, 23-25, 27-29, 31, 36, 38-40, 45-49, 52-53, 56, 58, 60-62, 64-65, 70-72, 77-78, 80-90, 93-94, 97-98, 100-101, 103-104, 107, 111, 113-114, 116, 118, 120, 122, 124-125, 127-128, 133-135, 137-138, 140, 142-146, 148-150, 153-154, 156-157, 159-160, 163, 167-169, 171-177, 179-184, 187-188, 190, 192-197, 200-201, 203-208, 210-211, 213-216, 218-219, 222, 224-228, 230, 232-233, 235-237, 239, 242, 244-252, 254-261, 263-265, 267-268, 270-271
Kelly, Ned, 232
Keynes, Maynard, 203
King and Empire, 5-7, 44, 55, 59, 62, 70, 72, 77, 82, 85, 99-100, 111, 114, 120, 123, 142-143, 155, 158, 168, 198, 208, 213, 246
King and Empire Alliance (KEA), 5-7, 55, 59, 70, 72,

77, 82, 85, 99, 114, 120, 123, 142-143, 155, 158, 168, 198, 208, 213, 246
King, Sir Kelso, 197
Kings School, The, 111, 260
Koteliansky, SS, 20, 87, 165, 205, 247
Krenkow, Hannah, 122
Labor Party, 58, 112, 173
Lacey, John, 44, 266
lagoon, 15-16, 37, 39-40, 267
Lascaris, Manoly, 230, 234
last chapter, 164, 177-178, 182-183, 189, 252
last page, 14, 191-193, 252, 263
Lawlor, Adrian, 130, 153, 196, 206-207, 258
Lawrence, Frieda, iii, viii, 11-12, 15-16, 18-19, 21-23, 28-32, 34-37, 41-45, 49, 53-54, 61, 75-78, 82-83, 95-99, 105, 107, 109, 115-118, 122, 127-132, 135, 145-147, 151-153, 158-159, 163-166, 169, 178-179, 184, 186, 189, 196-197, 205-206, 212-213, 216-223, 227-229, 233, 240, 245, 247-248, 251-253, 260, 268, 271
Lawson, Henry, 21, 68
League of Comrades, 80, 203
League of National Security, 207
Leithdale, 12, 22-25, 262
Leys, Simon, 261
Light Horse, 75-76
Lindsay, Jack, 139, 253
literary soiree, 83
Loddon Falls, 185
Lord and Master, 129, 132
love of comrades, 102
Lowell, Amy, 25
Macarthur-Onslow, Brigadier-General George, 75
Macquarie Street, 29-30, 32, 42-43, 45, 52, 141
Maggies, i, 5, 56, 64, 69-70, 72-73, 75-76, 80, 85, 88, 99, 110-111, 113, 117, 134, 167, 198, 210, 212, 222, 227, 244-246, 252
Mandrake Press, 139
Marchbanks, Mr & Mrs, 165
Martin Place, 30-31, 60, 62, 90, 139, 162-163, 253
mateship, 67-68, 112, 134, 200-203
May Day riot, 168
McQueen, Humphrey, 6, 245
Meanjin, 2, 196, 247-248
Mendes Chambers, 82, 142, 145, 243
Meridian, 256

INDEX

Military Intelligence, 59, 70
mis-pagination, 175
missing chapter, 10, 133, 222
Molesworth, Vol, 243
Monash, General Sir John, 86-87, 207
Moore, Dr Andrew, i, vii, 6, 13-14, 70, 83, 195, 207, 253-254, 256, 258, 265
Morrell, Lady Ottoline, vii, 1-2, 203, 241-242, 270
Mosman Bay, 55-56, 59, 63, 90, 92, 209, 256, 267
Mr Noon, 23, 53, 128, 208, 218
Mullumbimby, 58, 64, 110, 148, 178
Murdoch Street, 51, 8, 31, 46, 61, 79, 105, 151, 172, 243, 251
Murry, John Middleton, 149, 201, 205, 216, 247, 262
Mussolini, Benito, 64, 73, 76, 204, 210, 213
Naldera, 83, 248
Narrabeen, ii, 15-18, 35-36, 42, 44-45, 57, 80, 83, 107, 188, 205, 213, 250, 254, 267-269
National Library, 6, 198, 249
Navy League, the, 197
Nazi, 210

Nehls, Edward, iv, 49-50, 54, 164-166, 185-186, 240, 243
Neutral Bay, 8, 43, 45, 59, 61, 99, 103, 110, 143, 151, 243, 267
New Guard, iii, 3, 235, 242, 244, 246
New Jersey, 192
New Mexico, 20, 91, 179
New York Review of Books, 261
New Zealand, 162, 178, 188, 190, 193, 197
nightmare, 109-110, 143, 145, 148, 150
Nobel Prize, 231
Nolan, Sir Sidney, ii, vii, 118, 219, 230-236
nomenclature, 66, 266
North Shore, the, 59-60, 248, 256, 267
Northern Beaches, the, 34
Norwood, 189
Not I But the Wind, iii, 186, 271
Not the End of the Story, iii, 10, 182, 252, 263
Oatley, Andree Adelaide, 42, 181
Oatley, Major Dudley, 181, 200
Oatley, Peter, 244, 250
Old Guard, 3-6, 83, 197, 199, 235, 242, 244, 246,

259-260, 265
Orsova, SS, 11, 21
Osterley, RMS, 20
page 299, 129
page 305, 127, 129-130
Palace Gardens, 93, 140-141, 147
Pera-Hera, 44
Perry, Warren, 143, 243
Pollinger, Gerald, 1-2
Port Kembla steelworks, 151
Portrait of a Genius, But..., 205
Pringle, John Douglas, 200, 203, 237
Quadrant, 84, 143
Rananim, iv-v, 12, 17, 22, 24, 30, 45, 56-57, 74, 78, 84, 96, 107, 122, 206, 215, 236, 249, 252, 259-260, 263, 266-267
Rawson House, 248
Rawson, Don, 9, 167
Red Flag riots, 245, 249, 253
red wooden heart, 122, 124, 135-136, 216-218, 220-224
red-hot treason, 74, 143, 209
Rees, Sir Richard, 149
repetition, 64, 72, 76, 93, 169
revolution, 72, 113, 127, 182, 197-198, 211-212, 249
Richards, Bill, 245
Riemer, Professor Nicholas, 256
Roberts, Dr Warren, vi, vii, 1, 194, 241
Rosenthal, Major-General Sir Charles, ii, 5-7, 10, 14, 17, 62, 66, 70, 74-77, 80, 82, 84-88, 90-92, 94-104, 111-114, 116-117, 120, 122-123, 125, 127, 129-130, 134-136, 138, 140-150, 152, 155-156, 158, 167, 169-170, 181, 184-185, 195-198, 203, 209-210, 212, 216, 218-224, 235, 243-249, 253, 257, 261-262, 264, 266-267
Ross, Dr Charles, 241
Rossman, Dr Chuck, 264, 266
Rothwell, Sally, 244, 259
Ruffels, John, i, 7, 10, 20, 35, 42, 48, 97, 137, 140, 164, 195, 243, 248, 253-254, 256
Rugby League, 63-64
Russell, Bertrand (3rd Earl), 203
Sandon Point, 53, 95
Sands Directory, 82, 243
Saturday June 17, 99-100, 129, 150, 218
Savoy Hotel, 22
Schultz, Charles, 39
Scott & Broad, 243-244

Scott, William John (Jack) Rendell, ii, 3-9, 15-18, 29-30, 35, 39-42, 45, 55-59, 61-64, 66-67, 69-84, 86, 88-90, 92-93, 95, 97-99, 105-106, 109-114, 117, 120, 122-125, 127, 130, 133-134, 136, 141, 143, 145-146, 148, 151-152, 154-161, 165, 167-169, 172, 175, 178, 181, 184, 188, 195-196, 198-203, 209-213, 222, 242-251, 253-257, 259-260, 262-263, 266-267, 269

Scrivener, Captain Arthur, 251

Scrivener, Mrs Arthur, 248-249

Sculthorpe, Peter, 225

Sea and Sardinia, 24, 57, 208

Seaview Parade, 18, 42, 268

second notebook, 94

Seldes, Gilbert, 192

Seltzer, Thomas, 127, 146

setting-texts, 183, 189-190, 192

sex, 65, 93, 108, 117-118, 132, 159, 196, 215, 219, 235, 257

Shead, Garry, ii, 219, 225, 227

shell-shock, 181

Siebenhaar, William, 13, 24, 32, 127, 136, 173

silvery freedom, i, 184, 210, 233

singalong, 48, 65, 92, 108-109

Skinner, Miss MS (Mollie), 245, 262

Somers, Harriett, 15-16, 18, 28, 36, 41, 53, 55, 58, 79, 94-96, 100, 105, 128-133, 135-136, 145-146, 158-159, 177-178, 184, 186, 189, 212, 232

Somers, Richard Lovatt, 15, 23, 53, 208, 266

Sons and Lovers, 23, 53

Southall, Ray, 256

Southwell, Mrs Beatrice, 50

Speakers Corner, 5, 168

Spearitt, Peter, 243

Spry, Brigadier Sir Charles, 59, 148, 248

Spy Letters, iv, 196, 205-206

spy story, the, 205

Squires, Michael, 205

St Laurence of Rome, 179

Steele, Dr Bruce, iii, 13-14, 27, 40, 62, 70-71, 78, 80, 86-87, 102, 125-126, 130, 133, 150, 172-173, 176, 181-183, 190, 202, 207-208, 252, 256-258, 261, 263-265

Strangeways, Jack, 4, 84, 181, 262

Strathfield, 164, 243

streamers, 187, 232
Struthers, Willie, 80, 97, 100, 137, 140, 142, 145-146, 148, 173, 222, 257, 261
Struthers/Garden, 93, 173
stuck, 98, 116-117, 124-125, 127, 129-130, 133-134, 146, 160, 165, 167, 222
Studies in Classic American Literature, 25
Sublime Point, 131, 220
Sussex Street, 31
Sutherland, Joan, 231
Sutherland, Mike, 268
Svengali Press, The, iii, 197
Sydney Harbour, 3, 28, 35, 60, 235
Sydney Municipal Council, 85
Tahiti, 60, 162, 189, 252
Tahiti, SS, 139, 189
Take Me to Your Liedertafel, 12, 22, 107
Taos, ii, 20, 36, 52, 74, 93, 96, 100, 103, 116, 127, 133, 156, 161, 172, 179-180, 182-183, 186, 188-191, 193, 222, 229, 255, 266
Taronga Park Zoo, 162
Taylor, George Augustine, ii, 14-17, 56-57, 62, 74, 85, 88, 90, 114, 264, 266-267
telegram, 136, 190-191, 219, 221
teller, 75-76, 246
The Australian, 4, 6, 21, 85, 237, 244, 246, 250
The Basin, 268
The Beard of the Prophet, 3, 242
The Boy in the Bush, 24
The Bulletin, 11, 46, 56, 70, 86-87, 90, 126, 143, 152-153, 160, 173, 240, 247-248
The Butchers, 64
The *Daily Telegraph*, 126
The Death of Cooley, 177, 261
the end house, ii, 15, 17
The Fifth Sparrow, iv
The First, 101, 113, 148, 213
the last chapter, 176, 183, 252
The Lost Girl, 21, 23, 53
The Man Who Was Kangaroo, 84
The Man Who Wasn't There, 266
The Mystery of Kangaroo, 244
The Nightmare, ii, 109-110, 127, 145-147, 149-150, 207, 210, 224, 233
The Plumed Serpent, 207, 261
The Price of Vigilance, 6, 85, 197
The Priest of Love, 102

INDEX

The Quest for Cooley, iii, v, vii, 1, 9
The Rainbow, 23, 53, 196
The Rallying Point, iii, 3, 242, 244
The Roaring Twenties, 139, 253
The Row in Town, ii, 32, 114, 167, 261
The Secret Army and the Premier, 260
The Sequel, iv, 15, 62-63, 85, 88, 90, 114, 266-267
The Soldier, 267
The Spectral Visitor, 197
The storm, 183
The Sun, 98, 166, 168-169, 202
The Virgin and the Gypsy, 84-85
The White Peacock, 215
Thirroul, i, iii, 2, 12-13, 18-19, 25-26, 39-40, 43-45, 47-50, 52-55, 57-58, 60, 63-66, 70-71, 76, 78, 90, 92-94, 96-98, 102, 115-117, 125, 131, 135-136, 146, 151, 155, 163-166, 169-171, 177-179, 181, 183, 185, 187, 189, 195, 209, 211, 214, 219-222, 226-227, 230, 232, 237, 240, 242-243, 245-249, 251-252, 254-256, 258-261, 267

Thomas Cooks, 30
Thompson, Tom, 165
Torestin, 50, 58, 65, 79, 93-94, 107, 254
Toy, Bert, 31, 46, 56, 61, 153
Trades Hall, 32, 136-138, 140, 146-147, 155, 169, 172-173, 257, 261
transformation technique, 17, 39-40, 57, 61, 76, 81-82, 134, 169, 259
Trewheelar, Joshua, 40
Trewhella, James (Jaz), 4, 17, 39, 63, 66, 90, 92, 96-98, 105-107, 111-113, 116, 127, 138, 140, 147, 154, 159-160, 169, 177-179, 187-188, 200, 246, 251, 254-255
Trewhella, Matthew, 40
TS1, 100, 183, 189
TS1a, 161, 182-183, 186, 188-189
TS1b, 182-183, 186, 189
TS1bR, 100, 182-183, 188-193
Underhill, Nancy, 230, 235
Union Line, 162
Venice novel, 23, 208
Verga, Giovanni, 23, 78
Vernon, Miss Markie, 259-260
Viking edition, 188
volcanoes, 126
von Richthofen, Baroness

Frieda, 44
Waite, George, 243
Walker, Janet, 268
Wattle Day, 185
weekender, 39, 42, 65
Wellington, 188
Welsh rarebit, 105, 257
Western Australia, 12, 18, 20-25, 27, 78, 84, 173, 230, 261
White Australia policy, 173
White Guard, 4, 207, 244, 246
White, Patrick, ii, viii, 228-231, 234-235
Whitelaw, Robert, i-ii, 15-16, 267
Whiteley, Brett, 219, 225, 227, 229-230
Whitlam, Gough, 242
Williams, Evan, 242
Willis, Arthur, 173
Wilmott, Fred, 4
Wollongong, 151-152, 238, 256, 266
Wolloona, 151
Women in Love, 20, 23, 53, 89, 194, 201, 215, 241
Wood, Florence, 22
Worthen, Dr John, 21, 265
WS Friend & Co, 253, 259
Wycombe Road, 8-9, 43, 59, 61, 63, 99, 104-106, 109-110, 114, 117, 125, 136, 141, 145, 148, 155, 251, 260, 267
Wyewurk, i, 2, 12-13, 18-19, 43-44, 47-51, 53, 61, 63-66, 69, 74, 77-78, 81-82, 89-90, 92-93, 95, 105, 107-110, 116-120, 125-126, 131, 133-134, 143, 145-146, 152, 154-155, 164-166, 169, 175, 184-186, 211, 219-221, 225, 227-228, 232-233, 237, 239, 242, 245, 249, 251-252, 254, 256, 258, 260, 265
Wyewurrie, 18, 48, 65, 77, 108, 172, 249, 251, 254
Yeend, Peter, 13, 42, 112, 260-261, 263, 268
Young, Ken, 251
Zabel, Frances, 13, 22
Zennor, 40

www.ingramcontent.com/pod-product-compliance
Lightning Source LLC
Chambersburg PA
CBHW070742170426
43200CB00007B/617